CASENOTE LEGAL BRIEFS

PROPERTY

Adaptable to courses utilizing Casner and Leach's Casebook on Property

NORMAN S. GOLDENBERG, SENIOR EDITOR
PETER TENEN, MANAGING EDITOR
ROBERT J. SWITZER, EDITORIAL DIRECTOR

STAFF WRITERS

MATT HARDY

CLAUDIA NORBY

ROBERT SWITZER

RICH LOVICH

JAMES ROSENTHAL

JERRY SMILOWITZ

JAMES KOSNET

FRANK CARLEO

COURTNEY WALSH

PUBLISHED BY

CASENOTES PUBLISHING CO. INC.   P.O. BOX 3946   BEVERLY HILLS, CA 90212

ISBN 0-87457-115-4

FORMAT
FOR
THE CASENOTE LEGAL BRIEF

The following outline indicates the organization of a Casenote Legal Brief:

THE CASENOTE CASE CAPSULE: *This **bold face section** high-lights the procedural nature of the case, a short summary of the facts, and the rule of law. This is an **invaluable quick-review device** designed to **refresh the student's memory** for **classroom discussion** and **exam preparation.***

NATURE OF CASE: This section indicates the *form of action* (i.e., breach of contract, negligence, battery, etc.), the *type of proceeding* (i.e., demurrer, appeal from trial court's jury instructions, etc.) and the *relief sought* (i.e., damages, injunction, criminal sanctions, etc.).

FACT SUMMARY: The fact summary is included merely to *refresh the student's memory.* It is assumed that the student has already read the complete discussion of the facts and is familiar with them. This section is therefore not a complete and thorough presentation of the facts. It can be used to quickly recall the facts of the opinion when the student is chosen by an instructor to brief a case.

CONCISE RULE OF LAW: This portion of the brief, like the fact summary, is included to *refresh the student's memory.* This section is not intended to provide a full presentation of the rule and rationale in this case. Rather it should be used for instant recall of the court's holding and for classroom discussion or home review.

FACTS: Here the editors present a precise expression of all *relevant facts* of the case including the contentions of the parties and lower court holdings. It is written in a logical order to enable the student to have a clear understanding of the case. The plaintiff and defendant are indicated by their proper names throughout and are always labeled with a (P) or (D).

ISSUE: The issue is a *concise question which brings out the essence of the opinion* as it relates to the section of the book in which it appears. Both substantive and procedural issues are included if relevant to the decision.

ZAHN v. TRANSAMERICA CORPORATION
U.S. Cir. Ct. of Apls., 3d Cir. (1947) 162 F.2d 36.

NATURE OF CASE: Derivative action alleging breach of fiduciary duty.

FACT SUMMARY: Zahn (P), a holder of Axton-Fisher Class A stock, asserted that Transamerica (D), as majority stockholder in Axton-Fisher, breached a fiduciary duty it owed the minority when it got Axton-Fisher's board to engage in a pre-liquidation redemption of Class A stock so as to benefit Transamerica (D).

CONCISE RULE OF LAW: In exercising their right to control a corporation, the majority shareholders owe a fiduciary duty to the minority as well as the corporation.

FACTS: Transamerica (D) was the majority stockholder when Axton-Fisher's board of directors voted to engage in a redemption of Class A stock. Zahn (P), a Class A stockholder, insisted that Transamerica (D) violated its fiduciary duty by using its control over the board to bring about the redemption plan for its own benefit (based on the non-public knowledge it had that tobacco held by Axton-Fisher in storage had risen sharply in value). The plan, he charged, was to bring about a redemption of Class A shares, then liquidate Axton-Fisher so that Transamerica (D) (as the holder of most of the remaining non-preferred stock) would gain for itself most of the value of the warehoused tobacco. His suit was dismissed for failure to state a cause of action.

ISSUE: Do majority stockholders owe a fiduciary duty to the minority?

HOLDING AND DECISION: Yes. As a fiduciary relationship is imposed by law on the directors of a corporation in respect to the corporation and its stockholders, a similar relationship governs those who are in charge of the corporation's affairs by virtue of majority stock ownership or otherwise. The majority has the right to control, but in exercising that right it owes a fiduciary duty to the minority as well as to the corporation itself or its officers and directors. Although the act of the board of directors in calling the Class A stock could be legally consummated by a disinterested board, if the allegations made are true, it was effected at the direction of the majority stockholder in order to profit it. In such a case, an action would definitely lie, and Transamerica (D) would be liable for breach of its fiduciary duty to the minority. Reversed.

EDITOR'S ANALYSIS: This case points up one situation (liquidations) in which the law prohibits controlling shareholders from exploiting their position to the detriment of the minority. While the fiduciary duties of controlling shareholders (breach of which can give rise to liability) are not quite coextensive with the fiduciary duties of directors, at least in cases of self-dealing, the issuance of stock, interference with voting rights, dissolutions, and the sale of assets, most courts will hold the majority to a duty of good faith, care, and diligence in the protection of minority rights and interests. Note also that most courts today give special scrutiny to situations in which a sale of control is effected by a controlling shareholder. See Perlman v. Feldman, 219 F.2d 173.

HOLDING AND DECISION: This section offers a clear and in-depth discussion of the *rule of the case and the court's rationale.* It is written in easy-to-understand language. When relevant, the student is provided with a thorough discussion of the exceptions listed by the court, the concurring and dissenting opinions, and the names of the judges.

EDITOR'S ANALYSIS: This addition to the brief is a new innovation. It is a hornbook style discussion of how the case is relevant to the section of the book and to the entire course. It indicates whether the case is a majority or minority opinion. It compares the principle case with other cases in the casebook. It also provides analysis from restatements, uniform codes, legal encyclopedias and treatises. This section points out the history of the case, the type of transaction involved and ways to avoid problems the case presents for the lawyer. In other words, it gives the student a broad understanding of *where the case "fits in" with other cases in the section of the book and with the entire course.* The editor's analysis will prove to be invaluable to classroom discussion.

NOTE TO THE STUDENT

It is the goal of Casenotes Publishing Company, Inc. to create and distribute the finest, clearest and most accurate legal briefs available. To this end, we are constantly seeking new ideas, comments and constructive criticism. As a user of Casenote Legal Briefs, your suggestions will be highly valued. With all correspondence, please include your complete name, address, and telephone number, including area code and zip code.

Casenote Legal Briefs are printed on perforated, three-hole punched sheets for easy inclusion in ringed binders. To remove a page, first fold the page at the perforations and then tear the sheet using care not to rip the punched holes.

EDITOR'S NOTE: Casenote Legal Briefs *are intended to supplement the student's casebook, not replace it. The student must master the skill of briefing if he/she expects to succeed in the study of law. There is no substitute for the student's own mastery of this important learning and study technique. If used properly, Casenote Legal Briefs are an effective law study aid which serve to reinforce the student's understanding of the cases.*

SUPPLEMENT REQUEST FORM

REF. #1030-84-190

At the time this book was printed, a brief was included for every major case in the casebook and for every existing supplement to the casebook. However, if a new supplement to the casebook (or a new edition of the casebook) has been published since this publication was printed and if that casebook supplement (or new edition of the casebook) was available for sale at the time you purchased this Casenote Legal Briefs book, we will be pleased to provide you the new cases contained therein AT NO CHARGE when you send us a stamped, self-addressed envelope.

TO OBTAIN YOUR FREE SUPPLEMENT MATERIAL, **YOU MUST FOLLOW THE INSTRUCTIONS BELOW PRECISELY** OR REQUEST WILL NOT BE ACKNOWLEDGED!

1. Please check if there is in fact an existing supplement and, if so, that the cases are not already included in your Casenote Legal Briefs. Check the main table of cases as well as the supplement table of cases, if any.

2. *REMOVE THIS ENTIRE PAGE FROM THE BOOK.* You MUST send this ORIGINAL page to receive your supplement. This page acts as your proof of purchase and contains the reference number necessary to fill your supplement request properly. No photocopy of this page or written request will be honored or answered. Any request from which the reference number has been removed, altered or obliterated will not be honored.

3. Prepare a STAMPED self-addressed envelope for return mailing. Be sure to use a FULL SIZE (9 × 12) ENVELOPE (MANILA TYPE) so that the supplement will fit, and AFFIX ENOUGH POSTAGE TO COVER 3 OZ. **ANY SUPPLEMENT REQUEST NOT ACCOMPANIED BY A STAMPED SELF-ADDRESSED ENVELOPE WILL ABSOLUTELY NOT BE FILLED OR ACKNOWLEDGED.**

4. MULTIPLE SUPPLEMENT REQUESTS: If you are ordering more than one supplement, we suggest that you enclose a stamped, self-addressed envelope for each supplement requested. If you enclose only one envelope for a multiple request, your order may not be filled immediately should any supplement which you requested still be in production. In other words, your order will be held by us until it can be filled completely.

5. CASENOTES prints two kinds of supplements. A "*New Edition*" supplement is issued when a new edition of your casebook is published. A "*New Edition*" supplement gives you all major cases found in the new edition of the casebook which did not appear in the previous edition. A regular "*supplement*" is issued when a paperback supplement to your casebook is published. If the box at the lower right is stamped, then the "*New Edition*" supplement was provided to your bookstore and is *not* available from CASENOTES, however CASENOTES will still send you any regular "*supplements*" which have been printed either before or after the new edition of your casebook appeared and which, according to the reference number at the top of this page, have not been included in this book. If the box is not stamped, CASENOTES will send you any supplements, "*New Edition*" and/or regular, needed to completely update your Casenote Legal Briefs.

6. Fill in the following information:

    A. Full title of CASEBOOK ___PROPERTY___

    B. CASEBOOK author's name ___CASNER___

    C. Date of new supplement which you are requesting _ _ _

    D. Name and location of bookstore where this *Casenote Legal Briefs* was purchased

    E. Name and location of law school you attend _____

    F. Any comments regarding *Casenote Legal Briefs* _____

NOTE: IF THIS BOX IS STAMPED, NO *NEW EDITION* SUPPLEMENT CAN BE OBTAINED BY MAIL.

CASENOTES PUBLISHING, CO., INC.   **P.O. Box 3946**   **Beverly Hills, CA 90212-0946**

PLEASE PRINT

NAME _____ PHONE _____

ADDRESS/CITY/STATE/ZIP _____

New OUTLINE Series

CASENOTE LAW OUTLINES

NEW from CASENOTES — *the Ultimate Outline*

▶ **WRITTEN BY NATIONALLY RECOGNIZED AUTHORITIES IN THEIR FIELD.**

▶ **CONTAINS:** *TABLE OF CONTENTS; CAPSULE OUTLINE; FULL OUTLINE; PRACTICE ESSAYS; PRACTICE MULTI-STATE EXAM; SUBJECT GLOSSARY; TABLE OF CASES; TABLE OF AUTHORITIES; CASEBOOK CROSS REFERENCE CHART; INDEX.*

▶ **THE TOTAL LAW SUMMARY UTILIZING THE MOST COMPREHENSIVE STUDY APPROACH IN THE MOST EFFECTIVE, EASY-TO-READ FORMAT.**

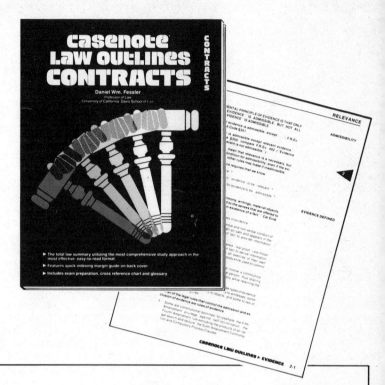

COMMON LATIN WORDS AND PHRASES ENCOUNTERED IN THE LAW

A FORTIORI: Because one fact exists or has been proven, that therefore a second fact which is related to the first fact must also exist. This term is most often used when making arguments based upon logic.

A PRIORI: From the cause to the effect. A term of logic used to denote that when one cause, fact, or position is shown to exist, another particular cause, fact or position must necessarily follow.

AB INITIO: From the beginning; a condition which has existed throughout, as in a marriage which was void *ab initio.*

ACTUS REUS: The guilty act; in criminal law, such action sufficient to trigger criminal liability.

AD VALOREM: According to value; an *ad valorem* tax is imposed upon an item located within the taxing jurisdiction calculated by the value of such item.

AMICUS CURIAE: Friend of the court. Its most common usage takes the form of an amicus curiae brief, filed by a person who is not a party to an action, but is nonetheless allowed to offer an argument supporting his legal interests.

ARGUENDO: In arguing. A statement, possibly hypothetical, made for the purpose of argument.

BILL QUIA TIMET: A bill to quiet title (establish ownership) to real property.

BONA FIDE: True, honest or genuine. May refer to the genuiness of a person's legal position (such as a bona fide purchaser for value), or a particular document (such as a bona fide last will and testament).

CAUSA MORTIS: With approaching death in mind. A gift causa mortis is a gift given by a party who feels certain that death is imminent.

CAVEAT EMPTOR: "Let the buyer beware," is the literal translation. This maxim is reflected in the rule of law that a buyer purchases at his own risk because it is his responsibility to examine, judge, test, and otherwise inspect what he is buying.

CERTIORARI: A writ of review. Petitions for review of a case by the United States Supreme Court are most often done by means of a writ of certiorari.

CONTRA: On the other hand. Opposite. Contrary to.

CORAM NOBIS: Before us; writs of error directed by a court to another branch of the same court.

CORAM VOBIS: Before you; writs of error directed by an appellate court to a lower court to correct a factual error.

CORPUS DELICTI: The body of the crime; the requisite elements of a crime amounting to objective proof that a crime has been committed.

CUM TESTAMENTO ANNEXO, ADMINISTRATOR (ADMINISTRATOR C.T.A.): With will annexed; an administrator c.t.a. settles an estate pursuant to a will in which he is not appointed.

DE BONIS NON, ADMINISTRATOR (ADMINISTRATOR D.B.N.): Of goods not administered; an administrator d.b.n. settles a partially settled estate.

DE FACTO: In fact; in reality; actually. Existing in fact but not officially approved or engendered.

DE JURE: By right; lawful. "As a matter of law" is what this term commonly connotes, in contrast to the term "de facto" (which generally connotes something existing in fact but not legally sanctioned or authorized). For example, *de facto* segregation would refer to segregation brought about by housing patterns, etc., while *de jure* segregation would refer to segregation created by law.

DE MINIMUS: Of minimal importance; insignificant; a trifle; not worth bothering with.

DE NOVO: Anew; a second time; afresh. A trial de novo is a new trial held at the appellate level as if the case originated there and the trial at a lower level had not taken place.

DICTA: Generally used as an abbreviated form of *obiter dicta,* a term describing those portions of a judicial opinion incidental or not necessary to resolution of the specific question before the court. Such nonessential statements and remarks are not considered to be binding precedent.

DUCES TECUM: Refers to a particular type of writ or subpoena requesting a party or organization to produce certain documents in their possession.

EN BANC: Full bench. Where a court sits with all justices present rather than simply a quorum.

EX PARTE: For one side or one party only. An ex parte proceeding is one undertaken for the benefit of only one party, and proceeds without notice to, or an appearance by an adverse party.

EX POST FACTO: After the fact. An ex post facto law is a law which retroactively changes the consequences of a prior act.

EX REL.: (abbr. for ex relatione) Upon relation or information. When the state brings an action in which it has no interest against an individual at the instigation of one who has a private interest in the matter.

FORUM NON CONVENIENS: Inconvenient forum. Although a court may have jurisdiction over the case, the action should be tried in a more conveniently located court, one to which parties and witnesses may more easily travel, for example.

GUARDIAN AD LITEM: A guardian of an infant as to litigation, appointed to represent the infant and pursue his rights.

HABEAS CORPUS: "You have the body" is the literal translation. The modern writ of *habeas corpus* is a writ directing that a person (body) being detained (such as a prisoner) be brought before the court so that the legality of his detention can be judicially ascertained.

IN CAMERA: In private, in chambers. When a hearing is held before a judge in his chambers or when all spectators are excluded from the courtroom.

IN FORMA PAUPERIS: In the manner of a pauper. A party who proceeds *in forma pauperis* because of his poverty may be allowed to bring suit without liability for costs.

INFRA: Below, under. The opposite of *supra,* above.

IN LOCO PARENTIS: In the place of a parent.

IN PARI DELICTO: Equally wrong; a court of equity will not grant requested relief to an applicant who is *in pari delicto,* or as much at fault in the transactions giving rise to the controversy as is the opponent of the applicant.

IN PARI MATERIA: On like subject matter or upon the same matter. Statutes relating to the same person or things are said to be *in pari materia.* It is a general rule of statutory construction that such statutes should be construed together, i.e. looked at as if they together constituted one law.

IN PERSONAM: Into or against the person. Jurisdiction over the person of an individual.

IN RE: In the matter of.

IN REM: A term that signifies an action against the *res,* or thing. An action *in rem* is basically one that is taken directly against property, in contradistinction to an action *in personam* or action against the person.

INTER ALIA: Amongst other things. Used to show that the whole of a statement, pleading, list, or statute, for example, has not been set forth in its entirety.

INTER PARTES: Between the parties. May refer to contracts, conveyances or other transactions having legal significance.

INTER VIVOS: Between the living. An inter vivos gift is a gift made by a living grantor, as distinguished from bequests contained in a will, which pass upon the death of the testator.

IPSO FACTO: By the mere fact itself.

JUS: Law or the entire body of law.

LEX LOCI: The law of the place; the notion that the rights of parties to a legal proceeding are governed by the law of the plac
where those rights arose.

MALUM IN SE: Evil or wrong in and of itself; inherently wrong. This term describes an act that is wrong by its very nature a
opposed to one which would not be wrong but for the fact that there is a specific legal prohibition against it (malu.
prohibitum).

MALUM PROHIBITUM: Wrong because prohibited, but not inherently evil. Used to describe something which is wrong becaus
it is expressly forbidden by law but which is not in and of itself evil, e.g. speeding.

MANDAMUS: We command. A writ directing an official to take certain action.

MENS REA: A guilty mind; a criminal intent. A term used to signify the mental state that accompanies a crime or other prohibite
act. Some crimes require only a general *mens rea* (general intent to do the prohibited act), but others (like assault with inte
to murder) require the existence of a specific *mens rea*.

MODUS OPERANDI: Method of operating; generally refers to the manner or style of a criminal in committing crimes, admissib
in appropriate cases as evidence of the identity of a defendant.

NEXUS: A connection to.

NISI PRIUS: The courts of first impression. The court where issues of fact are tried before a judge or jury.

N.O.V. (NON OBSTANTE VERDICTO): Notwithstanding the verdict. A judgment n.o.v. is a judgment given in favor of one par
despite the fact that a verdict was returned in favor of the other party, the justification being that the verdict either had n
reasonable support in fact or was contrary to law.

NUNC PRO TUNC: Now for then. This phrase refers to actions which may be taken, and then have full retroactive effect.

PENDENTE LITE: Pending the suit; pending litigation underway.

PER CAPITA: By head; beneficiaries of an estate, if they take in equal shares, take *per capita*.

PER CURIAM: By the court; signifies an opinion ostensibly written "by the whole court" and with no identified author.

PER SE: By itself; in itself; inherently.

PER STIRPES: By representation. Used primarily in the law of wills to show that when a person, generally because of death,
unable to take that which is left to him by the will of another, his heirs shall divide such property between them rather tha
take under the will individually.

PRIMA FACIE: On its face; at first sight. A *prima facie* case is one that is sufficient on its face, meaning that the evidenc
supporting it is adequate to establish the case until contradicted or overcome by other evidence.

PRO TANTO: For so much; as far as it goes. Often used in eminent domain cases when property owner receives partial payme
for his land without prejudice to his right to bring suit for the full amount he claims his land to be worth.

QUANTUM MERUIT: As much as he deserved. Today, this term refers to recovery based on the doctrine of unjust enrichment
those cases in which a party rendered valuable services or furnished materials that were accepted and enjoyed by anoth
under circumstances that would reasonably notify the recipient that the rendering party expected to be paid. In essenc
the law implies a contract to pay the reasonable value of the services or materials furnished.

QUASI: Almost like; as if; nearly. This term is essentially used to signify that one subject or thing is almost analogous to anoth
but that material differences between them do exist. For example, a quasi-criminal proceeding is one that is not strict
criminal but which shares so many of the same characteristics that it is sufficiently like a criminal proceeding to require tha
some of the same safeguards apply (e.g., procedural due process must be followed in a parol hearing).

QUID PRO QUO: Something for something. In contract law, the consideration, something of value, passed between the parties t
render the contract binding.

RES GESTAE: The things done; in evidence law, this principle justifies the admission of a statement, which otherwise would b
hearsay, when it is made so closely to the event in question   as to be said to be a part of it or with such spontaneity as not t
have the possibility of falsehood.

RES IPSA LOQUITUR: The thing speaks for itself. This doctrine gives rise to a rebuttable presumption of negligence when th
instrumentality causing the injury was within the exclusive control of the defendant, and the injury was one which does n
normally occur unless a person has been negligent.

RES JUDICATA: A matter adjudged. Doctrine which provides that once a court of competent jurisdiction has rendered a fin
judgment or decree on the merits, that judgment or decree is conclusive upon the parties to the case and their privies an
prevents them from engaging in any other litigation on the points and issues determined therein.

RESPONDEAT SUPERIOR: Let the master reply. This doctrine holds the master liable for the wrongful acts of his servant (or th
principal for his agent) in those cases in which the servant (or agent) was acting within the scope of his authority at the tim
of the injury.

STARE DECISIS: To stand by or adhere to that which has been decided. The common law doctrine of *stare decisis* attempts t
give security and certainty to the law by following the policy that once a principle of law as applicable to a certain set of fac
has been set forth in a decision, it forms a precedent which will subsequently be followed even though a different decisic
might be made were it the first time the question had arisen. Of course, *stare decisis* is not an inviolable principle, but
departed from in instances where there is good cause (e.g. considerations of public policy led the Supreme Court t
disregard prior decisions sanctioning segregation).

SUPRA: Above. A word referring a reader to an earlier part of a book.

ULTRA VIRES: Beyond the power. This·phrase is most commonly used to refer to actions taken by a corporation which a
beyond the power or legal authority of the corporation.

ADDENDUM OF FRENCH DERIVATIVES

IN PAIS: Not pursuant to legal proceedings.

CHATTEL: Tangible personal property.

CY PRES: Doctrine permitting courts to apply trust funds to purposes not expressed in the trust, but necessary to carry out th
settlor's intent.

PER AUTRE VIE: For another's life; in Property Law, an estate may be granted which will terminate upon the death of someor
other than the grantee.

PROFIT 'A PRENDRE: A license to remove minerals or other stone from land.

VOIR DIRE: Process of questioning jurors as to their predispositions about the case or parties to a proceeding and removir
those jurors displaying bias or prejudice.

CASENOTE LEGAL BRIEFS

PRICE LIST — EFFECTIVE JULY 1, 1990 ● PRICES SUBJECT TO CHANGE WITHOUT NOTICE

Ref. No.	Course	Adaptable to Courses Utilizing	Retail Price
1380	ACCOUNTING	FIFLIS, KRIPKE & FOSTER	7.50
1265	ADMINISTRATIVE LAW	BONFIELD & ASIMOW	11.00
1263	ADMINISTRATIVE LAW	BREYER & STEWART	14.00
1261	ADMINISTRATIVE LAW	DAVIS	10.00
1260	ADMINISTRATIVE LAW	GELHORN, B., S., R & S.	13.00
1264	ADMINISTRATIVE LAW	MASHAW & MERRILL	12.50
1262	ADMINISTRATIVE LAW	SCHWARTZ	13.00
1290	ADMIRALTY	HEALY & SHARPE	15.50
1291	ADMIRALTY	LUCAS	13.50
1350	AGENCY & PARTNER. (ENT. ORG.)	CONARD, KNAUSS & SIEGEL	15.00
1280	ANTITRUST	AREEDA & KAPLOW	14.50
1281	ANTITRUST (TRADE REG.)	HANDLER, B., P & G.	11.50
1282	ANTITRUST	OPPENHEIM, W. & M.	12.50
1610	BANKING LAW	SYMONS & WHITE	9.00
1303	BANKRUPTCY (DEBT.-CRED.)	EISENBERG	12.00
1440	BUSINESS PLANNING	HERWITZ	9.50
1040	CIVIL PROCEDURE	COUND, F., M. & S.	15.00
1043	CIVIL PROCEDURE	FIELD, K. & C.	14.00
1046	CIVIL PROCEDURE	LANDERS, MARTIN & YEAZELL	13.00
1041	CIVIL PROCEDURE	LOUISELL, HAZARD & TAIT.	14.00
1047	CIVIL PROCEDURE	MARCUS, REDISH & SHERMAN	15.00
1044	CIVIL PROCEDURE	ROSENBERG, S. & K.	15.00
1311	COMMERCIAL LAW	FARNSWORTH & HONNOLD	14.00
1312	COMMERCIAL LAW	JORDAN & WARREN	14.00
1310	COMMERCIAL LAW	SPEIDEL, SUMMERS & WHITE	14.00
1312	COMMERCIAL PAPER (COMM. LAW)	JORDAN & WARREN	14.00
1320	COMMUNITY PROPERTY	VERRALL & BIRD	13.50
1071	CONFLICTS	CRAMTON, CURRIE & KAY	13.00
1070	CONFLICTS	REESE, ROSENBERG & HAY	15.00
1082	CONSTITUTIONAL LAW	BARRETT, COHEN & VARAT	17.00
1086	CONSTITUTIONAL LAW	BREST & LEVINSON	12.00
1080	CONSTITUTIONAL LAW	GUNTHER	15.00
1084	CONSTITUTIONAL LAW	KAUPER & BEYTAGH	14.00
1081	CONSTITUTIONAL LAW	LOCKHART, K., C. & S.	14.00
1085	CONSTITUTIONAL LAW	ROTUNDA	16.00
1087	CONSTITUTIONAL LAW	STONE, S., S. & T.	15.00
1017	CONTRACTS	CALAMARI, PERILLO & BENDER	17.00
1014	CONTRACTS	DAWSON, H. & H.	14.00
1010	CONTRACTS	FARNSWORTH & YOUNG	14.00
1011	CONTRACTS	FULLER & EISENBERG	15.00
1100	CONTRACTS	HAMILTON, R. & W.	13.50
1013	CONTRACTS	KESSLER, GILMORE & KRONMAN	17.50
1016	CONTRACTS	KNAPP & CRYSTAL	15.50
1012	CONTRACTS	MURPHY & SPEIDEL	16.00
1018	CONTRACTS	MURRAY	16.00
1015	CONTRACTS	ROSETT	15.00
1019	CONTRACTS	VERNON	14.00
1501	COPYRIGHT	NIMMER	14.50
1218	CORPORATE TAXATION	LIND, S., L & R.	9.00
1050	CORPORATIONS	CARY & EISENBERG (ABR. & UNABR.)	14.00
1054	CORPORATIONS	CHOPER, MORRIS & COFFEE	16.50
1350	CORPORATIONS (ENT. ORG.)	CONARD, KNAUSS & SIEGEL	15.00
1053	CORPORATIONS	HAMILTON	13.00
1051	CORPORATIONS	HENN	15.00
1055	CORPORATIONS	JENNINGS & BUXBAUM	13.50
1056	CORPORATIONS	SOLOMON, SCHWARTZ & BOWMAN	15.00
1052	CORPORATIONS	VAGTS	12.00
1300	CREDITOR'S RIGHTS (DEBT.-CRED.)	RIESENFELD	15.00
1550	CRIMINAL JUSTICE	WEINREB	12.50
1020	CRIMINAL LAW	BOYCE & PERKINS	17.00
1024	CRIMINAL LAW	DIX & SHARLOT	12.00
1025	CRIMINAL LAW	FOOTE & LEVY	12.00
1027	CRIMINAL LAW	JOHNSON	17.00
1021	CRIMINAL LAW	KADISH & SCHULHOFER	14.00
1026	CRIMINAL LAW	KAPLAN & WEISBERG	12.50
1023	CRIMINAL LAW	LaFAVE	13.00
1022	CRIMINAL LAW	WEINREB	10.00
1200	CRIMINAL PROCEDURE	KAMISAR, LaFAVE & ISRAEL	14.00
1204	CRIMINAL PROCEDURE	SALTZBURG	12.00
1203	CRIMINAL PROCEDURE (PROCESS)	WEINREB	13.50
1303	DEBTOR-CREDITOR	EISENBERG	13.00
1302	DEBTOR-CREDITOR	EPSTEIN, LANDERS & NICKLES	12.00
1300	DEBTOR-CREDITOR (CRED. RTS.)	RIESENFELD	15.00
1301	DEBTOR-CREDITOR	WARREN & HOGAN	13.00
1304	DEBTOR-CREDITOR	WARREN & WESTBROOK	13.00
1223	DECEDENTS EST. (WILLS, T. & E.)	DUKEMINIER & JOHANSON	14.50
1224	DECEDENTS ESTATES	RITCHIE, ALFORD & EFFLAND	14.50
1222	DECEDENTS ESTATES	SCOLES & HALBACH	14.50
1231	DECEDENTS ESTATES (TRUSTS)	WELLMAN, W. & B.	13.00
1244	DOMESTIC RELATIONS (FAM. LAW)	AREEN	16.00
1242	DOMESTIC RELATIONS (FAM. LAW)	CLARK	13.00
1241	DOMESTIC RELATIONS (FAM. LAW)	FOOTE, LEVY & SANDER	17.00
1243	DOMESTIC RELATIONS (FAM. LAW)	KRAUSE	17.00
1240	DOMESTIC RELATIONS (FAM. LAW)	WADLINGTON	14.00
1350	ENTERPRISE ORGANIZATIONS	CONARD, KNAUSS & SIEGEL	15.00
1341	ENVIRONMENTAL LAW	FINDLEY & FARBER	14.00
1340	ENVIRONMENTAL LAW	HANKS, TARLOCK & HANKS	8.50
1254	EQUITY (REMEDIES)	LAYCOCK	14.50
1253	EQUITY (REMEDIES)	LEAVELL, LOVE & NELSON	15.00
1252	EQUITY (REMEDIES)	RE	18.50
1255	EQUITY (REMEDIES)	SHOBEN & TABB	16.50
1250	EQUITY (REMEDIES)	YORK, BAUMAN & RENDLEMAN	18.00
1217	ESTATE & GIFT TAXATION	BITTKER & CLARK	10.00
1214	ESTATE & GIFT TAXATION	KAHN & WAGGONER	12.00
1213	ESTATE & GIFT TAXATION (FED. WEALTH TRANS.)	SURREY, McDANIEL & GUTMAN	11.00
1090	ETHICS (PROF. RESPONSIBILITY)	PIRSIG & KIRWIN	10.00
1064	EVIDENCE	CLEARY, STRONG, BROUN & MOSTELLER	15.50
1065	EVIDENCE	GREEN & NESSON	13.00
1061	EVIDENCE	KAPLAN & WALTZ	14.00
1063	EVIDENCE	LEMPERT & SALTZBURG	7.00
1062	EVIDENCE	McCORMICK, SUTTON & WELLBORN	17.00
1066	EVIDENCE	MUELLER & KIRKPATRICK	13.00
1060	EVIDENCE	WEINSTEIN, M., A. & B.	15.50
1244	FAMILY LAW (DOMESTIC REL)	AREEN	16.00
1242	FAMILY LAW (DOMESTIC REL)	CLARK	13.00
1241	FAMILY LAW (DOMESTIC REL)	FOOTE, LEVY & SANDER	12.00
1243	FAMILY LAW (DOMESTIC REL)	KRAUSE	17.00
1240	FAMILY LAW (DOMESTIC REL)	WADLINGTON	14.00
1360	FEDERAL COURTS	BATOR, M., S. & W.	15.00
1362	FEDERAL COURTS	CURRIE	12.00
1363	FEDERAL COURTS	LOW & JEFFRIES	11.00
1361	FEDERAL COURTS	McCORMICK, C. & W.	15.00
1510	GRATUITOUS TRANSFERS	CLARK, LUSKY & MURPHY	13.00
1371	INSURANCE LAW	KEETON	15.00
1370	INSURANCE LAW	YOUNG & HOLMES	11.00
1392	INTERNATIONAL LAW	HENKIN, P., S. & S.	12.00
1390	INTERNATIONAL LAW	SWEENEY, OLIVER & LEECH	15.00
1460	JUVENILE JUSTICE	MILLER, D., D. & P.	12.00
1331	LABOR LAW	COX, BOK & GORMAN	14.00
1333	LABOR LAW	LESLIE	12.50
1332	LABOR LAW	MELTZER & HENDERSON	14.00
1330	LABOR LAW	MERRIFIELD, S. & C.	13.00
1471	LAND FINANCE (REAL ESTATE TRANS.)	AXELROD, BERGER & JOHNSTONE	13.00
1620	LAND FINANCE (REAL ESTATE TRANS.)	NELSON & WHITMAN	15.00
1470	LAND FINANCE	PENNEY, B. & C.	12.00
1450	LAND USE	WRIGHT & GITELMAN	16.00
1420	LEGISLATION	NUTTING & DICKERSON	12.00
1590	LOCAL GOVERNMENT LAW	VALENTE	16.00
1520	MEDICINE	SHARPE, FISCINA & HEAD	15.00
1600	NEGOTIABLE INSTRUMENTS	WHALEY	9.00
1570	NEW YORK PRACTICE	PETERFREUND & McLAUGHLIN	19.00
1541	OIL & GAS	KUNTZ, L, A & S.	13.00
1540	OIL & GAS	WILLIAMS, M., M. & W.	11.00
1560	PATENT LAW	CHOATE & FRANCIS	18.00
1431	PRODUCTS LIABILITY	KEETON, MONTGOMERY & GREEN	14.00
1430	PRODUCTS LIABILITY	NOEL & PHILLIPS	15.50
1090	PROF. RESPONSIBILITY (ETHICS)	PIRSIG & KIRWIN	10.00
1033	PROPERTY	BROWDER, C., N., S. & W.	15.50
1030	PROPERTY	CASNER & LEACH	16.00
1031	PROPERTY	CRIBBET, JOHNSON, FINLEY & SMITH	16.50
1035	PROPERTY	DUKEMINIER & KRIER	13.00
1034	PROPERTY	HAAR & LIEBMAN	14.50
1036	PROPERTY	KURTZ & HOVENKAMP	15.00
1032	PROPERTY	RABIN	14.00
1620	REAL ESTATE TRANSFER & FINANCE	NELSON & WHITMAN	15.00
1254	REMEDIES (EQUITY)	LAYCOCK	14.50
1253	REMEDIES (EQUITY)	LEAVELL, LOVE & NELSON	15.00
1252	REMEDIES (EQUITY)	RE	18.50
1255	REMEDIES (EQUITY)	SHOBEN & TABB	16.50
1250	REMEDIES (EQUITY)	YORK, BAUMAN & RENDLEMAN	18.00
1312	SECURED TRANS. (COMM. LAW)	JORDAN & WARREN	14.00
1270	SECURITIES REGULATION	JENNINGS & MARSH	14.00
1271	SECURITIES REGULATION	RATNER	13.00
1215	TAXATION (BASIC FED. INC.)	ANDREWS	14.00
1217	TAXATION (ESTATE & GIFT)	BITTKER & CLARK	10.00
1212	TAXATION (FED. INC.)	FREELAND, LIND & STEPHENS	13.00
1211	TAXATION (FED. INC.)	GRAETZ	12.00
1214	TAXATION (ESTATE & GIFT)	KAHN & WAGGONER	12.00
1210	TAXATION (FED. INC.)	KLEIN, BITTKER & STONE	13.50
1216	TAXATION (FED. INC.)	KRAGEN & McNULTY	11.00
1218	TAXATION (CORPORATE)	LIND, S., L & R.	9.00
1213	TAXATION (FED. WEALTH TRANS.)	SURREY, M. & G.	11.00
1281	TRADE REGULATION (ANTITRUST)	HANDLER, B., P & G.	11.50
1006	TORTS	DOBBS	16.00
1003	TORTS	EPSTEIN, GREGORY & KALVEN	16.50
1004	TORTS	FRANKLIN & RABIN	12.50
1001	TORTS	HENDERSON & PEARSON	14.50
1002	TORTS	KEETON, K., S. & S.	16.00
1000	TORTS	PROSSER, WADE & SCHWARTZ	18.00
1005	TORTS	SHULMAN, JAMES & GRAY	16.00
1230	TRUSTS	BOGERT & OAKS	14.50
1231	TRUSTS (DECEDENTS ESTATES)	WELLMAN, WAGGONER & BROWDER	13.00
1410	U.C.C.	EPSTEIN, MARTIN, H. & N.	10.00
1580	WATER LAW	TRELEASE & GOULD	14.00
1223	WILLS, TRUSTS & EST. (DEC. EST.)	DUKEMINIER & JOHANSON	14.50
1220	WILLS	MECHEM & ATKINSON	15.00

CASENOTES PUBLISHING CO. INC. ● P.O. BOX 3946 ● BEVERLY HILLS, CA 90212 ● (213) 475-1141

PLEASE PURCHASE FROM YOUR LOCAL BOOKSTORE.   IF UNAVAILABLE, YOU MAY ORDER DIRECT. *

4TH CLASS POSTAGE (ALLOW TWO WEEKS) $1.00 PER ORDER; 1ST CLASS POSTAGE $3.00 (ONE BOOK), $2.00 EACH (TWO OR MORE BOOKS)

* CALIF. RESIDENTS PLEASE ADD SALES TAX   (SERIES XXII)

CASENOTE LAW OUTLINES ®

At last... the Ultimate Outline

Chapter Headlines

ADMISSIBILITY

Quick-Reference Margin Headline

I. THE FUNDAMENTAL PRINCIPLE OF EVIDENCE IS THAT ONLY "RELEVANT EVIDENCE" IS ADMISSIBLE, BUT NOT ALL "RELEVANT EVIDENCE" IS ADMISSIBLE.

A. "All relevant evidence is admissible, except . . ."; F.R.Ev. 401.

Code & Case Citations

B. "No evidence is admissible except relevant evidence." Compare F.R.Ev. 402 ("Evidence which is not relevant is not admissible.")

Margin Index

2

C. These two rules mean that relevance is a necessary, but not a sufficient condition for admissibility; even if the evidence is relevant, other rules may make it inadmissible.

Concise Definitions & Issue Spotting

D. The rule of relevance requires that we know:

1. What is "evidence"?

2. What is required for "evidence" to be "relevant"?

Rules of Law

3. What does it mean for evidence to be "admissible"?

II. WHAT IS "EVIDENCE"?

EVIDENCE DEFINED

A. " 'Evidence' means testimony, writings, material objects, or other things presented to the senses that are offered to prove the existence or non-existence of a fact."

Margin Note Space

1. There are three basic types of evidence:

a) "Testimony" is the verbal and non-verbal conduct of a person who has taken an oath and appears in the presence of the trier of fact to provide information about the case.

Pages Numbered by Chapter

b) "Objects" (sometimes called "real proof") are those things that permit triers of fact to derive information from them solely through an exercise of their own senses; for example, the bloody knife used to commit a murder.

c) "Writings" are "objects" that involve a communicative effort on the part of some person, thus sharing some of the features of testimony while retaining the features of "objects."

Completely Typeset, Easily Rea◄ Outline Format. Pages Perfora◄ and 3-Hole Punched.

2. The rules of relevance apply to all three types of evidence, but some of the other rules apply only to witnesses, some only to writings, a few only to objects, and some to two of the three categories.

B. Not all of the legal rules that control the admission and exclusion of evidence are rules of evidence.

1. Some are constitutional doctrines; for example, the Fifth Amendment privilege against self-incrimination, the Fourth Amendment rule excluding the products of an illegal search-and-seizure, the Sixth Amendment Confrontation and Compulsory Process Clauses.

CASENOTE LAW OUTLINES CONTRACTS

DANIEL WM. FESSLER
Professor of Law
University of California, Davis

► The total law summary utilizing the most comprehensive study approach in the most effective, easy-to-read format.
► Features quick indexing margin guide on back cover.
► Includes assorted practice exams, flow chart and glossary keyed to subject.

► WRITTEN BY NATIONALLY RECOGNIZED AUTHORITIES IN THEIR FIELD.

► FEATURING A FLEXIBLE, SUBJECT-ORIENTED APPROACH.

► CONTAINS: TABLE OF CONTENTS; CAPSULE OUTLINE; FULL OUTLINE; EXAM PREPARATION; GLOSSARY; TABLE OF CASES; TABLE OF AUTHORITIES; CASEBOOK CROSS-REFERENCE CHART; INDEX.

► THE TOTAL LAW SUMMARY UTILIZING THE MOST COMPREHENSIVE STUDY APPROACH IN THE MOST EFFECTIVE, EASY-TO-READ FORMAT.

look for the book with t◄ distinctive black

TABLE OF CASES

TABLE OF CASES

TABLE OF CASES

PIERSON v. POST

SUP. COURT OF NEW YORK, 1805. 3 Caines 175

NATURE OF CASE: Action of trespass on the case.

FACT SUMMARY: Post (P) was hunting a fox. Pierson (D), knowing this, killed the fox and carried it off.

CONCISE RULE OF LAW: Property in wild animals is only acquired by occupancy, and pursuit alone does not constitute occupancy or vest any right in the pursuer.

FACTS: Post (P) found a fox upon certain wild, uninhabited, unpossessed waste land. He and his dogs began hunting and pursuing the fox. Knowing that the fox was being hunted by Post (P) and within Post's (P) view, Pierson (D) killed the fox and carried it off.

ISSUE: Has a person in pursuit of a wild animal acquired such a right to or property in the wild animal as to sustain an action against a person who kills and carries away the animal, knowing of the former's pursuit?

HOLDING AND DECISION: No. Property in wild animals is acquired by occupancy only. Mere pursuit vests no right in the pursuer. One authority holds that actual bodily seizure is not always necessary to constitute possession of wild animals. The mortal wounding of an animal or the trapping or intercepting of animals so as to deprive them of their natural liberty will constitute occupancy. However, here, Post (P) only shows pursuit. Hence there was no occupancy or legal right vested in Post (P) and the fox became Pierson's (D) property when he killed and carried it off. The purpose of this rule is that if the pursuit of animals without wounding them or restricting their liberty were held to constitute a basis for an action against others for intercepting and killing the animals, "it would prove a fertile source of quarrels and litigation."

DISSENT: The dissent feels that a new rule should be adopted: that property in wild animals may be acquired without bodily touch, provided the pursuer be in reach or have a reasonable prospect of taking the animals.

EDITOR'S ANALYSIS: The ownership of wild animals is in the state for the benefit of all its people. A private person cannot acquire exclusive rights to a wild animal except by taking and reducing it to actual possession in a lawful manner or by a grant from the government. After the animal has been lawfully subjected to control, the ownership becomes absolute as long as the restraint lasts. Mere ownership of the land that an animal happens to be on does not constitute such a reduction of possession as to give the landowner a property right in the animal, except as against a mere trespasser who goes on such land for the purpose of taking the animal.

KEEBLE v. HICKERINGILL

11 EAST 576, Cas. T. Holt 19, 11 Mod. 130

NATURE OF CASE: Action to recover damages caused by trespass.

FACT SUMMARY: Keeble (P) had prepared a decoy pond on his land which attracted wild fowl. With the intention of depriving Keeble (P) of the fowl, Hickeringill (D) drove the fowl away by shooting his gun.

CONCISE RULE OF LAW: A violent or malicious act to a person's occupation, profession, or livelihood, gives rise to a cause of action.

FACTS: Keeble (P) alleged that he had a decoy pond on his land which he had equipped with decoy ducks and nets for the purpose of capturing the wild fowl attracted to the pond. He further alleged that Hickeringill (D), with the intent of depriving Keeble (P) of the yearly profit he made from the pond, drove the fowl away by discharging his gun.

ISSUE: Will a violent or malicious act to a person's occupation, profession, or livelihood give rise to a cause of action?

HOLDING AND DECISION: Yes. Where a violent or malicious act is done to a person's occupation, profession, or livelihood, an action will lie. In this case, the decoy was a benefit to Keeble (P). Hickeringill's (D) action interfered with Keeble's (P) exercising of his trade. There would not be an action if Hickeringill (D) had damaged Keeble (P) by setting up a decoy on his land near Keeble's (P), since he has as much right to make and use a decoy as Keeble (P). If a person sets up the same trade as another in the same town, there is damage, but it is sine injuria, for it is lawful for him to set up the same trade. Judgment for Keeble (P).

EDITOR'S ANALYSIS: The court decided that this action was not brought for property but for Hickeringill's (D) interference with Keeble's (P) occupation, and so based its decision on those grounds. In Andrews v. Andrews, 242 N.C. 382, 88 S.E. 2d 88 (1955), the plaintiff complained that the decoy pond, set up by the defendant on a lot adjoining plaintiff's farm, attracted wild geese, who used the pond as a base for attacking plaintiff's crops. The court held that an action would lie in nuisance. The dissent argued that the case should be dismissed, since the defendant did not have ownership in the geese, or even possession of them, to make him responsible for their actions.

NOTES:

GHEN v. RICH
DISTRICT COURT OF UNITED STATES,
D. Mass., 1881, 8 Fed. 159

NATURE OF CASE: Admiralty action to recover the value of a whale.

FACT SUMMARY: Rich (D) purchased a whale at auction from a man who found it washed up on the beach. The whale had been killed at sea by the crew of Ghen's (P) whaling ship which left Ghen's (P) identifying bomb-lance in the animal.

CONCISE RULE OF LAW: When all that is practicable in order to secure a wild animal is done, it becomes the property of the securer who has thus exercised sufficient personal control over the wild animal.

FACTS: Due to the problems involved in capturing whales for commercial use in nineteenth century New England, a trade usage arose as follows: when the crew of a whaling ship killed a whale using its identifying bomb-lance, the ship's owner by custom was considered to be the owner of that whale. When the whale washed ashore, the finder could identify the owner by the bomb-lance and would send notice of the find to the whaling center, Provincetown, Massachusetts. The finder would be paid a reasonable salvage fee. In this case, Ellis, the finder, did not notify Provincetown, but, rather, sold the whale at auction where Rich (D) purchased it. Rich (D) removed the blubber which he had processed into oil. Ghen (P) claimed to be the owner of the whale under the trade usage and sued Rich (D) for the value of the whale.

ISSUE: By the trade usage, was the whale placed under sufficient control by the capturing whaler so that it became his property?

HOLDING AND DECISION: Yes. Ghen (P) through the use of the identifying bomb-lance did all that was practicable in order to secure the whale. While local trade usages should not set aside maritime law, the custom can be enforced when it is embraced by an entire industry and has been concurred in for a long time by everyone engaged in the trade. This particular trade usage was necessary to the survival of the whaling industry for no one would engage in whaling if he could not be guaranteed the fruits of his labor.

EDITOR'S ANALYSIS: Under the common-law rule, for a wild animal to be reduced to a possession, it must be placed under the control of the one who makes capture. Here, two major considerations modified the application of the rule to the situation. First, all that was practicable to secure the whale was done. Second, the trade usage was industry-wide, necessary to the survival of the industry, and fair to all parties (including the whale's finder who received a reasonable salvage fee). Note, also, that the rule here was not being applied to a sport such as hunting or fishing, but, instead, to an industry. Economic interests were certainly important in the holding of this case.

YOUNG v. HICHENS
QUEEN'S BENCH, 1844.
1 Dav. & Mer. 592; 6 Q.B. 606

NATURE OF CASE: Action to recover damages for trespass.

FACT SUMMARY: Young (P) circled a school of fish with its net. Hichens (D) rowed its boat through an open space in the net and captured all of the fish.

CONCISE RULE OF LAW: In order to have possession or custody of a wild animal, a person must have actual power over the animal.

FACTS: Young's (P) boat let out its nets around a large school of fish. The net was in a semicircle around the school. There was an open space in the net which was between seven and ten fathoms. In this opening, Young's (P) fishermen were splashing and disturbing the water so that the fish would not escape. Hichens' (D) boat rowed through this space, let out its net, and captured all of the fish. Hichens (D) contends that Young (P) did not show possession of the fish and so cannot maintain an action in trespass.

ISSUE: Must a person have actual power over a wild animal in order to possess the animal?

HOLDING AND DECISION: Yes. There can be no custody or possession of a wild animal until a person has actual power over the animal. In this case it does appear that Young (P) would have had possession of the fish but for Hichens' (D) act. However, Young (P) did not have actual control over the fish and so cannot be said to possess them. The court says that Hichens (D) may have acted unjustifiably in preventing Young (P) from obtaining such power, but that would only show a wrongful act for which he might be liable in some other type of action. The other two judges concurred.

EDITOR'S ANALYSIS: This case demonstrates the rule that as long as wild animals are not reduced to possession, they are public property. Not even the owner of the soil over which a stream containing fish flows owns the fish in the stream. Also, as demonstrated here, the fact that a particular person is engaged in the business of taking fish, does not give him any property in the fish prior to taking.

NOTES:

HANNAH v. PEEL

KING'S BENCH DIVISION, 1945. (1945) 1 K.B. 509

NATURE OF CASE: Action to recover chattel (article of personal property).

FACT SUMMARY: Hannah (P), a soldier who found a diamond brooch in a house temporarily requisitioned by the British Army, sought to recover the brooch from the owner of the land, Peel (D), who claimed it even though he had not previously been aware of its existence nor knew the true owner.

CONCISE RULE OF LAW: The finder of a chattel, clearly lost, has rights to possession superior to everybody except the true owner; the place of finding is of no consequence.

FACTS: Peel (D) owned a house he had never occupied. Hannah (P), a soldier stationed in the house after the Army had requisitioned it, found a diamond brooch covered with cobwebs and dirt loose in a crevice on the top of a windowpane. Hannah (P) turned the brooch over to the police who, in turn, gave it to Peel (D). Peel (D) neither knew previously of the brooch's existence nor its true owner. The true onwer not having been found, Peel (D) sold the brooch. Even though Peel (D) offered Hannah (P) a reward for finding the brooch, Hannah (P) refused it, and sued Peel (D) for the return of the brooch or its value and damages for its retention.

ISSUE: Does the finder of a chattel have a superior right to possession over everybody except the true owner, even when the chattel is found on the land of a third person?

HOLDING AND DECISION: Yes. The court initially notes that, in surrendering up the brooch, Hannah (P) did not intend to waive his claim to the article, and suggests that if the discovery had never been communicated to the defendant, the real owner of the brooch could never have had a cause of action against the defendant simply because it was found in his home. Since Peel (D) never had custody over the brooch, he had come under no responsibility, as he would have been had the brooch been intentionally deposited in his home. The circumstances under which the brooch was found indicate it was lost in the ordinary sense of the word. Furthermore, Peel (D) could claim no prior possession. The court distinguishes earlier cases which held that a man possesses everything which is attached to or under his land by noting that the same principle does not embrace things lying unattached on the surface of a man's land even though no one else has possession.

EDITOR'S ANALYSIS: Following a traditional approach, Hannah (P) would probably not have prevailed had the brooch been classified as misplaced, treasure trove or abandoned. A chattel is misplaced if voluntarily placed by the owner and then neglected or forgotten. Under this category, the land owner is in a better position to return the article to its true owner than a finder who takes the article off the premises. However, in this case, it is unlikely that the true owner would have placed the brooch intentionally into the remote crevice from which it was recovered. Similarly, it is not likely the brooch was a remnant of some treasure trove which in English common law meant it was intentionally hidden or secreted and therefore reverts to the Crown. The brooch is a single item of jewelry found uncovered and unenclosed. In this country, the finder has a superior right to treasure trove even over the State. Once again, the spot in which the brooch was found suggests that it was not abandoned. A land owner who must suffer abandoned property should have possession of it if he chooses.

NOTES:

QUEEN v. ASHWELL

CROWN CASE RESERVED, 1885. 16 Q.B.D. 190

NATURE OF CASE: Appeal from conviction for larceny of a sovereign.

FACT SUMMARY: Ashwell (D) requested Keogh to lend him a shilling (12 pence), but Keogh unknowingly gave him a sovereign (240 pence) instead, yet although Ashwell (D) soon thereafter realized he had received the wrong coin, he refused to return it.

CONCISE RULE OF LAW: While a finder of a lost chattel commits larceny where he has taken and carried away the chattel, not believing that it has been abandoned, the recipient of transferred goods who at the time of receipt is mistaken as to their real value or nature lacks the requisite felonious intent.

FACTS: Ashwell (D), promising to quickly repay, requested Keogh to loan him a shilling (12 pence). Instead, Keogh gave Ashwell (D) a sovereign (240 pence) which neither man at the time realized to be the wrong coin. The following day, Keogh, after becoming aware of his error, informed Ashwell (D), and asked for return of the sovereign. At first, Ashwell denied having received the sovereign, yet later admitted he had, and would not return it since he had only asked to be loaned a shilling. The trial court found that Ashwell (D) did not know of the mistake at the time he received the coin, but soon discovered the real nature of his receipt. Since Ashwell (D) could have easily restored the coin to Keogh, but chose to appropriate it for his own use, and thereafter deny receiving a sovereign, the trial court found that Ashwell (D) had evidenced a bad mental state, and so convicted him of larceny.

ISSUE: Has a man committed larceny when he has received more money than he asked to be loaned and appropriated it for his own use, even though at the time of receiving the sum he is unaware of its real value, and only forms a fraudulent intent after the transfer has been completed?

HOLDING AND DECISION: No. In order for larceny to be proved, two requisite elements of the crime must be shown. First, there must be a taking and carrying away of the chattel against the will of the owner. The coin here was not taken against the will of Keogh (P) since he freely meant to deliver the coin to Ashwell (D) and, in fact, did so. The coin was never actually lost — Keogh (P) knew where it was at all times — so the law of finders has no real application here. Rather, what is involved is a mistake as to the coin's real value. While a finder of a lost chattel may be held guilty of larceny, the same cannot be said for those instances where the owner has not "lost" anything. Secondly, for larceny to be proved, at the time of taking, the taker must have a felonious intent in his mind. Here, Ashwell (D), at the time he received the coin, honestly thought he was getting only what he asked for — a shilling.

DISSENT: Since the law speaks of intelligent delivery, the taking of the coin by Ashwell (D) did not occur until he realized that he had received a sovereign instead of a shilling, and it was at the same identical moment that he decided to misappropriate it for his own use.

EDITOR'S ANALYSIS: Since this is a larceny case, involving a criminal conviction, the primary issue presented is when Ashwell (D) formed the intention to appropriate the shilling to his own use. Ordinarily, in situations involving the delivery of fungible (e.g., money bonds) as opposed to tangible goods, a bailment may result even if the same article is not to be returned. Even so, although Ashwell (D) may have become Keogh's (P) bailee, his liability goes only so far as the understanding he has with the bailor on the scope of duty in taking the goods. Ashwell (D), at the moment of taking, indicated he would only take possession of a shilling, and not a sovereign.

NOTES:

PEET v. THE ROTH HOTEL COMPANY

SUPREME COURT OF MINNESOTA, 1934.
191 Minn. 151, 253 N.W. 546

NATURE OF CASE: Action to recover value of lost ring.

FACT SUMMARY: Peet (P), desirous of having a jeweler repair a unique ring, left it with the cashier at the Hotel (D) the jeweler was staying in, but the cashier, not being aware of the ring's expense, carelessly left it lying about, whereupon it was either lost or stolen.

CONCISE RULE OF LAW: The delivery and acceptance of a chattel constitutes the receiver a bailee (one who receives goods to be held in trust for a limited time and a specific purpose) although he may not have appreciated or been aware of the chattel's true value. Hence, should the bailee lose the chattel, he is liable for its true value.

FACTS: Peet (P) wanted to have Hotz, a jeweler, repair a unique, expensive ring of hers. Peet (P) left the ring at the St. Paul Hotel, owned by the Roth Hotel Company (D), where Hotz was staying. Taking the ring off in the presence of the hotel's cashier, Peet (P) asked her to give it to Hotz. Peet (P) gave the ring to the cashier who then placed it in an envelope with Hotz' name written on it. The cashier placed the envelope with the ring in it on top of the front desk where it was either lost or stolen. Peet sued the Hotel (D) successfully for $2,500, the value of the ring, over the Hotel's (D) defense that there was no bailment because Peet (P) failed to disclose the unusual value of the ring.

ISSUE: Did the hotel become Peet's (P) bailee with respect to the ring and thus liable for the ring's true, undisclosed value?

HOLDING AND DECISION: Yes. A bailment, generally, is the rightful possession of goods by one who is not the owner with physical control of the goods and an intent to exercise that control. No bailment will exist where the goods are concealed from the alleged bailee; in this case, however, the Hotel knew it accepted a ring, the only question being as to its real value. The degree of care owed by a bailee is dependent upon whether there is benefit for both parties, or only for the bailor (one who delivers the goods into the trust of the bailee). If the former is the case, only slight care is owed; no liability is attached to the bailee for other than gross negligence. Here, the Hotel had accepted the ring in the ordinary course of its business and so, because of mutual benefit, its liability is formed following an ordinary standard of negligence. Following the law in its jurisdiction, the court holds that the burden of proof is on the Hotel to show that it was NOT negligent in losing the ring once it is established that the Hotel was acting as a bailee.

EDITOR'S ANALYSIS: The majority of courts differ from the opinion here by holding that the bailor has the burden of persuasion in proving the bailee negligent, and that the bailor's presumption of negligence disappears once the bailee presents some evidence to rebut this presumption.

COWEN v. PRESSPRICH

SUPREME COURT OF NEW YORK, APPELLATE TERM, 117 Misc. 663, 192 N.Y.S. 242, Reversed 202, App. Div. 796, 194 N.Y.S. 926

NATURE OF CASE: Action in conversion to recover value of lost bond.

FACT SUMMARY: Cowen's (P) messenger delivered bond to Pressprich's (D) office, but Pressprich's (D) employee, discovering that wrong bond had been delivered, mistakenly returned the bond to a boy, not the messenger, who then absconded with it.

CONCISE RULE OF LAW: It is the duty of the bailee to deliver the bailed article to the right person, and that delivery to the wrong person is not capable of being excused by any possible showing of care or good faith or innocence. No involuntary bailee (a person who receives goods placed under his control without his consent or knowledge) will be obligated to assume this duty unless he assumes dominion over the goods whereupon his duty to care for the goods becomes absolute.

FACTS: Cowen's (P) messenger delivered a bond to Pressprich's (D) office by dropping it through a door slot. An employee of Pressprich's (D), noticing that the bond was not the one ordered by Pressprich (D) opened the door and called out for the messenger. A boy appeared and the employee, not knowing Cowen's (P) messenger on sight, delivered the bond to him. This boy, who had no connection with Cowen (P), absconded with the bond. Cowen (P) successfully sued Pressprich (D) to recover the value of the bond.

ISSUE: Is an involuntary bailee absolutely liable for goods lost or damaged which were misdelivered to him but which he attempted to return?

HOLDING AND DECISION: Yes. The only distinction between a voluntary bailee (one who receives goods placed under his control with his consent and knowledge) and an involuntary bailee (one who receives goods placed under his control without his consent or knowledge) relates solely to the degree of care the bailee owes to the sender of the goods in returning or redelivering them to the right person. With respect to delivery, the duty is absolute. So long as the bailee neither attempts to assume control over the goods nor accepts them as his own, he is under no duty at all to care for the goods. Once, however, he takes dominion over them, his duty is absolute to see that they are delivered in the same condition to the right person. Pressprich's (D) employee could have telephoned Cowen (P) or sent the bond back via one of Pressprich's (D) own messengers.

DISSENT: No. Where a person has goods thrust upon him which he neither sought nor has any clear idea how to handle, he should have no affirmative duty to care for them. An absolute liability will arise only when a person in possession of another's property does some act inconsis̲ with the idea that he does not accept the posses̲ refuses to surrender the goods to the ba̲ wilfully destroys it, or uses it for hi̲ Pressprich's (D) employee very the misdelivery. By casting himself as an involuntary bailee, Pressprich's (D) employeed used means which, under the circumstances, were reasonable and proper to return the chattel. His duty is only one of simple care.

EDITOR'S ANALYSIS: The dissent in this case represents the position adopted by the great majority of courts. Virtually all courts are unanimous in maintaining that a misdelivery of goods by a bailee to an individual not approved or authorized by the bailor makes out a case for conversion — the degree of care exercised being immaterial. Most courts carve out an exception for the involuntary bailee who is held liable only for negligent action.

NOTES:

GILLESPIE v. DEW
SUP. CT. OF ALA., 1827, 1 Stew. 229

NATURE OF CASE: Action for trespass.

FACT SUMMARY: Dew (D) entered upon land that Gillespie (P) had title to but was not actually occupying, and cut and removed some trees.

CONCISE RULE OF LAW: A person who has title to real estate, although not actually in possession, may still maintain an action in trespass.

FACTS: Dew (D) entered upon Gillespie's (P) land where he cut down some trees and carried them off. At the trial, Gillespie proved that although he had title to the land when the trespass occurred, no one was actually in possession. The trial judge charged the jury that unless the evidence showed that the plaintiff was in actual possession of the land, by himself or through his agents, the jury must find for the defendant. Gillespie (P) objected to this charge.

ISSUE: Must a person having title to real estate be in actual possession of the land in order to maintain an action for trespass?

HOLDING: No. The trial judge's charge to the jury stated the common law rule. There was ample rationale for this rule in a country such as England where virtually all the land is occupied. However, the common law rule has little application in a developing country with a sparse population such as the United States in 1827. If an action could not be maintained, one would have the possibility of a wrong without a remedy.

EDITOR'S ANALYSIS: The court here really decided the case on the grounds of convenience. This is simply a convenient way to supply a remedy for the wrong. The court in part of the opinion states the rule in the form: Where there is no adverse possession, the title to land carries with it CONSTRUCTIVE possession, so as to sustain the action of trespass. The rule is stated thus because even an adverse possessor may bring an action for trespass. The situation is complicated where you have both an adverse possessor and a true owner. As between the two of them, who has the right to bring an action of trespass? The court did not discuss this point because there was no adverse possessor.

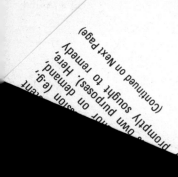

...ssion, ...not on demand, (e.g. ... own purposes). Here, ... prompty sought to remedy (Continued on Next page)

STATE v. SCHINGEN
SUP. CT. OF WIS., 1865. 20 Wis. 79

NATURE OF CASE: Criminal action for larceny.

FACT SUMMARY: While acting as an employee Schingen (D) took some merchandise that had been entrusted to him and converted it to his own use.

CONCISE RULE OF LAW: The crime of larceny may be committed when a servant (employee) converts goods which have been entrusted to him to his own use.

FACTS: Schingen (D) was an employee of Buhler. He had been instructed by Buhler to take a wagon and some horses and deliver some beer to Omro and Waukau, and to return the same day with the money by way of Eureka. Schingen (D) disposed of most of the beer in the first city he was supposed to visit. What beer he did not sell he simply threw away and drove off with the wagon and horses to a third city where he sold the harness and tried to sell the horses.

Schingen (D) wanted a jury charge that unless the goods were taken while in the actual possession of the owner, there could be no trespass and without a trespass there could be no larceny. Schingen (D) contends that since he had possession of the goods when he decided to abscond with them, there could be no trespass and therefore no larceny.

ISSUE: Must a person take goods from the actual possession of the owner for an action in trespass to lie?

HOLDING AND DEC ISION: No. Schingen (D) never had possession of the beer and wagon. Since he was a mere employee (servant), he had custody, not possession. Larceny is a crime against possession. Since possession lay in Buhler, Schingen (D) did commit the crime of larceny when he took the beer and wagon beyond the place he was supposed to go and converted them to his own use.

EDITOR'S ANALYSIS: This case expands the legal fiction of constructive possession further. The crux of the court's rationale is convenience. If the court agreed with the defendant they would create a situation of a wrong without a remedy.

This case also points out the distinction between custody and possession. A servant to whom goods are demurred by the master to be used in his business is held not to be a bailee of the goods, but only to have custody. The master is still said to be in "constructive possession."

Another way to look at this case is the distinction between larceny and embezzlement. A servant who takes goods from his master's business and fraudulently disposes of them is guilty of larceny. Even where the master delivers the goods into the actual physical custody of the servant, if the servant sells or otherwise disposes of them contrary to the master's interests, the offense is larceny, and not embezzlement.

The above can be somewhat simplified: "A servant (employee) has custody; the master (employer) has possession.

EWING v. BURNET
36 U.S. (1 Pet.) 41 (1837)

NATURE OF CASE: Appeal from denial of order of ejectment.

FACT SUMMARY: Ewing (P) contended that because his title to a lot was issued prior to the title issued to Burnet (D) from a common grantor, he had good title even though Burnet (D) had used and exercised open and notorious dominion and control over the property for over 21 years.

CONCISE RULE OF LAW: Title to land based on adverse possession may be obtained where the possessor performs acts of ownership for over 21 years without interruption, with the knowledge of an adverse claimant.

FACTS: Symmes conveyed title to a parcel of land to Forman in 1798. In 1803, he executed a deed to the same lot to Burnet (D). Forman conveyed his title to Williams, who knew of Burnet's (D) adverse claim, but did not act on it and did not exercise control of the land. For over 21 years, the statutory period for adverse possession in Ohio, Burnet (D) controlled the land, granting leases for the use of its gravel, using the gravel himself, and prosecuting trespassers. He did so openly and notoriously. Williams died in 1824, and Ewing (P) succeeded to the land. He brought suit in ejectment, and the jury found Burnet (D) had obtained title by adverse possession. Ewing (P) appealed.

ISSUE: Does the open and notorious exercise of ownership and control over land continuously for over 21 years permit a party to assert title by adverse possession?

HOLDING AND DECISION: (J. Baldwin) Yes. A party may obtain title to land by adverse possession if he execises open and notorious control over land for over 21 years, to such an extent as to evidence an assertion of ownership over that of a knowing adverse claimant. The determination whether the acts of open ownership were sufficient to establish adverse possession was a determination of fact. In this case, the use of the gravel, the granting of leases, and the prosecution of trespassers clearly support the jury's finding of sufficient ownership and control, and therefore such findings must be upheld on appeal. Affirmed.

EDITOR'S ANALYSIS: The time period included in adverse possession statutes, usually 20 years, is a special type of statute of limitations. It requires a landowner to bring suit to remove an encroaching party within the time period or forfeit the cause of action, and with it, the title to the land. The reason for allowing a party to obtain title by adverse possession is to induce the full use of land. An owner who allows his land to lie dormant for extended periods is not aiding society by exploiting his land. To induce full use of lands, society threatens the owner with loss of title to a party who will use the land productively.

BRUMAGIM v. BRADSHAW

SUP. CT. OF CAL., 1870. 39 Cal. 24

NATURE OF CASE: Action of ejectment.

FACT SUMMARY: Brumagim (P) alleged that his administratrix had been in possession of a tract of land for many years which was bounded on three sides by natural boundaries and on the fourth by a wall and which he had used for pasturing. He alleged that Bradshaw (D) had entered and remained upon the property.

CONCISE RULE OF LAW: In cases where the enclosures consist wholly or partially of natural barriers, it is for the jury to decide whether or not the acts of dominion relied upon, considering the size of the tract, its peculiar condition, and appropriate use, were of such a character as usually accompany the ownership of lands similarly situated, so as to give notice to the public of appropriation and possession.

FACTS: A certain tract of land called the Potrero is a peninsula containing about 1,000 acres. It is bounded on three sides by bays and creeks and on the fourth side by a wall. In 1850, the owner of the Potrero, Treat, repaired the wall so that it was adequate to enclose cattle, and began to use the land for pasturage. Treat continued to so use the land until 1852, when he conveyed to Dyson, by deed, all his interest in the property. Dyson used the land for pasturage until the time that Bradshaw (D) entered. Dyson died after this action was brought, and Brumagim (P), his administrator, was substituted as plaintiff. The court takes judicial notice that the Potrero in the year 1850 was separated from the City of San Francisco only by Mission Creek and Bay, and that it is now a portion of the city, divided into lots, blocks and streets. The court instructed the jury that if they were satisfied that Treat entered upon the enclosed Potrero in 1850, and that he made a complete enclosure sufficient to protect stock and that he used such enclosure for that purpose up to the time of the conveyance to Dyson, and that he deeded the same to Dyson, and that Dyson used the land for pasturage, and that the land was suitable for pasturage, and that Bradshaw (D) entered adversely and subsequent to the completion of said enclosure and while the land was being so used, they would find for Brumagim (P) against Bradshaw (D) pr~~ovi~~ded Bradshaw (D) occupied the premises at the c~~ommenc~~ement of this suit.

ISSUE: In c~~ases where e~~nclosures consisting of natural boundaries~~ is it for the jury~~ to decide, considering the quantity~~, quality and character of~~ the land, whether or not the a~~cts of dominion were of suc~~h character as usually acc~~ompany the ownership of lands sim~~ilarly situated so as t~~o give notice to the public~~

~~HELD: Yes. The rule in regard to acts~~ of ownership ~~which are relied upon as sufficien~~t to consti~~tute possession vary with the c~~ondition, ~~locality and use of the land. The general~~ prin-

ciple is that the acts of dominion must be adapted to the particular land, its condition, locality and appropriate use. The basis of this principle is that by such acts the party proclaims to the public that he asserts an exclusive ownership over the land. However, in cases involving natural barriers, this rule must be varied according to the circumstances of each particular case. In such cases the acts of dominion which establish possession must correspond, in a reasonable degree, with the size of the tract, its condition and appropriate use, and must be such as usually accompany the ownership of land similarly situated. In such cases it is the province of the jury to decide whether or not the acts of dominion relied upon, considering the size of the tract, its peculiar condition and appropriate use, were of such a character as usually accompany the ownership of similar lands. In this case the court should have instructed the jury that if all the facts hypothetically stated in the instruction were true, it was for the jury to decide, considering the quantity, quality and character of the land, whether or not these acts of dominion were sufficient to give notice to the public that Treat, first, and Dyson, as his successor in interest, had appropriated the land and claimed the exclusive dominion over it. The judgment for Brumagim (P) is reversed, for these reasons, and a new trial is ordered.

EDITOR'S ANALYSIS: It is not essential to the acquisition of title to land by adverse possession that it be enclosed, or fenced, in the absence of statutory requirement. However, enclosure is evidence of possession, and, either by itself or in connection with other acts of ownership, may be sufficient basis for a claim of adverse possession. Where enclosure is essential or is relied upon as the evidence of possession it must be complete and so open as to give notice of ownership. The enclosure should also be appropriate to fit the premises to the purposes to which they are adapted or to be used. It has been held in some jurisdictions that title cannot be acquired merely by fencing land without grazing it or farming it or putting it to other use.

NOTES:

MENDONCA v. CITIES SERVICE OIL COMPANY OF PENNSYLVANIA

SUP. JUDICIAL COURT OF MASSACHUSETTS, 1968.
Mass. 237 N.E. 2d 16

NATURE OF CASE: Bill in equity brought to obtain an injunction and to recover damages for trespass.

FACT SUMMARY: Mendonca (P) claims to have acquired a strip of Cities Service Oil Co.'s (D) land by adverse possession.

CONCISE RULE OF LAW: The one asserting title through adverse possession must prove such title and must show that his possession was actual, open, continuous, and under a claim of right or title.

FACTS: Mendonca (P) and Cities Service Oil Co. (D) own adjoining lots. Record title to a parcel of land including the disputed 24-foot strip bordering Cities' lot has been in Cities Service Oil Co. (D) since 1936, and taxes on the whole parcel have been assessed to and paid by Cities Service Oil Co. (D) since 1936. In 1951, Cities Service Oil Co. (D) rebuilt the gas station on its property. During this renovation work the contractor used the disputed area for storage for a period of three or four weeks. As part of the work the contractor tore down a fence which Cities (D) had erected parallel to the 24-foot disputed strip. He also tore down a fence that Mendonca (P) had built on the strip. A new fence was erected across the lot parallel to and about 24 feet from the boundary line between the parcels. Since 1936, Mendonca (P) and some of their predecessors made use of the strip for various purposes without protest or objection by Cities (D).

ISSUE: Can a claim for adverse possession be defeated by showing that the person who had record title to the claimed property used it for three weeks during the twenty years required for adverse possession?

HOLDING AND DECISION: Yes. The one asserting title through adverse possession must prove such title and included in the burden of proof is the obligation of showing that his possession was actual, open, continuous, and under a claim of right or title. If any of these elements is left in doubt, the claimant cannot previal. In this case, Mendonca (P) cannot prevail because Cities (D) use of the strip in 1951, broke the requisite element of continuity of possession. Any adverse use subsequent to 1936 was interrupted before twenty years had lapsed, and adverse use since 1951 falls short of the required twenty years. The removal of fences and use of the strip in 1951 were acts of dominion by Cities (D) consistent with its title of record.

EDITOR'S ANALYSIS: It has been said that if there is one element more distinctly material than another in conferring title by adverse possession, it is the existence of a continuous adverse possession. It is held that there must be such continuity of possession as will furnish a cause of action for every day during the whole period required to perfect title by adverse possession. The moment the possession is broken, it ceases to be effectual.

ARMORY v. DELAMIRIE

KING'S BENCH, 1722, 1 Strange 505

NATURE OF CASE: Action in trover to recover the value of personal property.

FACT SUMMARY: Armory (P) found a jewel which he took to Delamirie (D), a goldsmith, for appraisal, but Delamirie's (D) apprentice removed the stones which Delamirie (D) refused to return.

CONCISE RULE OF LAW: A finder of chattel has title superior to all but the rightful owner upon which he may maintain an action at law or in equity.

FACTS: Armory (P), a chimney sweeper's boy, found a jewel which he took to Delamirie's (D) goldsmith shop to learn what it was. Delamirie's (D) apprentice, under the pretense of weighing the jewel, removed the stones from the setting and told his master the value. Delamirie (D) offered Armory (P) three halfpence for the stones, but he refused. Delamirie (D) returned the setting without the stones.

ISSUE: Could Armory (P), who lacked legal title to the chattel, maintain an action to recover its value?

HOLDING AND DECISION: Yes. The finder of lost property, although he does not acquire absolute ownership, does acquire title superior to everyone else except the rightful owner. Such title is a sufficient property interest in the finder upon which he may maintain an action against anyone (except the rightful owner) who violates that interest. Additionally, Delamirie (D) was liable as he was responsible for the actions of his apprentice. As for the measure of damages, if Delamirie (D) did not show the stones were not of the finest value, their value would be so determined.

EDITOR'S ANALYSIS: As to ownership, the finder is in a position similar to that of a bailee. The finder does not obtain absolute ownership, but does have the right of ownership against everybody except the true owner. Here, the chattel, the jewel, was subsequently converted against the finder. Yet the finder, if he should subsequently lose the chattel, may reclaim it from a subsequent finder. The finder has a choice of remedies. He may recover the chattel in specie if it is still in the converter's possession, or he may recover full value from the wrongdoer. Notice that an action in trover, which is an action at law, is to recover the value of the chattel. If it is desired to have the item returned, an action in replevin must be brought in equity.

NOTES:

THE WINKFIELD

COURT OF APPEALS, 1901 (1902), P. 42

NATURE OF CASE: Action by bailee for damages for destruction of bailed property.

FACT SUMMARY: After the Winkfield collided with and sank the Mexican and its owners admitted liability for half the loss of the Mexican, the Postmaster-General, amongst others, fired claims for damages. The Postmaster sued for the loss of mail bags and parcels, for parcels whose owners had authorized the Postmaster to represent them, and for the value of letters and parcels whose owners did not make claim, but were lost in the accident.

CONCISE RULE OF LAW: As the possessor of property has absolute title to that property against all except the rightful owner, the possessor may maintain an action against anyone who violates that title (except for the rightful owner).

FACTS: The owners of the Winkfield, which collided with and sank the Mexican off the coast of South Africa, admitted liability for half the loss to the Mexican and paid into court 32,514 pounds. The Postmaster-General filed claim for the loss of a substantial amount of mail aboard the mexican as follows: (1) 105 pounds for mail bags and parcels which were property of the crown; (2) 5,041 pounds for parcels whose owners authorized the Postmaster to represent them; and (3) 1,726 pounds estimated value of letters and parcels whose owners had not filed claim nor instructed the Postmaster, but who undertook to distribute this claim amongst them. While recovery was had on the first two claims, recovery was disallowed on a third ground as the Postmaster-General concededly was not liable to the senders or addressees for their loss.

ISSUE: Where a bailee brings an action against a wrongdoer who violated the title to bailed property held by the bailee, can the bailee recover the loss against the wrongdoer although he has no liability to the bailor?

HOLDING AND DECISION: Yes. A person possessed of goods as his property has absolute title against all but the rightful owner. One who violates that title, having no title in himself, is a wrongdoer and cannot defend himself by showing that title was in a third person, "For against a wrongdoer, possession is title." The right of the possessor to recover full damages cannot be made to depend upon the extent of his liability to the true owner as that question of liability is not relevant as between the possessor and wrongdoer. Between a bailee and a stranger, possession gives title, an absolute and completed ownership, and a right to receive the complete equivalent for his loss. Once full damages have been paid to the bailee, the wrongdoer has answered any claim by the bailor.

EDITOR'S ANALYSIS: In Armory v. Delamirie, 1 Strange 505 (1722), it was established that the possessor of property has absolute title against all except the rightful owner, and that the possessor can maintain an action against anyone who violates his rights of possession. Early cases had established the right of a bailee to sue a wrongdoer on the basis of the bailee's liability to the bailor for the loss of the bailment. In this case, the bailee had no liability to his bailors. In fact, the bailors could not necessarily be established. Even so, as the bailee had the right to possession, he had all the rights inherent in possession against all except the rightful owner(s). Thus, it became irrelevant to the wrongdoer's argument that the bailee was not liable to his bailor. The issue was defendant's wrongful action alone. No argument could be interposed which was irrelevant to that issue. In those cases where the bailee is liable to his bailor, the bailee's recovery against the wrongdoer terminates the wrongdoer's liability. The bailor must seek his recovery against the bailee.

NOTES:

ZIMMERMAN v. SHREEVE

CT. OF APPEALS OF MARYLAND, 1882. 59 Md. 357

NATURE OF CASE: Action of quare clausum fregit (recovery of damages for unlawful entry upon another's land).

FACTUAL SUMMARY: Zimmerman (D) unlawfully cut and removed timber on land claimed by Shreeve (P) as life tenant under his mother's will.

CONCISE RULE OF LAW: A life tenant of land may recover damages against a third party who unlawfully trespasses on his land only to the extent of his interest.

FACTS: Mary E. Shreeve devised an outlying, unenclosed mountain lot in her will to her children as life tenants. Upon the death of any child, his share would go to his children in fee simple. Shreeve, a son (P), purchased from his brothers and sisters their interest in the land so that upon his own death, only his children would stand to gain a complete interest in the land in fee simple. Zimmerman (D) unlawfully cut and removed timber from the mountain lot. Shreeve (P) sued Zimmerman (D) and, at trial, the court instructed the jury that Shreeve (P) could recover the full amount of Zimmerman's (D) damage to the lot. When the jury rendered judgment for Shreeve (P) for the full amount of damage, Zimmerman (D) appealed the court's instructions.

ISSUE: Is a life tenant entitled to recover only to the extent his interest in land which has incurred damage by a third party?

HOLDING AND DECISION: Yes. A life tenant may recover no greater damages to land in which he maintains an interest than to that share of the estate he has a claim to. If this was otherwise, a life tenant whose interest was about to expire (e.g., he is near death) might get extravagant damages. If all persons who had an interest in the land could recover complete damages against the tort feasor, this would be unfair for the tort feasor would have to pay out for a single act in multiple suits against him. A tenant for life, in fee, or in tail, may sue and recover only insofar as his individual right to possession and enjoyment is concerned. The life tenant may cut only such timber, himself, from the land while he is actually on it; he cannot destroy or dispose of the timber nor cause any permanent injury. Because of the land's remoteness involved here, the land's only real value is its timber, and Shreeve (P) certainly is entitled to some recovery.

EDITOR'S ANALYSIS: Where the life tenant has, in some way, obligated to protect, preserve, or maintain the property against a third party, courts will permit him a recovery greater than his actual estate in the land. Persons who stand to gain an interest in the land at some future point in time may also sue a tort feasor but only if the tort feasor has caused the existence of a permanent condition or injury to remain on the land.

ROGERS v. ATLANTIC, GULF & PACIFIC CO.

COURT OF APPEALS OF NEW YORK, 1915. 213 N. Y. 246, 107 N. E. 661

NATURE OF CASE: Action in tort for damages.

FACT SUMMARY: Rogers (P), a life tenant, was awarded a judgment for all the damage to his land which resulted from the fire negligence of Atlantic, Gulf & Pacific Co. (D).

CONCISE RULE OF LAW: A life tenant is entitled to recover for all of the damages inflicted on his land by a third party.

FACTS: Rogers (P), a life tenant, recovered a judgment for all of the damage, both to his life estate and to the interest of those who stood to inherit the entire estate, caused by a fire set by Atlantic, Gulf & Pacific Co. (D), a canal contractor, on adjoining lands, and negligently allowed to spread to Rogers' (P) land.

ISSUE: May a life tenant recover all of the damages neligently inflicted on his land by a third party?

HOLDING AND DECISION: Yes. A life tenant's recovery is not limited to the extent of his own limitedinterest. The usual reason advanced for this rule is that the life tenant is liable to the remaindermen (those who stand to possess the estate upon his death) for any injury to their inheritance not caused by them, the act of God or the public enemy. If this were the rule, Rogers' (P) liability must be based on some notion of permissive waste (permitting the fire to spread). However, the court rejects this rationale. A life tenant is not liable to his remainderman for injuries done to his land by a negligent third party. In New York, nonetheless, the life tenant can sue on his own without asserting the rights of any remainderman. The wrongdoer cannot be allowed to assert the rights of third parties under whom he does not claim to limit his liability. Since the court can fashion an appropriate remedy to protect the interests of remaindermen, the only legitimate concern of the wrongdoer is in being protected from multiple suits for the same act. As a result, since the life tenant may recover all the damages, such a recovery will bar an action by the remaindermen against the wrongdoer.

EDITOR'S ANALYSIS: See Zimmerman v. Shreeve for a jurisdiction which arrived at the opposite result. Also, in disagreement with the New York court's result is Restatement of Property Section 118, which states: "The measure of the damages recoverable by the owner of the estate for life is the difference between the value of the estate for life before and its value after the violation."

NOTES:

TAPSCOTT v. COBBS
COURT OF APPEALS OF VIRGINIA, 1854.
82 Va. 172, 11 Grat. 172

NATURE OF CASE: Action of ejectment to regain possession of real property.

FACT SUMMARY: Lewis, who never had title to the land of which she was in possession until her death, bequeathed that land to Cobbs (P). Without any pretense of title, Tapscott (D) took possession of the land. Cobbs (P) sued to eject Tapscott (D).

CONCISE RULE OF LAW: One in possession of land has title superior to all others except the actual, rightful titleholder.

FACTS: Anderson, the original owner of the land in question, devised it to his executors to sell after his death. The executors contracted to sell to Mrs. Lewis in about 1820, but it appeared that she never paid the purchase price or received a deed to the land. Despite this, Mrs. Lewis entered the land, took possession, built upon it, and remained in possession until her death in 1835. Mrs. Cobbs (P), Mrs. Lewis' lessor and heir, brought this action to eject Tapscott (D) who entered and took possession of the land without pretense of title.

ISSUE: Can one in mere possession of land without title maintain an action against another also without title who attempts to take possession away?

HOLDING AND DECISION: Yes. Cobbs (P), as prior possessor, had the right to possession "against all except him who has the actual right to the possession." The defendant, who without title or authority to enter and who attempts to oust the prior possessor, cannot defend his action on the ground that title is outstanding in another. Instead, to successfully defend, Tapscott (D) had to show he had either title or authority to enter under the title. Being herir to Lewis' possessory interest, Cobbs (P) was presumed to be in rightful possession at the time she was ousted by Tapscott (D) even though there was no evidence of Lewis (P) being in possession.

EDITOR'S ANALYSIS: The court states that the general rule is that the right of the plaintiff in ejectment "rests on the strength of his own title," and that the defendant may defend by simply showing that title is not in the plaintiff, but in another. But this case is an exception. After reviewing the English and American cases, prior possession was found to be good against the whole world except the rightful owner. In ejectment, the question is the right to possession and prior peaceful possession is a protected interest. Mrs. Cobbs (P) was in adverse possession of the land. In most jurisdictions, one who is in uninterrupted adverse possession, usually for a period of twenty years, acquires title to the land. While the time of possession was not clear here, the issue was not argued.

NOTES:

WINCHESTER v. CITY OF STEVENS POINT
SUP. CT. OF WIS., 1883. 58 Wis. 350, 17 N.W. 3

NATURE OF CASE: Action to recover damages for injury to real property.

FACT SUMMARY: Winchester (P) alleged that she was the owner and in possession of certain property which she claims was damaged by a dike built by City of Stevens Point (D). Winchester (P) was not able to prove a complete chain of title.

CONCISE RULE OF LAW: Where a party seeks to recover as owner of land, for an injury to the land, he must prove his title, and such title, will not be presumed from evidence under claim of title.

FACTS: Winchester (P) alleged that she owned certain property which she had been in possession of for more than one year before the commencement of this lawsuit. She claims that City of Stevens Point (D) built a dike so as to seriously impair her ingress and egress and cause water to back up on her land. Winchester (P) attempted to trace her title from an original U. S. patent to herself. Two of the deeds in this chain of title were not entitled to be recorded because they were attested by only one witness. City of Stevens Point (D) objected to their being admitted into evidence, and one of them was excluded. Hence, Winchester (P) was not able to prove a complete chain of title.

ISSUE: Must a party in possession of certain property prove his title to the property in order to recover for an injury to the property?

HOLDING AND DECISION: Yes. If a party who seeks to recover for an injury to certain property is not the owner of the property, he should not recover for injury to the property. In this case, Winchester (P) did not seek recovery for injury to her possession. She sought to recover for injury to the property itself. Hence, she had to prove ownership. Since two of the deeds were not entitled to be recorded, she could not prove her title. There are authorities which hold that a plaintiff's seizin is proved prima facie by evidence of actual possession under claim of title. However, Winchester (P) offered evidence which overcame the presumption arising from the fact of her possession. The court states that the case is much like condemnation proceedings and should be governed by the same rule. The plaintiff must show title, and title will not be presumed from evidence of possession under claim of title.

DISSENT: The dissenting judge believes that a mere trespasser, having no title and not claiming under a third person having a title, who intrudes upon the actual peaceable possession of one claiming title, cannot defend by questioning the possessor's title. However, he agrees that the lower court's judgment in Winchester's (P) favor should be reversed, because she was permitted to recover damages to which she was not entitled, if she had established a perfect title. He feels that City of Stevens

Point's (D) acts constitute a continuing trespass or a nuisance, and the rule in such actions is that the plaintiff may not recover damages he may sustain in the future but only such damages as he has already sustained.

EDITOR'S ANALYSIS: As this case demonstrates, generally, one asserting title has the burden of establishing it. Under the common law, a rebuttable presumption of ownership arises from possession of real property. However, if the custody and possession of property are shown to be equally consistent with an outstanding ownership in a third person, no presumption of ownership arises solely from possession. Also, a presumption of ownership from possession is not allowable against ascertained and established facts to the contrary.

NOTES:

LASALLE COUNTY CARBON COAL CO. v. SANITARY DISTRICT OF CHICAGO

SUP. COURT OF ILLINOIS, 1913.
260 Ill. 423, 103 N.E. 175

NATURE OF CASE: Action for damages for permanent damage to real property.

FACT SUMMARY: LaSalle (P) was in adverse possession of farmland which was permanently damaged by sewage which overflowed from Sanitary's (D) sewage channel.

CONCISE RULE OF LAW: A cause of action for permanent damage to land does not accrue to one who has a mere possessory interest in the land at the time the cause arises even if he acquires valid title afterwards.

FACTS: To end the dumping of sewage into Lake Michigan, Sanitary (D) began a project which reversed the flow of the Chicago River. This resulted in city sewage flowing into several other rivers. An Illinois statute placed liability on Sanitary (D) for damage caused by sewage overflows. In 1900, a sewage overflow occurred permanently damaging LaSalle's (P) land. At the time the damage occurred, LaSalle (P) was in adverse possession of the land for 15 years. In 1905, LaSalle's (P) adverse possession ripened into absolute title under Illinois' 20-year adverse possession statute. Having title, LaSalle (P) brought suit for damages and had judgment against Sanitary (D).

ISSUE: Can one recover for damage to land which was in his adverse possession at the time the cause of action arose?

HOLDING AND DECISION: No. The right to recover for damage to real property accrues to the titleholder of that property at the time the cause of action arises. At the time the cause of action arose, LaSalle (P) was merely in adverse possession. The one who suffered the damage, the titleholder, is the only one who could maintain an action against the wrongdoer. That LaSalle (P) acquired title after the cause of action arose, even though it was in possession at the time the action arose, placed it in no different postion than if it had not been in possession but acquired title by conveyance after the action accrued. If a titleholder to land suffers damage to his land at the fault of another, his cause of action does not pass to his grantee should he transfer the land. A grantee takes the land as he finds it. It is presumed the price paid takes into account the depreciation in the land's value.

EDITOR'S ANALYSIS: Only the titleholder to land can sue on a cause of action which accrues to the land. A mere possessory interest is insufficient. Even though LaSalle (P) was on the land and had possession of it for 15 years, it did not have title when the damage was done. LaSalle's (P) subsequent acquisition of title five years later under the adverse possession statute still did not transfer the cause of action. Notice that LaSalle (P) apparently believed the action accrued to it upon its acquisition of title as it was not until then that suit was brought.

ILLINOIS & ST. LOUIS R.R. & COAL CO. v. COBB

SUP. CT. OF ILL., 1879. 94 Ill. 55

NATURE OF CASE: Action to recover damages for trespass.

FACT SUMMARY: Cobb (P) took possession of an island which formed in a river. Subsequently, accretion caused the island to join with the mainland. Illinois & St. Louis R.R. & Coal Co. (D) tore down the fence Cobb (P) had erected and laid a track down across the land.

CONCISE RULE OF LAW: A person in possession of property can recover damages for injury to the property, as well as to the possession, from a trespasser, even though title to the property is in a third person.

FACTS: Cobb (P) took possession of an island formed by accretion in the Mississippi River. He built a house on it. According to the state law, the island belonged to the owners of the shore who did not make any claim. The island grew and joined with the mainland at its two ends. Cobb (P), claiming ownership of the island, leased it to a tenant. Later he fenced part of it for pasturage. Illinois & St. Louis R.R. & Coal Co. (D) tore down the fence, laid a track and switch across the land and began to remove soil from it. Cobb (P) brought an action against Illinois (D) and recovered damages for trespass. Illinois (D) tore down his fence two more times. Cobb (P) brought this action. Illinois (D) gave evidence tending to prove an outstanding title to the property in the village of Cahokia.

ISSUE: Can a person in possession of property recover damages for injury to the property, as well as to the possession, from a trespasser, even though title to the property is in a third person?

HOLDING AND DECISION: Yes. A trespasser cannot avoid paying damages for all beyond the injury to the possession by proving a defect in the possessor's title. To hold that the trespasser could mitigate the damages by proving title in a third person would be a harsh and unjust rule. A possessor's title might be clearly equitable, unclaimed and unchallenged by the person holding legal title and yet, if such a rule should prevail, the equitable owner and occupant might have his property destroyed and only recover nominal damages. In this case, the fact that evidence was introduced tending to show title in one other than Cobb (P) does not affect the amount of damages Cobb (P) can recover. He, as possessor, is entitled to recovery for damages caused by Illinois (D) to both the property and his possession.

EDITOR'S ANALYSIS: The opposing rule to the one demonstrated by this case is that the possession of land with title in a third person does not authorize a recovery for injury to the freehold. Further possession and equitable title do not authorize recovery for injury to the freehold. Nor does possession of land under a contract for purchase authorize such recovery under that rule. The recovery is limited by the extent of plaintiff's right. Hence, a tenant can recover only damages to his estate whether he is a life tenant or a tenant for years and a co-owner cannot recover damages for the others.

IRONS v. SMALLPIECE

CT. OF KING'S BENCH, 1819, 106 English Reports 467

NATURE OF CASE: Action in trover for claim to personal property.

FACT SUMMARY: Irons (P) claimed that his father had promised to give him two colts which had passed to Smallpiece (D), the father's executrix, upon father's death 12 months after his making the promise of gift. Father never gave Irons (P) physical possession of the colts.

CONCISE RULE OF LAW: In order to transfer property by gift, there must be either a deed or instrument of gift or an actual delivery of the thing to the donee.

FACTS: One year before his death, Irons' (P) father promised to give to Irons (P) two colts. Father kept physical possession of the colts up until his death. As the colts remained in father's possession at the time of his death, they passed to Smallpiece (D), father's executrix and residuary legatee. Smallpiece (D) refused to turn over the colts to Irons (P).

ISSUE: Did father's failure to give up physical possession of the items of the gift defeat the gift?

HOLDING AND DECISION: Yes. In order to transfer property by gift, there must be either a deed or instrument of gift, or an actual delivery of the thing to the donee. There must be an actual change of possession or physical evidence of a change of possession.

EDITOR'S ANALYSIS: A verbal gift is not completed until the donor gives and the donee accepts delivery. The donee, after the act, has prima facie evidence in favor of the gift. Physical delivery makes significant to the donor his act of gift. Physical delivery is an unequivocal act to the witnesses of it. Other forms of gift or grant of a chattel are by deed and by sales contract where the parties intend for the property to pass before delivery.

NOTES:

NEWELL v. NATIONAL BANK OF NORWICH

SUP. CT. OF N.Y., APLT. DIV., 1925, 212 N.Y.S. 158

NATURE OF CASE: Action to reclaim a gift of personal property.

FACT SUMMARY: Upon what appeared to be his deathbed, Reynolds, Bank's (D) testator, gave Newell (P), his closest friend, a diamond ring. As Reynolds recovered, Newell (P) returned the ring, but Reynolds insisted it was Newell's (P) and consented to wear it again only if it was understood the ring was Newell's (P). Upon Reynolds' death, the Bank (D), executor of Reynolds' estate, refused to recognize the gift.

CONCISE RULE OF LAW: A gift inter vivos may be made in apprehension of death as long as the donor intends that the gift shall remain the donee's no matter whether he lives or dies.

FACTS: Reynolds, Bank's (D) testator, on what appeared to be his deathbed, gave Newell (P), his closest and most intimate friend, a diamond ring. Reynolds recovered and lived another four years. After his recovery, Newell (P) insisted that Reynolds take back the ring, but he refused and would only agree to again wear the ring if it was understood that the ring remained Newell's (P), and that it would be returned to Newell (P) upon Reynolds' death. Reynolds remained in possession of the ring until his death. Reynolds' executor, Bank (D) refused to return the ring to Newell (P).

ISSUE: Can a gift inter vivos be made upon one's deathbed?

HOLDING AND DECISION: Yes. The circumstances surrounding the gift indicate that Reynolds, during his illness, gave the gift of the ring to Newell (P) irrespective of whether he lived or died, although, at the time, Reynolds was in apprehension of death. Whether a gift is made inter vivos or causa mortis is not the fact alone that the donor expects to die, but whether the donor intended the gift to take effect presently, irrevocably, and unconditionally, whether he lives or dies. Reynolds' refusal to accept the ring after his recovery reflected his mental attitude at the time of his illness when he delivered the ring to Newell (P), although insufficient in itself to constitute a gift as Reynolds retained possession of the gift. If Reynolds' purpose was to give Newell (P) the ring no matter whether he lived or died, then absolute title vested in Newell (P). Reynolds' subsequent use and possession was merely as bailee.

EDITOR'S ANALYSIS: A gift inter vivos is made when the donor intends upon his giving physical possession of the gift to the donee for the donee to have present, irrevocable, and unconditional ownership whether the donor lives or dies. A gift causa mortis is made in fear or present apprehension of death. The donor intends that the donee shall retain the gift only if the donor dies. Should the donor not die, the gift is ineffective, and the item of gift is returned to the donor. Accordingly, it can be understood that even though the donor may be in present apprehension of death, he can still intend for the donee to retain the gift permanently.

GRYMES v. HONE

COURT OF APPEALS OF NEW YORK, 1872, 49 N.Y. 17

NATURE OF CASE: Action to establish validity of a gift causa mortis.

FACT SUMMARY: The donor, before his death, rather than physically handing over the gift to the donee, gave it to his wife to hold for the donee until his death.

CONCISE RULE OF LAW: For a valid gift causa mortis, it must be made with a view to the donor's death; the donor must die of his present ailment or peril; and there must be delivery of the object of gift.

FACTS: The decedent by a signed and witnessed writing gave twenty shares of stock of the Bank of Commerce of New York to his favorite granddaughter, Grymes (P). He kept the paper but later gave it to his wife to hold with his will until his death as he was unsure of what might happen to himself and whether he would need the shares. Decedent, at the time of gift, was in a state of "failing health" and so remained until his death five months later. Grymes (P) sued to effect a transfer of the shares to her name as a valid gift causa mortis.

ISSUE: Was there an effective delivery of the object of gift to Grymes (P)?

HOLDING AND DECISION: Yes. Three things are required to make a valid gift causa mortis. The donor must make the gift in view of his impending death. The donor must die of the ailment or peril under which he made the gift. There must be a delivery. Here, the donor, knowing he was in failing health, made the gift and ultimately died from his general state of failing health. While delivery of the writing was not made directly to Grymes (P), the donee, it was sufficient that the donor parted with the writing to his wife, who held the writing as agent for the donee. Thus, a sufficient delivery to make an effective gift causa mortis occurred.

EDITOR'S ANALYSIS: Generally, the three conditions stated above are agreed upon as being all that are necessary to effect a valid gift causa mortis. The donor does not have to be suffering from an illness. Rather, he could be facing peril of death (e.g., in combat during wartime). There is no time limit as to when the donor must die as long as it is from the peril or ailment suffered. Here, death did not occur for five months. Delivery is sufficient as long as donor physically parts with the gift. Delivery can thus be to a third person for the benefit of the donee.

NOTES:

MEYERS v. MEYERS

COURT OF CHANCERY OF NEW JERSEY (1926), 134 A. 95

NATURE OF CASE: Action attacking the validity of a gift causa mortis.

FACT SUMMARY: The decedent signed and acknowledged a deed assigning to his 15-year-old son (D) his interest in a bond and mortgage prior to undergoing surgery and left that deed with his attorney with instructions to record it in case of his death.

CONCISE RULE OF LAW: The delivery of a deed to the object or subject of the gift is equivalent to physical delivery of the gift.

FACTS: The decedent was about to undergo surgery. He instructed his attorney to draw up a deed to the decedent's two-thirds interest in a mortgage and bond. The decedent signed and acknowledged the deed and told his attorney to record the deed for his 15-year-old son in case of his death as a result of the surgery. Upon the decedent's death after surgery, his administratrix (P) sought to set aside the assignment as an incomplete gift causa mortis.

ISSUE: Can a delivery of the subject of a gift causa mortis be made by deed?

HOLDING AND DECISION: Yes. A gift is valid if made by deed and the deed is delivered with donative intent, though the subject does not accompany the deed. A delivery of the deed is equivalent to a delivery of the subject of the gift. The deed is rather a symbolical delivery of the gift. It was sufficient a transfer to strip the father of all ownership and control of his interest in the bond and mortgage. While the donor had held the belief he could revoke the gift, such belief was of no matter as the right to revoke is a condition of a gift causa mortis.

EDITOR'S ANALYSIS: Here, the decedent made the gift on account of an illness by which he feared death, and he died from that illness. Thus, the first two requirements of a gift causa mortis were met. The only question was as to the effectiveness of the delivery. Historically, a gift by deed is equivalent to physical delivery of the subject of the gift. Note that the major issue of Grymes v. Hone, 49 N.Y. 17 (1872) is not really raised. That is, delivery to a third person for the donee is matter of factly accepted by the court. Notice, too, that it was alleged that the gift was actually testamentary in character and failed to satisfy the statute of wills. That is, if there was not an effective gift causa mortis, the the decedent's failure to make the deed in form to satisfy the signature and witnessing requirements of a will would cause the subject of the gift to remain a part of the decedent's estate which apparently would then pass to the decedent's widow, who happened to be the administratrix (P), thus, perhaps, revealing the true motive behind this case.

INNES v. POTTER

SUP. COURT OF MINNESOTA, 1915.
130 Minn. 320, 153 N.W. 604

NATURE OF CASE: Action by administrator to recover personal property for the estate.

FACT SUMMARY: Potter, deceased, endorsed a stock certificate in favor of his daughter, Potter (D), but gave it to a third person to deliver to his daughter upon his death.

CONCISE RULE OF LAW: A gift of personal property can be made by delivering the subject of the gift to a third person who will deliver the gift to the donee upon the death of the donor.

FACTS: Potter, a man of advanced years (and deceased at the time of this action), desired to give his daughter a gift of 1,000 shares in his company. He endorsed the certificate and gave it along with a writing to Casey. The writing instructed Casey to hold the certificate for Potter (D) until the elder Potter's death when Casey was to deliver the certificate by registered mail. Casey delivered as instructed. Innes (P), the administrator of Potter's estate, seeks to recover the 1,000 shares, alleging the gift to be invalid and testamentary in character.

ISSUE: Can an effective gift of personal property be made where the donor gives the subject of gift to a third person to deliver it to the donee upon the death of the donor?

HOLDING AND DECISION: Yes. The deceased relinquished all control over the stock and all rights in it; he intended to give and gave the stock to Potter (D); and intended for the gift to take effect upon delivery to Casey. Beneficial enjoyment by the donee was delayed until the death of the donor. Such has been the rule for gifts of real property, and the court sees no reason for a distinction between a gift of real property and a gift of personal property. Delivery of the gift was made to a third person and some interest vested upon delivery. As a present interest was transferred and the donor relinquished all control in the gift, an effective, irrevocable gift inter vivos was made.

EDITOR'S ANALYSIS: Historically, there was no question as to the effectiveness of a gift of the nature of the one here as to real property. As real property could not be consumed, it could be held without it being lost. The trend in equity was away from any distinction between the gift in real property and personal property. The court here simply said there was no distinction of merit. The gift was inter vivos. The gift could not be causa mortis for the obvious reason that the donor was not ill or in any peril of death. The gift was not made in contemplation of death. As intent to transfer a present interest in the gift was found, an effective gift inter vivos was upheld.

TYGARD v. McCOMB

COURT OF APPEALS OF MISSOURI, 1893. 54 Mo. App. 85

NATURE OF CASE: Action to establish ownership to deposited funds.

FACT SUMMARY: Wilson, deceased, deposited sums in a bank in an account in the name of his two minor daughters, but treated the funds as his own, raising a question as to whether he had actually and irrevocably given the money to his daughters at the time of his death.

CONCISE RULE OF LAW: For an effective gift inter vivos, there must be an absolute and unequivocal intention by the donor to pass title and possession to the subject of gift to the donee at once.

FACTS: Wilson, deceased, opened a bank account in the names and to the joint credit of his two minor daughters. Wilson kept possession of the passbook and made deposits and withdrawals from time to time, always in the names of his daughters. In addition, he made a loan of $600 to one Hill in money withdrawn from the account. Wilson died in a mine accident before the loan was repaid. Tygard (P), guardian of Wilson's minor daughters, seeks a declaration of the daughters' right to the note Hill gave on the loan, while McComb (D), Wilson's administrator, seeks a declaration of the right of the estate to the funds remaining in the bank.

ISSUE: Did the deceased intend to pass title and possession to the gift over to the donees at once?

HOLDING AND DECISION: No. For an effective gift inter vivos, there must be an absolute and unequivocal intention by the donor to pass title and possession over at once to the donee. The deceased maintained possession and control of the sum on deposit as evidenced by his use of the funds and his continued possession of the passbook. If Wilson did not intend at once to part with title and possession, but simply deposited the money "to take effect as a kind of post mortem benefaction" to become the daughters' if anything should happen to him, the gift was testamentary in nature and not a valid gift inter vivos.

EDITOR'S ANALYSIS: When one attempts to make a gift in form but does not complete it in substance, it will not be upheld. While Wilson placed the money in the names of the donees, he retained possession and control over it. While he may have appeared to have made the gift, he did not meet the conditions of a gift inter vivos. Naturally, there was no gift causa mortis as while he may have actually intended there to be a gift upon his death, he was not ill or in peril of death at the time.

NOTES:

MATTER OF TOTTEN
COURT OF APPEALS OF NEW YORK, 1904.
179 N.Y. 112, 71 N.E. 748

NATURE OF CASE: Action to establish ownership to the proceeds of a trust.

FACT SUMMARY: Fannie Lattan, deceased, established several savings accounts in the Irving Savings Institution of New York in trust for various individuals including her nephew, Emile Lattan (P). Emile did not know of the trust account in his favor during Fannie's lifetime and sued, more than a year after her death, to establish ownership to the money in the account, which Fannie had withdrawn before her death.

CONCISE RULE OF LAW: A deposit by one person of his own money in his own name as trustee for another, standing alone, does not establish an irrevocable trust during the lifetime of the depositor unless he completes the gift by some unequivocal act or declaration. If the depositor dies before he can complete the gift, the presumption arises that an irrevocable and absolute trust was created as to the balance at hand at the death of the depositor if the beneficiary is still living.

FACTS: Fannie Latten opened several savings accounts in trust for various individuals at the Irving Savings Institution of New York. There were several accounts which were opened and closed at different times by Fannie with many changes in named beneficiaries. At the time of Fannie's death, there were four trust accounts to which her administrator handed over the passbooks to the beneficiaries, including Emile Latten (P). Emile (P) did not know until about a year after Fannie's death that there had been other trust accounts to which he was named beneficiary but had been closed before Fannie's death. He sued to establish his ownership to the funds that had been withdrawn from those trust accounts to which he was the named beneficiary. During her lifetime, Fannie maintained control over the accounts by retaining possession of the passbooks and making deposits and withdrawals as she pleased.

ISSUE: Did Emile (P) have a right to possession of the money deposited in trust for him without his knowledge by Fannie and subsequently withdrawn by her before her death?

HOLDING AND DECISION: No. For there to be a trust, there must be an explicit declaration of trust or circumstances which show beyond a reasonable doubt that a trust was intended to be created. Here, Fannie made no express declaration to create a trust. Emile, in fact, never knew of certain trusts which had been created but later withdrawn. To infer a gift from the form of deposit alone would, too often, impute an intention which never existed and defeat the real purpose of the depositor. A deposit by one person of his own money, in his own name as trustee for another, standing alone, does not establish an irrevocable trust during the lifetime of the depositor. It is a tentative trust merely, revocable at will, until the depositor dies or completes the gift in his lifetime by some unequivocal act or declaration, such as delivery of the passbook or notice to the beneficiary. In case the depositor dies before the beneficiary without revocation, or some decisive act or disaffirmance, the presumption arises that an absolute trust was created as to the balance on hand at the death of the depositor.

EDITOR'S ANALYSIS: The rule is simply that where one as trustee deposits money for another as beneficiary without completing the gift during his lifetime by some decisive act, there is a revocable trust. However, should the trustee die before the beneficiary, there is an irrevocable trust as to the money still on deposit. This landmark case is an exception to the law of trusts. The property in trust is unknown until the death of the trust's creator. A "Totten" trust is nothing more than money on deposit in the name of another. For there to be a Totten trust, two conditions must be met: (1) the depositor must die before the beneficiary, and (2) there must be some money still on deposit. An intent to create a trust by the depositor's depositing money in another's name alone cannot be found as people have many different reasons for creating such accounts such as hiding the value of their personal holdings.

NOTES:

MALONE v. WALSH

SUP. JUDICIAL COURT OF MASSACHUSETTS, 1944.
315 Mass. 484, 53 N.E. 2d 126

NATURE OF CASE: Action to determine ownership to the proceeds of a savings account.

FACT SUMMARY: The decedent, Mary Ryan, who desired to keep her funds from passing to most of her relatives, including her husband, after her death, placed her money in three joint deposits in her name and in the name of her brother, Patrick Walsh (D). Malone (P), administrator of Ryan's estate, sues to establish ownership of the joint deposits for the estate.

CONCISE RULE OF LAW: The deposit of funds in joint tenancy vests a present interest in each of the joint tenants which will ripen into complete ownership and enjoyment for the surviving joint tenants upon the death of the joint tenant who made the initial deposit.

FACTS: Mary Ryan, deceased, made several arrangements in order to keep her money from falling into the hands of her husband upon her death. At first she deposited about $15,000 jointly with her sister, Catherine. As she believed her relatives were eagerly awaiting her demise, Mary decided to withdraw the deposit with her sister and redeposit the funds jointly with her brother, Patrick Walsh (D). Walsh (D), who lived in Ireland, signed deposit cards which Mary sent to him and which he returned to her in the United States. The new joint deposit removing Catherine was made without Catherine's knowledge. Mary died intestate (without a will). The administrator of her estate, Malone (P), sued to determine ownership to the funds on joint deposit which Walsh (D) claimed to be his.

ISSUE: As Mary maintained control over the funds on joint deposit in order to influence the distribution of those funds upon her death, was there a present completed gift vesting the right to ownership in the joint deposit in Walsh (D)?

HOLDING AND DECISION: Yes. There was a present completed gift. While the time of enjoyment of the gift was delayed until Mary's death, Walsh's (D) interest in ownership vested upon deposit. Without vesting of a present interest in Walsh (D), Mary's desire to disinherit her husband and sister would be defeated. Her reservation of a right to withdraw income and principal and to revoke the joint tenancy was not inconsistent with a perfected creation inter vivos of a joint tenancy. Mary's intention to disinherit her husband was not unlawful; and as to the original joint tenancy with her sister, Mary impliedly reserved the right to revoke the joint deposits.

EDITOR'S ANALYSIS: The reason Mary deposited the money in joint tenancy was because of the most important characteristic of a joint tenancy, the right of survivorship. Upon the death of a joint tenant, the entire ownership remains in the surviving joint tenant(s). The interest of the deceased joint tenant simply dissolves. Upon his death, his joint interest does not descend to his heirs or pass under his will. Obviously, disinheritance is easily achieved in this manner. A person who makes a gift by way of joint intestacy places a present interest of ownership (a vested interest) in the donee joint tenant. The donor can reserve the right to revoke the joint tenancy and can delay the enjoyment of the gift to the donee until the death of the donor. Many states consider bank accounts to be a special kind of joint tenancy, and the student should make himself aware of the legislation in his state. What is basically the major point of this case is that Mary Ryan's (as donor and joint tenant) reserving control over the gift did not prevent the vesting of a present interest in the donee joint tenant. Thus, the retention of the donee's right of enjoyment until her death did not make the gift testamentary in nature and a violation of the statute of wills for failure to conform to the rules pertaining to formalities for wills.

NOTES:

SMITH'S ESTATE

SUP. COURT OF PENNSYLVANIA, 1891.
144 Pa. St. 428, 22 A. 916

NATURE OF CASE: Action to establish the validity of a trust.

FACT SUMMARY: Thomas Smith, deceased, purchased $13,000 in bonds for his nephew and recorded the purchase and collection of interest in his memorandum book for the benefit of his nephew. He also told his nephew's father that he had "appropriated" some bonds for the nephews.

CONCISE RULE OF LAW: The intention to create a trust though not expressly declared can be found in the words and actions of the creator of the trust.

FACTS: Thomas Smith, deceased, purchased 13 $1,000 bonds of the Pensacola & Atlantic Railroad Company. He recorded the purchase and the collection of $390 in interest for the benefit of his 13-year-old nephew, Thomas Smith Kelly, as belonging to him. Though Kelly's parents were living, he had lived with and was educated by his uncle since the age of three. Smith purchased the bonds on January 28, 1882, and died May 20, 1883. Kelly lived with Smith's family until 1887. When Smith purchased the bonds, he told his nephew's father that he had "appropriated" certain bonds for the boy, and, in his own handwriting and over his signature, had written in his memoranda book that the bonds were "property of his nephew," "belonged to him," "bought for," and "held for him." Upon his death, Smith's executor (D) claimed there was not a sufficient declaration of trust when Kelly's guardian (P) sued to recover the bonds. Smith never used the express words "in trust."

ISSUE: Was there a sufficient declaration to create a valid trust?

HOLDING AND DECISION: Yes. First, it is clear that intention to create a trust existed. While the express words "in trust" were never used, it is "so obvious and certain" that that was Smith's intention by his written words. The declaration of the intention to create a trust need not be made to the beneficiary. It is sufficient if made to other persons under circumstances indicating the donor's intention to make a declaration of trust. The declaration cannot be said aloud to oneself as that is nothing more than an expression of mere intention and cannot be proved. Neither can a hidden writing alone accomplish the requirement as it can be destroyed by the donor. Here, however, Smith did tell the nephew's father that he had "appropriated" some bonds for the boy. Additionally, the purpose of his written notes seemed to be for the eyes of others expressing his intention as to the bonds. The court need not consider whether or not Smith might have revoked the declaration as the right to revoke a trust can be expressly reserved by the donor.

EDITOR'S ANALYSIS: It is quite obvious that the court was reaching in order to sustain an ambiguous trust. Equity will not take an imperfect gift, a gift where the donor fails to transfer legal title to the donee, and treat it as a trust. Otherwise, all imperfect gifts would be treated as trusts. A trust is created when the donor places legal title to the subject of trust (the trust res) in a trustee and equitable title in the donee, the beneficiary. No writing is necessary to create a trust in personal property. An oral declaration is sufficient to create the trust. Here, the donor did not expressly declare orally to the father that he intended to create a trust. However, it might be considered, although the court passed over it briefly, that Smith's having shown the memoranda book to another nephew who had drawn a line through an entry at Smith's request may have been a clearer declaration of his intent than his simply leaving the book with its entries for the eyes of others in the future. But Smith's leaving the book open to view, not hiding it, and, actually, carefully preserving it, seems to have gotten the court around the rule against a hidden, written trust declaration.

NOTES:

HESSEN v. IOWA AUTOMOBILE MUTUAL INSURANCE COMPANY

SUP. COURT OF IOWA, 1922. 195 Iowa 141, 190 N.W.150

NATURE OF CASE: Action to recover on an insurance policy.

FACT SUMMARY: Hessen's (P) automobile, which unbeknownst to him was a stolen car when he purchased it, was stolen. Mutual (D), the insurer of the car, refused to satisfy Hessen's (P) claim.

CONCISE RULE OF LAW: A bona fide purchaser cannot acquire title to goods or chattel as against the owner from whom it was stolen.

FACTS: Hessen (P) purchased what he believed to be a 1919 Buick from a corporation now dissolved. He insured the auto with Mutual (D). The auto was stolen within the term of the policy, and Hessen (P) alleged a loss of $1,350. It was then learned that Hessen's (P) auto was a stolen auto at the time he had purchased it, although he had never known that. On that basis, Mutual (D) refused to pay Hessen's claim alleging that he had no insurable interest in the auto, which was actually a 1916 model.

ISSUE: Could Hessen (P), a bona fide purchaser, have an insurable interest in an auto that was stolen at the time of purchase?

HOLDING AND DECISION: No. If one has no legal or equitable interest in the thing insured, the contract is viewed as a "mere wager" and will not be enforced. A person can have no insurable interest in a thing where his right arises under a contract which is unenforceable or void either at law or equity. As Hessen (P) could only acquire an interest under the sales contract, and the vendor had nothing more than possession of a stolen car to transfer, no valid title could be transferred. Only the owner of a chattel or his lawful representative can convey valid title to that chattel. In addition, the insurance contract expressly provided that the contract was void if Hessen (P) was not the unconditional and sole owner. Judgment for Hessen (P) reversed.

EDITOR'S ANALYSIS: Professor Casner states that while it is true that the bona fide purchaser cannot acquire title to stolen property, it does not follow that a bona fide purchaser could have no insurable interest. The court ignores the concept of relativity of title where one could have title against the first person but not against the second. While Hessen (P) may have had good title against his vendor, it must be remembered that the vendor, a corporation, had since dissolved. Even so, he still had good title against the rest of the world except for the actual owner. Neither should it automatically follow that a "sole and unconditional ownership" clause should defeat Hessen's claim. (There is case authority to that effect but subsequent to the date of this case.) If the reason for such a clause is to prompt the insured into preserving the insured property, it would appear that a bona fide purchaser would naturally have such an interest. The major basis of this decision appears to be that as an insurance policy is a contract, it would be contrary to public policy for one to acquire a policy to something in which he has no legal or equitable interest.

NOTES:

MORGAN v. HODGES

SUPREME COURT OF MICHIGAN, 1891.
89 Mich. 404, 50 N. W. 876

NATURE OF CASE: Action in trover to recover value of a horse.

FACT SUMMARY: After innocently buying a horse, buggy, etc. from Seaman, Hodges (D) is confronted by Morgan (P), who claims to be the real owner of the property.

CONCISE RULE OF LAW: The forbearance to assert a colorable claim of title to goods is sufficient consideration to support a settlement offer where the ownership of the property has neither been proven nor conceded.

FACTS: Hodges (D) purchased two horses, buggies, harnesses, etc. from Seaman. One of the horses, buggies, etc. had actually been rented by Seaman from Morgan (P). Hodges (D) sold the horse belonging to Morgan (P), but kept the remainder of Morgan's (P) property. Hodges (D) had no reason to know or suspect that this property did not actually belong to Seaman. Five months later, Morgan (P) traced the property to Hodges (D). According to Hodges' (D) testimony, Morgan (P) explained that Seaman had rented a horse, buggy, etc. from him (Morgan), and that Hodges (D) knew of their whereabouts. Hodges (D) stated that he had bought two horses, buggies, etc. from Seaman but that he had already sold the horses. Morgan (P) said that if the remainder of the property were returned to him he would let the horse go and would "call it square." Hodges (D) immediately returned the remainder of Morgan's (P) property. Morgan (P) then instituted an action in trover for the value of the horse. Morgan (P) denied the existence of the settlement agreement and contended that even if there were such an agreement it was void for want of consideration because there was nothing in dispute and no controversy had arisen. The judge in the lower court instructed the jury that if Hodges (D) did not concede Morgan's (P) ownership, no determination of ownership was made, and Morgan (P) made the settlement offer, then it would be binding on the parties. The jury found for Hodges (D).

ISSUE: Was the return of the remaining property without a concession or determination of ownership sufficient consideration to support a settlement offer?

HOLDING AND DECISION: Yes. Where a third party is innocent of any wrongdoing or negligence in the original transaction and does not misrepresent the situation to the rightful owner. The law will uphold the settlement agreement if ownership has neither been conceded or determined. This is a policy decision since the law favors out-of-court settlements of this kind. The court stresses that there was no admission by Hodges (D) that the property was Morgan's (P). Silence was not tantamount to a concession of ownership. The court implied that the consideration was supplied by the release of Hodges' (D) colorable claim to the property.

DISSENT: Hodges (D) only did what he had to do by surrendering the property. There was no consideration for the promise by Morgan (P) to settle.

EDITOR'S ANALYSIS: Implicit in the court's decision is the concept that a seller can convey no better title than he himself had. Therefore, there was never any question in the court's mind that Morgan (P) had an absolute right to the property. The only question was whether or not they should enforce the purported settlement agreement. The majority appeared to feel that it was. They decided the issue on policy grounds. It is difficult to believe that Hodges' (D) immediate return of the property was not a concession of ownership. The majority was obviously struggling to justify their decision. Under contract law (the settlement agreement was a contract), the forbearance to assert a claim, if believed to be legitimate at the time, will be considered adequate consideration to support a settlement offer, even though the claim later proves to be invalid. Here, there is no showing that Hodges (D) believed his claim to be valid. His immediate surrender of the property seems to lead one to the exact opposite conclusion. If the claim was not believed legitimate at the time the property was given up, there is no consideration.

NOTES:

22

DONALD v. SUCKLING
COURT OF QUEEN'S BENCH, 1866.
L. R. 1, Q. B. 585

NATURE OF CASE: Action in detinue for the value of four debentures and damages for their detention.

FACT SUMMARY: Simpson assigned four debentures given to him as security by Donald (P) to Suckling (D) (Simpson's creditor) prior to the due date of Donald's (P) note.

CONCISE RULE OF LAW: Property given to a pledgee as security, when coupled with a right of disposal upon default, may be assigned or even sold prior to pledgor's default without destroying the security interest in the property.

FACTS: Donald (P) delivered four debentures to Simpson as security for a bill of exchange. Donald (P) agreed that Simpson should have full power to sell or otherwise dispose of them if the bill was not paid when due. Simpson, prior to the note's due date, assigned the debentures to Suckling (D), one of Simpson's creditors. Donald (P) then defaulted on the note. Donald (P) never paid or offered to pay the note and Simpson's debt to Suckling (D) remained unpaid. Donald (P) brought suit in detinue for the debentures and damages, claiming that the assignment by Simpson to Suckling (D) voided the security agreement, and therefore, Suckling (D) was detaining the property unlawfully.

ISSUE: Did the assignment of the pledged property prior to Donald's (P) note being due extinguish the security lien on the debentures?

HOLDING AND DECISION: No. While a right of lien is a personal right incapable of assignment, delivery of the chattel coupled with the right to sell or dispose of the property upon default creates a special property right in the pledgee. The pledgee or pawnee only has the duty to safeguard the property and to return it when the underlying debt is paid. Since the debt had not been paid, Donald (P) did not have the right to have the property delivered to him (the basis of an action of detinue); therefore, the action failed. The wrongful transfer of the debentures was not sufficiently grave so as to destroy the underlying security interest in the property. Since Suckling (D) received the same interest in the debentures as Simpson had, he could legally hold them until the note was paid.

EDITOR'S ANALYSIS: At common law, a pledge involved the delivery of property to a creditor or bailee to be held as security for the repayment of a debt. The pledgor retained title and the creditor (pledgee) had constructive possession of the property. Upon default, the pledgee could foreclose by a bill in equity praying for sale of the pledge. Until the granting of the bill, his only right to the property was constructive possession. This case holds that where the creditor (pledgee) has the contractual right to dispose of the property upon default, he has a property right in the property which is akin to that of a pawnor. It has gone beyond mere constructive possession and is capable of being sold or assigned to a third party even before the note is due. The purchaser or assignor receives the same interest in the property as the pledgee had, and the property would have to be returned to the original pledgor if the debt were repaid. The dispute in this case would now probably be covered by U.C.C. 9-305 and 9-302. U.C.C. 9-305 states that when the secured goods are in the creditor's possession, his security interest is perfected. U.C.C. 9-302(2) seems to indicate that assignments of these interests are permitted and that the interest is not extinguished (see Official Comment 7).

NOTES:

THE SHERER-GILLETTE COMPANY v. LONG

SUPREME COURT OF ILLINOIS, 1925.
318 III. 432, 149 N.E. 225

NATURE OF CASE: Action of replevin for a display counter.

FACT SUMMARY: Long (D) purchased a display counter from Taylor, not knowing that the title to it was held by the Sherer-Gillette Company.

CONCISE RULE OF LAW: Where goods are sold by a person who is not the owner thereof, and who does not sell them under the authority or with the consent of the owner, the buyer acquires no better title to the goods than the seller had, unless the owner of the goods is, by his conduct, precluded from denying the seller's authority to sell.

FACTS: The Sherer-Gillette Company (P) sold a display counter to Taylor on a conditional sales contract. It was to retain title to the counter until the contract was paid. Two days later, Taylor sold the counter to Long (D) without telling him of the title reservation. Long (D) paid one hundred dollars for the counter. The Sherer-Gillette Company (P) brought an action of replevin against Long (D) to recover the counter.

ISSUE: Is a bona fide purchaser for value protected against an undisclosed reservation of title?

HOLDING AND DECISION: No. Section 23 of Illinois' Uniform Sales Act states that, "... (w)here goods are sold by a person who is not the owner thereof, and who does not sell them under the authority or with the consent of the owner, the buyer acquires no better title to the goods than the seller had, unless the owner of the goods is, by his conduct, precluded from denying the seller's authority to sell." This was a statutory departure from common-law decisions. Prior to the enactment of the Uniform Sales Act an undisclosed reservation of title on a conditional sales contract was considered a constructive fraud on an innocent third party purchaser because the conditional vendee had been given the indicia of ownership (possession of the property). A policy of statutory construction is that when the legislature passes a statute which is in derogation of the common law, the courts should give force to its natural and common meaning, not strain it to fit previous decisions. While possession is one indice of ownership, it is not conclusive. The court cites bailees and lessees as examples. Therefore, the mere granting of possession, without additional acts by the original seller, is insufficient to estop the Sherer-Gillette Company (P) from asserting its title.

EDITOR'S ANALYSIS: Two conflicting public policies are represented in this case. First, how can innocent third parties be protected in similar situations? Secondly, if all conditional sales contracts had to be perfected by filing, the cost in time, money and manpower would be staggering. The Uniform Commercial Code has attempted to take an approach in between the two extremes presented in this case. U.C.C. 9-301(1)(c) gives the bona fide purchaser for value, without notice, superior title to the unperfected security holder if the transaction involved goods, instruments, documents and chattel paper and was not a bulk transfer or made in the ordinary course of business. U.C.C. 9-301(1)(d) gives the bona fide purchaser for value, without notice, superior title in the case of accounts and intangibles. The secured party has ten days to file after the debtor receives possession of the property (U.C.C. 9-301[2]) if he is to protect himself against an immediate reconveyance by the debtor (as was the situation in this case). U.C.C. 9-302 presents numerous exceptions to this filing requirement. The most notable are where possession is retained by the secured party and a purchase money security interest in consumer goods other than motor vehicles or fixtures is involved. Long (D) might have prevailed under the Uniform Commercial Code if he could have shown that the display counter was not a consumer good (or was a fixture) or was not bought in the normal course of business. He would have to further prove that the Sherer-Gillette Company had not perfected their security interest within ten days of delivering the counter to Taylor.

NOTES:

O'CONNOR, ADMX., v. CLARK

SUPREME CT. OF PA., 1895. 170 Pa. St. 318, 32 A. 1029

NATURE OF CASE: Replevin to recover a horse and wagon.

FACT SUMMARY: O'Connor (P) directed his employee George Tracy to place the words "George Tracy, Piano Mover" on the side of O'Connor's wagon, after which Tracy sold the wagon as his own to Clark (D).

CONCISE RULE OF LAW: While the general rule is that a vendee of personal property takes only such title or interest as his vendor has and is authorized to transfer, a well-recognized exception states that where (1) the owner has so acted with reference to his property as to clothe the person (vendor) assuming to dispose of the property, with the apparent title to or authority to dispose of it, and (2) the person taking from the vendor has acted and parted with value upon the faith of such apparent authority, the owner will be estopped from asserting title to his property over such bona fide purchaser.

FACTS: O'Connor (P) was in the wagon renting business. One of his employees, George Tracy, had previously been in that business, as a piano mover. In order to retain Tracy's former customers, O'Connor (P) ordered him to paint the words "George Tracy, Piano Mover" on the side of a new wagon which O'Connor (P) was having built. Subsequently, Tracy sold the wagon and the horse with it to Clark (D). To convince Clark (D) that he (Tracy) was, in fact, the owner, he took him down to the local police station and had himself identified as George Tracy, which, of course, matched the name on the wagon. O'Connor (P), now deceased, sues through the administratrix of his estate to recover possession of his property from Clark (D). The trial court instructed the jury that if the jury believed the testimony that the wagon belonged to O'Connor (P) and that Tracy sold it without his permission, no title was conveyed to Clark, and O'Connor (P) must therefore be allowed to recover. From judgment for O'Connor's Administratrix (P), Clark appeals, contending that the above instruction was error.

ISSUE: May the owner of personal property, by his own conduct, be estopped from asserting his title to such property held by a bona fide purchaser for value?

HOLDING AND DECISION: Yes. While the general rule is that a vendee of personal property takes only such title or interest as his vendor has and is authorized to transfer, a well-recognized exception states that where (1) the owner has so acted with reference to his property as to clothe the person (vendor) assuming to dispose of the property with the apparent authority to dispose of it; and (2) the person taking from the vendor has acted and parted with value upon the faith of such apparent authority, the owner will be estopped from asserting title to his property over such bona fide purchaser. If there were nothing more in this case than the facts alluded to by the trial judge in his instruction ([1] that O'Connor [P] owned the wagon, and [2] that Tracy sold it without his permission), the general rule here would apply and the instruction would be correct. Other facts were established at trial, however. Clark (D) bought the wagon from Tracy in the good faith belief that he was the actual owner. This reliance was justified both by the name on the side of the wagon and the police identification of Tracy as Tracy. The name was put on the side of the wagon on the instructions of O'Connor (P) for the obvious purpose of inducing in the public the impression that Tracy was, in fact, its owner. Under such conditions it would be inequitable to permit O'Connor (P) having participated in deluding Clark (D) to now assert title to the wagon to Tracy's detriment. The decision must be reversed and remanded for a new trial with proper instructions.

EDITOR'S ANALYSIS: This case points up the generally accepted application of the equitable theory of estoppel to bona fide (good faith) purchaser cases. Note closely that there are two essential elements which the purchaser must prove for estoppel to be invoked. (1) Words or conduct by the owner that leaves the impression that the vendor has authority to sell, and (2) good faith reliance by the purchaser. In such cases, equity applies the maxim that "... wherever one of two innocent persons must suffer by the acts of a third, he who has enabled such third persons to occasion the loss must sustain it." Note finally that replevin was the common-law form of action to recover goods from a person ex delicto (i.e., out of fault as opposed to on contract).

NOTES:

PHELPS v. McQUADE
COURT OF APPEALS OF NEW YORK, 1917.
220 N.Y. 232, 115 N.E. 441

NATURE OF CASE: Replevin to recover goods.

FACT SUMMARY: Gwynne bought jewelry from Phelps (P) on a false representation of identity and credit, then resold it to McQuade (D), who bought in good faith.

CONCISE RULE OF LAW: Although a vendor may be deceived as to the identity of the person with whom he is dealing, title to any goods he sells will nevertheless pass if he is found to have intended to sell those goods to the person with whom he is dealing.

FACTS: J. Walter Gwynne, a criminal, represented himself to be Baldwin J. Gwynne, a respectable citizen from Cleveland, in order to induce Phelps (P) a vendor of jewelry, to sell him (as Baldwin J. Gwynne) some on credit. Gwynne immediately thereupon resold it to McQuade (D), who purchased it believing it, in good faith, to be Gwynne's legally. Upon discovering the fraud, Phelps (P) filed an action of replevin to regain the goods which McQuade (D) had purchased. McQuade (D) pleaded that, as a bona fide purchaser, he should be permitted to keep the jewelry. Phelps (P), however, contends that since Gwynne gained possession of the jewelry by larceny, title could not have passed to him to sell to McQuade (D). As such, McQuade (D) could never have "purchased" title to the jewelry. Judgment was for McQuade (D), but was reversed on appeal. This appeal followed that one.

ISSUE: Does the vendor of personal property lose title to that property when he is deprived of it by larceny?

HOLDING AND DECISION: Yes. Although a vendor may be deceived as to the identity of the person with whom he is dealing, title to any goods he sells will nevertheless pass if he is found to have intended to sell those goods to the person with whom he is dealing. It is the intention of the vendor which is controlling. If he intends to pass title, it is deemed passed. It is true that, prior to the change in the criminal statutes (recognizing larceny by trick in which possession but not title was passed), the question of passing of title was material to the question of whether the property had been wrongfully (i.e., criminally) taken, as must be proven in replevin actions. This is no longer true. The taking was wrongful, and the only material question is whether the vendor intended to pass title. Here, he clearly did. The original judgment for McQuade (D) is affirmed. He took good title from Gwynne.

EDITOR'S ANALYSIS: This case points up another exception to the general rule that a vendor without title can confer no title on any purchaser including a bona fide purchaser for value. To understand it, however, basic criminal theft law must be reviewed. Larceny, at common law, was the "trespassory taking" and carrying away of the personal property of another with the intent to steal it.

Since where fraud was involved no actual physical "trespass in the taking" could be found in a theft, different categories were formed. Where the fraud was found to induce the owner to part with possession but not title to his property (e.g., rent) the crime is still larceny, of course, since there was a constructive trespass in the taking of the owner's title interest. Where, as here, however, the owner intended to pass title, no trespass occurred in the taking itself so larceny did not occur. In such cases, though the transfer was voidable, it was not void per se as criminal. It was at this point that the exception which states that a voidable title taken by a transferee, since it is valid until voided, can serve as the basis for a bona fide purchaser taking consistent with the general rule above (i.e., a vendor without title cannot confer it on any purchaser) came into play. When the crime of false pretenses was created statutorily (as alluded to above) to cover the above situation, such conduct as criminal meant the title transferred was void ab initio, in criminal law terms, so no title could be transferred subsequently by the vendee. The court here, however, merely points out that the criminal law considerations, though once analogous, were now immaterial to property law. The important question in whether or not title was passed was the intention to pass title by the owner. Intention rules all else.

NOTES:

HURD v. BICKFORD
SUPREME JUDICAL COURT OF MAINE, 1892.
85 Me. 217, 27 A. 107

NATURE OF CASE: Action in trover.

FACT SUMMARY: Bickford (D) returned a promissory note to Gross in return for a horse and sleigh which Gross had fraudulently bought from Hurd (P).

CONCISE RULE OF LAW: A vendee becomes a bona fide purchaser if it is shown that (1) he acted in good faith upon the apparent title of the seller, ignorant of any prior fraud, and (2) that the purchase was made for a valuable consideration, but a valuable consideration must be something more than the discharge of a debt that revives when the consideration for its discharge fails.

FACTS: Gross purchased a horse and sleigh from Hurd (P), in a manner which was found by a court to be fraudulent. Gross thereupon exchanged the horse and sleigh for a promissory note he had given Dr. Bickford (D) for medical services rendered (prior to the purchase from Hurd [P]). Upon discovering the fraud, Hurd (P) filed an action of trover to recover the horse and sleigh against Bickford (D). From a judgment for Hurd (P), Bickford (D) excepted, contending that he was a bona fide purchaser and should be permitted to retain title thereby.

ISSUE: May the good faith purchaser of items fraudulently acquired by the seller retain such goods where they were accepted as payment of an antecedent debt?

HOLDING AND DECISION: No. A vendee becomes a bona fide purchaser if it is shown that (1) he acted in good faith upon the apparent title of the seller, ignorant of any prior fraud, and (2) that the purchase was made for a valuable consideration; but a "valuable consideration" must be something more than the discharge of a debt that revives when the consideration for its discharge fails. It is true that the discharge of an antecedent debt is, for most purposes, a valuable consideration, but, if the title to the goods (in the vendor-vendee relationship) fails for the vendee, then the discharge of the debt fails as well, and he has lost nothing by allowing the defrauded owner to recover his property. It would be inequitable to hold otherwise. The judgment must be affirmed.

EDITOR'S ANALYSIS: This case points up the two basic elements of a "bona fide purchaser": good faith and valuable consideration. Such a bona fide purchaser is permitted to retain title to goods even over the claim of the original owner. It is felt to be inequitable to deprive him of goods honestly purchased. The refusal here to permit retention of the goods is, of course, an example of the general rule that one who has no title to goods cannot pass title to even a purchaser in good faith. Bona fide purchasers "for value" are permitted to retain purchased goods, however, in certain specific cases. Five such exceptions arise: (1) sales in the market overt, which is recognized only in England, which stated that anything bought on calendar "market days" was presumed to be a valid sale; (2) transfer of money and negotiable instruments, since recognition of them is so essential to the free flow of commerce; (3) transfers of goods with voidable as distinct from void titles; (4) transfers where the owner is estopped by his own conduct (in granting apparent authority to sell to his vendor) from asserting ownership; (5) transfers under conditional sales contracts in jurisdictions following the Uniform Conditional Sales Act Section 9. Note, finally, the definitions of terms used in these cases. A vendor is any person who transfers property by sale. Trover is a common-law form of action to recover property wrongfully interfered with or detained.

NOTES:

HIGGINS v. LODGE

Ct. OF APPLS. OF MARYLAND, 1888. 68 Md. 229, 11 A. 846

NATURE OF CASE: Replevin to recover goods from an auctioneer.

FACT SUMMARY: Higgins (D), an auctioneer, advanced money to Levy for goods fraudulently acquired from Lodge (P).

CONCISE RULE OF LAW: A purchaser of goods will not qualify as a "bona fide purchaser for value" if (1) he had knowledge of circumstances calculated to put a man of ordinary prudence and caution upon inquiry as to whether the seller had acquired the goods involved by fraud; and (2) he fails to make such an inquiry.

FACTS: Levy had commenced a jobbing business on June 15, 1885. On August 21, he bought $6,000 worth of goods from Lodge (P), to be paid for on October 10. Even prior to this purchase, Levy had been sending goods to Higgins (D), an auctioneer, for sale. One week before September 5, he had an inventory of $15,000, but on September 5, he had sent all but $400 or $500 worth of stock to Higgins (D), who advanced him money for the stock, for sale. Levy realized over $6,400 from the auction sale. On September 7, he withdrew all his money from his bank account and changed the business to his wife's name. Lodge (P) sued Higgins (D) to recover the transferred stock of goods. At trial, it was established that Levy's actions were fraudulent. The judge instructed the jury that (1) Higgins' (D) status as a bona fide purchaser for value could be lost if it were established that he failed to take precautions he should have, but (2) if Higgins (D) acted without any notice or knowledge of the circumstances by which Levy acquired the goods in question, he must be allowed to retain them. From a judgment for Lodge (P), Higgins (D) appeals challenging the first above instruction.

ISSUE: May the purchaser of goods fraudulently acquired by the seller be precluded from retaining them as a bona fide purchaser for value merely because he should have known they were fraudulently acquired?

HOLDING AND DECISION: Yes. A purchaser of goods will not qualify as a "bona fide purchaser for value" if (1) he had knowledge of circumstances calculated to put a man of ordinary prudence and caution upon inquiry as to whether the seller had acquired the goods involved by fraud, and (2) he fails to make such an inquiry. It is well settled that the purchaser of fraudulently acquired goods may retain them against the claim of the original owner if it is proved that the purchase was in good faith and for valuable consideration. Here, the circumstances surrounding the sale of goods to Lodge (P) should have put him on inquiry as to whether they had been fraudulently acquired by Levy. His failure to do so prevents a finding of good faith. The judgment must be affirmed.

EDITOR'S ANALYSIS: This case points up an exception to the "bona fide purchaser for value" exception to the general rule that a vendor may not transfer something to which he lacks good title. Simply, a vendee/purchaser's failure to inquire into suspicious circumstances surrounding the title of his vendor is viewed as abrogating good faith in the purchase. Note, of course, that both questions of the existence of such circumstances and the failure of the vendee to sufficiently investigate them are questions of fact for the jury to determine. Levy's actions above are consistent with a common criminal scheme wherein a group buys a business with a good credit rating, buys a great deal of merchandise on credit, sells it at a low discount rate, then disappears before the bill from its creditors comes due. A person in the same business should, by the low discount prices offered by the criminals, know that something unusual is going on.

NOTES:

WOODENWARE COMPANY v. UNITED STATES
SUPREME COURT OF THE UNITED STATES, 1882.
106 U.S. 432, 1 S. Ct. 398

NATURE OF CASE: Action in the nature of trover for damages.

FACT SUMMARY: Woodenware (D) bought lumber which had been illegally cut on United States (P) Indian lands.

CONCISE RULE OF LAW: In an action for damages for property unlawfully appropriated by a seller against a purchaser who had no notice of any wrongdoing by such seller (but still failed to qualify as a "bona fide purchaser for value"), the measure of damages is the value of the property, improved or not, at the time of purchase.

FACTS: An unnamed trespasser cut and removed timber from United States public land (Oneida Indian Reservation) and sold them to Woodenware (D). The United States (P) sued Woodenware for damages for the timber. At trial, it was evidently proved that Woodenware (D) did not have a claim as a bona fide purchaser for value. Judgment was for the United States (P). Woodenware (D), however, challenges the measure of damages used by the trial court. It was proven at trial that, at the time of felling, the timber was worth $60.71 on the ground. After cutting them and transporting them, they brought a price of $850 from Woodenware (D). The trial court used the latter as the measure of damages. Woodenware (D) objects on the grounds that the United States (P) suffered no damage from the improvements made by the trespasser (cutting and transporting) which resulted in the higher sale value.

ISSUE: May the owner of misappropriated property recover the sale value of his property from a subsequent purchaser?

HOLDING AND DECISION: Yes. In an action for damages for property unlawfully appropriated by a seller, against a purchaser who had no notice of any wrongdoing by such seller (but still failed to qualify as a "bona fide purchaser for value"), the measure of damages is the value of the property, improved or not, at the time of the purchase. It is true that in cases where the trespass involved is innocent (either by the defendant in the case or by his vendor), the labor and expense of the defendant (here the price paid for cutting and transporting by the guilty trespasser if he were innocent) may be deducted from damages. But to allow a purchaser of property from a wrongdoer to retain that increment of value which was added by the wrongdoer after misappropriation, would, in light of the fact that the total value of the goods to the purchaser is so heavily made up of such increment ($790 of the $850), destroy any deterrent now existing against wrongdoers misappropriating others' property. The judgment must be affirmed.

EDITOR'S ANALYSIS: This case points up the general rule for damages recoverable from a bona fide purchaser. If a bona fide purchaser establishes his claim, he, of course, is not liable for damages for having asserted dominion over the property of another. Frequently, however, his claim will be found to be subordinate to that of the original owner. In such case he is liable for the taking. Two other concepts should be noted: accession and confusion. Accession occurs when the purchaser of property converts the specie of the property by his own work and labor (lumber into furniture), and gains a clear title to it thereby. Confusion of goods results when personal property belonging to two or more owners becomes intermixed to the point where the property of any of them no longer can be identified except as part of a mass of like goods. In such cases, all owners have equal pro rata interests in the mass.

NOTES:

RICHTMYER v. MUTUAL LIVE STOCK COMMISSION COMPANY

SUPREME COURT OF NEBRASKA, 1932.
122 Neb. 317, 240 N.W. 315

NATURE OF CASE: Action for conversion.

FACT SUMMARY: A thief took cattle from Richtmyer (P) and then sold them to Mutual Live Stock (D) who resold them innocently as regular beef cattle instead of more valuable pure breds which they were.

CONCISE RULE OF LAW: The general rule for the measure of damages for conversion (even against innocent purchasers) is the value of the property at the time and place of conversion with interest from that date, but the "time and place of conversion" must be determined by examining the acts of the purchaser in dealing with the property rather than the act of original taking in which the purchaser took no part.

FACTS: Cattle were stolen from Richtmyer (P) and sold to the Mutual Live Stock Commission Co. (D). Though they were pure bred hereford cattle valued at $3,500, they were resold by Mutual Live Stock (D) as ordinary beef cattle worth $1,000. Conceding that Mutual Live Stock (D) could not be charged with culpability, Richtmyer (P) nevertheless sues to recover the damage sustained upon the loss of the cattle. The trial court found for Richtmyer (P) and awarded as damages the value of the cattle at the time of their original taking ($3,500). Mutual Live Stock (D) appeals, contending that the trial court erred in not permitting evidence of their subsequent sale of the cattle ($1,000) to be admitted to the question of damages.

ISSUE: Is the "time of conversion" for damages in an action for conversion necessarily the time of the original wrongful taking?

HOLDING AND DECISION: No. The general rule for the measure of damages for conversion (even against innocent purchasers) is the value of the property at the time and place of conversion, with interest from that date; but, the "time and place of conversion" must be determined by examining the acts of the purchaser in dealing with the property rather than the act of original taking in which the purchaser took no part. In Woodenware Co. v. U.S., the U.S. Supreme Court held that the measure of damages, where value had increased at the time of resale, should be the time of such resale, to avoid officially recognizing the value increase earned by the thief himself. Here, the opposite situation has occurred. The value of the property here decreased by the time of resale. Whatever the rights of the parties in this case, it is clear that the court should have admitted evidence on the conduct of Mutual Live Stock (D) in their resale of the goods. Though Richtmyer (P) must be fully compensated for his loss, the court must examine Mutual Live Stock's (D) conduct as well. The judgment must be reversed.

EDITOR'S ANALYSIS: This case points up the general rule for determining time of conversion in cases where an innocent purchaser who does not qualify as a bona fide purchaser for value (and is insulated from liability thereby). The rule is really only consistent with the cause of action involved. It is only logical that an action for conversion by a subsequent purchaser should focus upon the time of conversion by that purchaser and not the time of acquisition by the thief/seller. To find otherwise would imply culpability for the purchaser. The purchase of stolen goods is in an analagous position criminally. The crime of receiving stolen goods "knowing them to be stolen" imposes criminal culpability upon one who knows or has reason to know that the goods he is purchasing are stolen.

NOTES:

STRONG v. WOOD
306 N.W 2d 737 (Iowa 1981)

NATURE OF CASE: Appeal from judgment affirming validity of deed.

FACT SUMMARY: Ruby Strong (P), the widow of the decedent, attempted to have a deed conveying her husband's farm to his children cancelled, on the grounds of fraud.

CONCISE RULE OF LAW: The fraudulent effects of a transferor's actions are determinative on the issue of actual fraud.

FACTS: Sometime in 1976, Philander L. ("Mike") Strong and Ruby Esterley (P) became acquainted. At that time Mike was a 76-year-old farmer who had lived by himself since the death of his previous wife, and Ruby (P) was a 66-year-old widow living in Minneapolis, Minnesota. Their relationship progressed to the point Mike proposed to her (P) in October 1976; Ruby (P), however, did not make up her mind to marry Mike until December 1976. On December 29, Mike called his children to a meeting at his lawyer's office, where it was agreed that the lawyer would draw up a warranty deed which, after reserving to Mike a life estate, would transfer Mike's interest in the farm to his three children. Mike and Ruby (P) married on January 26, 1977, and after his death on December 3, 1978, Ruby (P) brought this action against Mike's three children (D), requesting that the deed be cancelled and annulled, and that she be granted a one-third share of the farm on the grounds of fraud in inducing her into marriage. The district court found in favor of the children (D), and Ruby (P) appealed.

ISSUE: Are the fraudulent effects of a transferor's actions determinative on the issue of actual fraud?

HOLDING AND DECISION: (J. Larson) Yes. The fraudulent effects of a transferor's actions are determinative on the issue of actual fraud. The establishment of a claim of fraud should turn on proof of the following elements: (1) a transfer made during a contract to marry or under such other circumstances, including its proximity to the marriage, indicating it was made in contemplation of marriage; (2) lack of adequate consideration for the transfer; (3) lack of knowledge of the transfer on the part of the prospective spouse; (4) fraudulent intent on the part of the transferor; and (5) reliance by the prospective spouse upon the transferor's interest in the transferred property as an inducement to marriage. A presumption of fraudulent intent may be allowed on the part of the transferor upon establishment of the first three elements. Here, despite the existence of some evidence tending to show Mike's intent to defraud Ruby (P), including his failure to reveal the transfer prior to marriage and its proximity in time to the marriage, the existence of an engagement or contract of marriage at the time of the transfer was not established. Thus, there is no showing that she relied on her prospective property rights as an inducement to marriage. Affirmed.

EDITOR'S ANALYSIS: "There has been some conflict of authority over the fraudulent character of a voluntary conveyance of property by one engaged to marry where the conveyance is merely not revealed, no resort being made to any active expedient to mislead or keep the intended spouse ignorant with respect to the conveyance. One view is that the conveyance is actually fraudulent. . .Another view is that such a conveyance, though prima facie good, must be judged by its own particular surroundings, purposeful concealment, however, being evidence evidence of purposeful fraud. Still a different view is that such a conveyance is prima facie fraudulent, but the parties holding thereunder may show that no fraud was intended or practiced on the party complaining. . . ." 41 Am Jur. 2d Husband and Wife § 198, at 174(1968).

NOTES:

KERWIN v. DONAGHY
317 Mass. 559, 59 N.E.2d 299(1945)

NATURE OF CASE: Appeal from order to transfer and deliver stocks and bonds.

FACT SUMMARY: Kerwin (P), the widow of the decedent, contended that an inter vivos trust, under which all of the marital property has been transferred to Donaghy (D), the decedent's daughter, should not be held to be valid, so as to deny Kerwin (P) her share of the marital estate.

CONCISE RULE OF LAW: A husband has an absolute right to dispose of any or all of his personal property in his lifetime, without the knowledge or consent of his wife.

FACTS: Kerwin (P), the widow of William J. Kerwin, brought this petition in equity in the Probate Court against his daughter Gladys M. Donaghy (D) and the executors of his will to recover for the estate a large number of stocks, bonds and deposits in banks, standing in the name of or held by Donaghy (D), but owned, it was alleged, by the estate of William Kerwin. Testimony at trial showed that William Kerwin, after having an argument with his wife, went to his attorney and told the lawyer that he wished to make sure that at his death Donaghy (D) would own all the property that she was then holding for him. The evidence further established that, during his lifetime, Kerwin would have his children hold their father's property in their name, as a means of defrauding the federal government. The lawyer advised a trust, and two formal trust agreements were drawn up and executed by Kerwin and Donaghy (D). The trial judge, viewing the circumstances, concluded that Kerwin had not intended to disinherit his wife and entered a decree ordering Donaghy (D) to transfer and deliver the stocks, bonds and bank deposits held in trust to the executors. Donaghy (D) appealed.

ISSUE: Does a husband have an absolute right to dispose of any or all of his personal property in his lifetime, without the knowledge or consent of his wife?

HOLDING AND DECISION: (J. Lummus) Yes. A husband has an absolute right to dispose of any or all of his personal property in his lifetime, without the knowledge or consent of his wife, with the result that it will not form part of his estate for her to share under the statute of distributions. That is true even though his sole purpose was to disinherit her. Here, the trust agreements furnish incontrovertible internal evidence that they were intended to express the whole transaction between Donaghy (D) and her father. His apparent purpose was to render a will practically unnecessary, and his reserved power to alter, amend or revoke the trust did not make the trust testamentary in its nature. As a matter of law, the trust instruments must be taken as intended to accomplish the very purpose of the so-called parole evidence rule, that of fixing beyond all question the rights of the parties to those agreements in accordance with their terms, and to preclude resort to extrinsic evidence. It is true that a written contract or other instrument may be invalidated by extrinsic proof that it was executed as a joke or even in some instances as a pretense, with no intention on the part of either party that it should create any legal right or obligation. However, an inference of fact could not properly be drawn that the trust agreements were intended merely as shams. The evident purpose at the time was to disinherit Kerwin (P). Affirmed in part; reversed in part.

EDITOR'S ANALYSIS: The parol evidence rule, although concerning the admissibility of evidence, constitutes a rule of substantive law. As Professor Scott notes: "Under the parol evidence rule, if the manifestation of intention of the settlor is integrated in a writing, that is, if a written instrument is adopted by him as the complete expression of his intention, extrinsic evidence, in the absence of fraud, duress, mistake, or other ground for reformation or rescission, is not admissible to contradict or vary it." Scott, Trusts(1039), §§38,164.1.

NOTES:

SWADA v. ENDO
561 P. 2d 1291 (1977)

NATURE OF CASE: Action to set aside conveyance of real property.

FACT SUMMARY: Endo (D) and his wife conveyed tenancy-by-the-entirety property to their son after Endo (D) had been sued.

CONCISE RULE OF LAW: Tenancy-by-the-entirety property may not be reached by the separate creditors of either spouse.

FACTS: Endo (D), who had no liability insurance, severely injured Helen (P) and Masako Swada (P). Suits for personal injuries were filed against Endo (D). Endo's (D) only real asset was real property held as a tenant by the entirety with his wife. This was conveyed to their son, for no consideration, shortly after the Swadas (P) had filed suit. Endo (D) and his wife continued to live on the land even though they had not reserved an estate in it. The Swadas (P) each recovered a judgment against Endo (D), but were unable to satisfy it. The Swadas (P) subsequently brought an action to set aside the conveyance of Endo's (D) property to the son, alleging that it was fraudulent. Endo's (D) wife had died prior to the action. Endo (D) alleged that the conveyance could not be deemed fraudulent because the separate creditor of either spouse may not reach property held as tenants by the entirety.

ISSUE: May the separate creditor of either spouse reach property held in tenancy by the entirety?

HOLDING AND DECISION: No. While this is a question of first impression, and there are four separate views, we hold that the separate creditors of either spouse cannot reach property held as a tenancy by the entirety. The other views are that: (1) the creditor may reach the entire property subject to the wife's contingent right of survivorship if the husband is the debtor; (2) the creditor may reach the property subject only to the other spouse's right of survivorship; and (3) the right of survivorship may be levied upon. Tenancy-by-the-entirety property is generally the family residence and public policy considerations of promoting family solidarity, as well as stare decisis, favor the result reached herein. Since the Swadas (P) could not have reached the property, the conveyance to the son was not fraudulent. Dismissed.

DISSENT: (J. Kidwell) Under the Married Women's Act there is equality between the spouses. I would, on this basis, choose to allow creditors of either spouse to reach their right of survivorship.

EDITOR'S ANALYSIS: In Hurd v. Hughes, 12 Del. Ch. at 193, the court stated in support of its decision not to allow creditors of one spouse to reach tenancy-by-the-entirety property, "But creditors are not entitled to special consideration. If the debt arose prior to the creation of the estate, the property was not a basis of credit, and if the debt arose subsequently, the creditor presumably had notice of the characteristics of the estate which limited his right to reach the property."

PICO v. COLUMBET

SUPREME COURT OF CALIFORNIA, 1859. 12 Cal. 414

NATURE OF CASE: Bill in equity for an accounting.

FACT SUMMARY: Columbet (D), by his own labor and money, profited from the use of property owned by tenancy in common with Pico (P).

CONCISE RULE OF LAW: One tenant in common has no remedy against the other who exclusively occupies the premises and receives the entire profits unless (1) he is ousted of possession (when ejectment may be brought) or (2) the other is acting as bailiff for his interest by agreement (where an action for an accounting will lie).

FACTS: Columbet (D), by his own labor and money, profited from the use of property which he owned with Pico (P) by tenancy in common. Pico (P) contributed neither labor nor money to the enterprise. Pico (P), nevertheless, now demands an accounting for his share of the profits. He avers (1) a tenancy in common, (2) sole possession and occupancy by Columbet (D), (3) receipt by Columbet (D) of all rents, profits and issues, (4) refusal to account by Columbet (D), and (5) $84,000 due him as his share. A demurrer to Pico's (P) bill was overruled, but, it was dismissed on its merits after trial. He appeals.

ISSUE: Does a tenant in common have a cause of action against a fellow tenant in common who has taken all profits from and exclusively occupied their premises?

HOLDING AND DECISION: No. One tenant in common has no remedy against the other who exclusively occupies the premises and receives the entire profits therefrom unless (1) he is ousted of possession (when ejectment may be brought) or (2) the other is acting as bailiff for his interest by agreement (where an action for accounting will lie). Each tenant in common is entitled to occupation of the premises, neither can exclude the other. To allow one to hold the other liable for profits accrued during that other's sole occupation of the premises would be to defeat the right to occupation of the premises by permitting the extortion of a de facto rent. Here, Columbet (D) was entitled to occupancy of the premises involved. Whatever he gains from his labor and money on such premises is his alone. Though the original demurrer here should have been sustained, the subsequent dismissal is certainly affirmed.

The court points out in dicta that if the so-called Statute of Anne were in force in California, the decision here would be different. That statute gave a co-tenant a right to recover from another co-tenant any increment of rent over and above that other's proportional share by treating all co-tenants as bailiffs. This statute was never adopted in California, however.

EDITOR'S ANALYSIS: This case points up the general rule that a tenant in common is not under any duty to account for his use and occupation of common property. A duty to account does exist, however, with respect to rents and profits received from a stranger to the title (non co-tenant). Tenants in common have an equal, exclusive right to possession. No charge for that right can be made by another co-tenant.

This case also points up the two general exceptions to this rule. (1) If one tenant in common is dispossessed or excluded from possession by another tenant in common, he may be restored to possession by an ejectment (from his interest) action. In such cases, the dispossessed tenant may recover damages for use of the land by the other tenant in common. (2) Where by agreement a bailor/bailee arrangement is established between tenants in common, an accounting may be had.

Note, finally, that when an owner of land dies intestate (no will) his land passes to his heirs as tenants in common.

NOTES:

McKNIGHT v. BASILIDES

SUPREME COURT OF WASHINGTON, 1943.
19 Wash. 2d 391, 143 P. 2d 307

NATURE OF CASE: Action for partition and accounting for real property.

FACT SUMMARY: Alice Basilides died intestate (no will) with two children by a former marriage, one child by a current marriage and her current husband surviving her; and, as owner with her husband as tenants by entirety of two houses, which he has since controlled.

CONCISE RULE OF LAW: A claim by a tenant in common of adverse possession against co-tenants will not be effective until the co-tenants have acquired actual knowledge of repudiation of their rights by the claimant; and, such co-tenant owes an accounting to the other co-tenants for: (1) any rents received from third parties and (2) rents which would be received from third parties but for such co-tenants' own occupancy of the premises (if such notice has not occurred).

FACTS: Alice Basilides had two children by a former marriage (Alice McKnight [P] and Fred King [P]) when she married Charles Basilides (D). By him, she had a child, Ruth Allison. During their marriage, they acquired two parcels of property with houses on them (hereinafter referred to as "big house" and "little house). She died intestate (no will). By state law, her property passed one half to her husband and one half to her children, all as tenants in common of the estate. After her death and prior to this action, Charles Basilides (D) remained in occupancy in big house and rented out little house, upon which he also made certain repairs and improvements. At no time, however, did he ever assert or otherwise indicate his intention to take the houses by adverse possession from his other co-tenants. McKnight (P) and King (P) now sue for (1) partition of their one-sixth interest in the property in question, (2) a proportionate share of the rents collected from little house and rents which would have been collected on big house; and, (3) a lien against Basilides' share of the property until their judgment is satisfied. From a judgment for McKnight (P) and King (P), Basilides (D) appeals, contending complete ownership by adverse possession.

ISSUE: May a co-tenant in common assert a right to rents, etc., from third parties by declaring that he has gained adverse possession of the property involved by mere exclusive control of the property?

HOLDING AND DECISION: No. A claim by a tenant in common of adverse possession against co-tenants will not be effective until the co-tenants have acquired actual knowledge of repudiation of their rights by the claimant; and such co-tenant owes an accounting to the other co-tenants for (1) any rents received from third parties, and (2) rents which would be received from third parties but for such co-tenant's own exclusive occupancy of the premises (if such knowledge of adverse possession has not occurred). Whether title to property may be secured by a tenant in common through adverse possession depends upon the notoriety of the acts of adverse possession (they must show an "actual, uninterrupted, open, notorious, hostile and exclusive possession . . . under claim of right") and the intent with which they were done. Here, the facts of (1) no indication of any adverse claim of right ever being made by Basilides (D), and (2) no notice to or knowledge by the children of Alice that Basilides (D) intended to claim by adverse possession, both require a finding that no adverse possession took place. Since Basilides (D) was therefore never more than just another co-tenant in common, he owes the others an accounting for all rents which he collected or should have collected from third parties. As a result, he owes the others for the rent collected on little house (minus an offset for the improvements he made and whatever rents can be attributed to those improvements) and for reasonable pro rata rental value of big house which he occupied himself, instead of renting out.

DISSENT: The dissenting judge objects to the charging of rent for the occupancy of big house. He points out the generally accepted rule that a tenant in common is not chargeable for rent for exclusive occupancy of premises since he has a right to occupy at all times.

EDITOR'S ANALYSIS: This case points up the majority rule for adverse possession by tenants in common, and for accountings by tenants in common for rent received from third parties. It points up the decided minority rule for accountings for exclusive occupancy by co-tenants, however. The general rule is that a co-tenant is under no duty to account for use and occupancy of common property except for rents received from third parties. Perhaps the majority view above was somehow predicated upon a theory of ejectment. The majority may have believed that the exclusive holding of the property by Basilides (D) constituted a wrongful dispossession of the other co-tenants. While there is no evidence that Basilides (D) so dispossessed them by his occupancy, if such had been found, he would be liable for any damages (lost profits) from his use of the land.

NOTES:

CITY BANK & TRUST CO. v. MORRISSEY
454 N.E. 2d 1195 (1983)

NATURE OF CASE: Appeal from the distribution of trust assets.

FACT SUMMARY: Henry (D) contended the trial court erred in applying the Rule in Shelley's Case to a trust distribution, and therefore the real property of the trust should have been distributed in the same manner as the personal property in the trust.

CONCISE RULE OF LAW: The Rule in Shelley's Case applies only where: (1) a freehold estate is granted to an ancestor; (2) a remainder is limited to his heirs; and (3) the two estates are of the same quality.

FACTS: In 1952, Margaret Tyne died testate, establishing by her will a trust. The trust directed Henry (D) as trustee to distribute upon the death of William Tyne, the beneficiary, to his heirs at law, all the assets of the trust either in kind or after conversion into cash. Subsequently, Henry (D) resigned as trustee and City Bank (P) suceeded her. In 1980, William Tyne died testate. City Bank (P) sought judicial determination of the real and personal property distributions among Henry (D) and the other heirs at law of William Tyne, and Appleman (D) and the other residuary legatees under William Tyne's will. The trial court held that the Rule in Shelley's Case applied requiring distribution of the real property to Appleman (D) and the residuary legatees and the personal property to both the residuary legatees and the heirs at law. Henry (D) and the heirs appealed, contending that because William's interest was in realty and the legatees were required to receive the property in cash, the two estates were not of equal quality and the Rule in Shelley's Case did not apply. Therefore, they argued, the real and personal property should be distributed in the same manner.

ISSUE: Must the two estates created by a grant to the ancestor and his heirs be equal in quality in order for the Rule in Shelley's Case to apply?

HOLDING AND DECISION: (J. Nash) Yes. The Rule in Shelley's Case applies only where: (1) a freehold estate is granted to an ancestor; (2) a remainder is limited to his heirs; and (3) the two estates are of the same quality. In this case there was no dispute as to the first two requirements. As to the third, the trustee was specifically given the option either to distribute the trust property in kind or to convert to cash and then distribute it. In such a case, where the direction to convert the property to cash is not made mandatory, no duty to sell arises and therefore no equitable conversion of the real property into personal property occurs. As a result, the estates were equal as the trust did not create an equitable conversion of the real property into personalty upon William's death. Consequently, the Rule in Shelley's Case was properly applied, and the trial court's distribution was correct. Affirmed.

EDITOR'S ANALYSIS: The Rule of Shelley's Case has been abolished by statute or judicial decision in a vast majority of jurisdictions. The Rule, in essence, provides that where an instrument creates a freehold estate in one person and also attempts to create a remainder in his heirs, the remainder becomes a fee simple, if both estates are either legal or equitable. By illustration, O grants to X for life, remainder to X's heirs. The Rule of Shelley's Case will apply to make the conveyance read: "to X for life, remainder in fee simple to X." It is important to note that this is all the Rule does. It is only through application of the doctrine of merger that the conveyance will ultimately read: "to X in fee simple."

ESTATE OF ANNIE I. KERN
274 N.W.2d 325(Ia.-1979)

NATURE OF CASE: Appeal from decision distributing an estate.

FACT SUMMARY: The collateral heirs of Kern's deceased husband (P) contended that the doctrine of worthier title should not be applied in cases involving antilapse statutes.

CONCISE RULE OF LAW: The doctrine of worthier title is inapplicable in antilapse statute situations.

FACTS: Annie I. Kern and her predeceased husband had but one descendant, their son, Ralph Kern. Annie made a will giving all of her property to Ralph, who thereafter died unmarried. Annie died subsequent to Ralph's death, and her will was admitted to probate. The collateral heirs of Annie's deceased husband claimed that Annie's property was to be divided among Ralph's heirs. If so, half of the property would go to collateral heirs of Ralph's father, and half to the collateral heir of Annie, pursuant to an antilapse statute. Annie's collateral heirs (D) contended that the property was to be divided entirely among them under the judicially-created worthier title doctrine. Under that doctrine, a devise in the same quantity and quality as the devisee would take by descent is void. If the devisee survives the testator, he takes as heir. If he does not so survive, the property goes as though the devise had never been made. As a result, the worthier title doctrine operated to nullify the application of the antilapse statute. The probate court held that the property passed entirely to Annie's heirs, and Ralph's heirs on the father's side (P) appealed.

ISSUE: Is the doctrine of worthier title inapplicable in antilapse statute situations?

HOLDING AND DECISION: (J. Uhlenhopp) Yes. The doctrine of worthier title is inapplicable in antilapse statute situations. The doctrine of worthier title originally had a practical purpose. Under the feudal system, if real property passed by law, the lord retained benefits which were lost if the property passed by will. A rule was accordingly developed that they could only take from their ancestors by inheritance. A title thus acquired was considered a "worthier title." However, it is difficult to square the worthier title doctrine with the strong language of the antilapse statute. The statute makes no express exception for the case of the devisee who is an heir of the testator. To uphold the worthier title doctrine in that framework, the doctrine must be held to be the only exception to the antilapse statute. Accordingly, the doctrine of worthier title should no longer be applicable in situations involving the antilapse statute. The worthier title doctrine, if otherwise applicable, applies to other wills. Reversed.

EDITOR'S ANALYSIS: Professor Morris, in a law review article discussing the worthier title doctrine, states that: "What meritorious arguments can be made in favor of the. . .worthier title doctrine?. . .The rule invites litigation, ensnares the unwary draftsman and frustrates the wary draftsman. As a rule of law it applies to devises made to people who are the most natural objects of the testator's bounty. To the writer's knowledge, every man who has taken up the pen to write on the policy aspects of the rule has concluded that it has no place in our law." See, 54 Michigan Law Review 451,495.

NOTES:

JEE v. AUDLEY
1 Cox 324, 29 Eng. Rep. 1186 (1787)

NATURE OF CASE: Bill to secure the future benefits of a will.

FACT SUMMARY: The daughters of John & Elizabeth Jee (P) sought a declaration that their interests under a will were not void under the Rule Against Perpetuities.

CONCISE RULE OF LAW: The 21-year vesting period of the Rule Against Perpetuities must be satisfied at the time the gift is created; the use of subsequent events to satisfy the Rule is not permitted.

FACTS: Edward Audley (D) set up a will bequeathing the interest of £1,000 to his wife for life and then to his niece, Mary Hall and her lawful issue. If Mary died "in default of" lawful issue, the gift was to be divided equally among the daughters, then living, of John and Elizabeth Jee. At the time of the testator's death, the Jees were quite old and had four daughters (P). Mary Hall was unmarried and 40 years old. The Jee daughters (P) filed this bill to ascertain their rights.

ISSUE: May events occurring subsequent to the creation of an interest be used in determining the applicability of the Rule Against Perpetuities?

HOLDING AND DECISION: (Kenyon, J.) No. The time at which the Rule's vesting period must be satisfied is the time the interest is created. The fact that the Jees were of an advanced age at the time of the testator's death and were not likely to have after-born children is not relevant to the case. If at the time the interest is created, there is any possibility of vesting after the 21-year period, no matter how remote the possibility might be, the interest must fail. Had the testator limited the gift to the daughters alive at his death, the gift would have been good. But as it stands, there is the possibility of inclusion of after-born daughters and therefore the gift is in violation of the Rule Against Perpetuities and is void. Bill dismissed.

EDITOR'S ANALYSIS: A key to understanding Jee v. Audley is the definition of the term "default of issue" used in Audley's will. An individual is in default of issue when all of her descendants are dead. Because of the possible remoteness in such an event occurring, none of the potential measuring lives could be used and a Rule Against Perpetuities problem arose.

NOTES:

TEITELBAUM v. DIRECT REALTY CO.
SUPREME COURT, NASSAU COUNTY, 1939.
172 Misc. 48, 13 N.Y.S. 2d 886

NATURE OF CASE: Action to recover damages for failure to provide premises under a lease.

FACT SUMMARY: Direct Realty (D) executed a lease with Teitelbaum (P), but was unable to deliver possession of the premises on time because of a wrongful holdover by a prior tenant.

CONCISE RULE OF LAW: The extent of a landlord's implied agreement with his lessee is that he has good title by which he can give an unencumbered lease for the term demised; so, if at the time of commencement of the term, possession is held by a trespassing holdover, the landlord is under no duty to oust him.

FACTS: Direct Realty Co. (D) executed a lease with Teitelbaum (P) for certain commercial premises. Teitelbaum (P) had gotten out of a lease with another landlord so he could take possession of the premises in July and open up business in August. On July 1, however, the Fergangs, who had occupied the Direct Realty (D) premises as tenants up to that date, refused to move out. (They claimed a right of renewal under their lease, but subsequently defaulted in proceedings by Direct Realty (D) to oust them.) They did not move out, in fact, until January of the following year. Teitelbaum (P) sued to recover damages (consideration paid to be released from the other lease, etc.) for Direct Realty's (D) failure to oust the holdovers from the premises by the time of the commencement of the term. Direct Realty (D) moves for a dismissal of the complaint.

ISSUE: Does a landlord owe a duty to remove all wrongful holdovers and trespassers from his premises before commencement of the term of a lease?

HOLDING AND DECISION: No. The extent of a landlord's implied responsibility to his lessee is that he has good title by which he can give an unencumbered lease for the term demised; so, if at the time of commencement of the term, possession is held by a trespassing holdover, the landlord is under no duty to oust him. As such, the failure to do so does not render a landlord liable for damages. It is true that if the holdover tenant does by the authority of the landlord (prior "effective" lease, etc.), such landlord will be held for resultant damage to a lessee. Here, however, such is not the case. The Fergangs, by defaulting, admitted that they wrongfully held over, that they were trespassers. As such, Direct Realty (D) more than met its responsibilities to Teitelbaum (P) when it commenced the action to which the Fergang's defaulted. Direct Realty (D) had no duty to break. The complaint must be dismissed.

EDITOR'S ANALYSIS: A landlord merely covenants that a lessee will have a legal right to possession and quiet enjoyment of his premises. This is the overwhelming American rule although a minority of states do follow the English rule. In England, the landlord also implicitly covenants to deliver possession of the premises to the lessee at the commencement of the lease.

FRANKLIN v. BROWN
NEW YORK COURT OF APPEALS, 1889. 118 N.Y. 110, 23 N.E. 126

NATURE OF CASE: Action to recover rent.

FACT SUMMARY: Brown (D) leased a dwelling house from Franklin (P) but was unable to occupy the house because of noxious odors coming from an adjoining stable.

CONCISE RULE OF LAW: Absent evidence of fraud or express covenant or warranty to repair, a landlord will not be held to any implied covenant that the demised premises are (1) suitable for occupation, (2) suitable for the purpose the tenant intends to use them for, or (3) even in a safe condition.

FACTS: Brown (D) leased a furnished dwelling house from Franklin (P) for a term of one year. She had fully inspected the premises before entering the agreement. Subsequently, the odors from an adjoining livery stable rendered the premises unfit for human habitation. (The stable was owned by a third party.) As a result, Brown (D) refused to pay the last three months' rent. Franklin (P) sued to recover this rent; Brown counterclaimed for damages arising from the uninhabitability of the premises. After a finding of fact as per above, the referee found for Franklin (P). Brown (D) appeals.

ISSUE: May a tenant be relieved of responsibility to pay rent by means of showing a failure by a landlord to meet an implied warranty of habitability of the premises?

HOLDING AND DECISION: No. Absent evidence of fraud or express covenant or warranty to repair, a landlord will not be held to any implied covenant that the demised premises are (1) suitable for occupation, (2) suitable for the purpose the tenant intends to use them for, or (3) even in a safe condition. A lessee of real property must run the risk of its condition, unless he has an express agreement with the lessor covering that subject. The tenant hires at his peril, in a manner similar to the doctrine of caveat emptor. He has the responsibility of seeking out defects in the premises and protecting himself against them (by not leasing or taking action to correct them). If he accepts the lease, however, he cannot later complain about what he has accepted. Here, Brown (D) inspected the premises prior to leasing them. The odor, which was in no way the responsibility of the landlord, Franklin (P) may not be used to relieve him of liability for rent. The judgment must be affirmed.

In dicta, the court points out that, of course, if the nuisance was caused by Franklin (P), then Brown (D) could recover damages for it.

EDITOR'S ANALYSIS: This case points up the majority but disfavored rule. This is based primarily on the common-law view of a lease as the purchase of an interest in land as opposed to a contract. The trend of authority (Wisconsin, District of Columbia, California) is contra this, however. Recognizing the modern contractual nature of a lease, many jurisdictions are recognizing an implied warranty of habitability in each lease, the breach of which by the landlord relieves the tenant of a duty to pay rent. In California, by statute, a tenant may deduct from rent any necessary repair costs which the landlord refuses to assume. This latter is the modern, better view.

NOTES:

MILHEIM v. BAXTER
SUPREME COURT OF COLORADO, 1909.
46 Colo. 155, 103 P. 376

NATURE OF CASE: Action for damages for constructive eviction.

FACT SUMMARY: Baxter (P) was forced to move from premises leased from Milheim (D), because of an adjoining house of prostitution, also owned by Milheim (D).

CONCISE RULE OF LAW: All leases carry an implied covenant for the quiet enjoyment of the leased premises; and any act wilfully done by a landlord which breaches this covenant and forces the tenant to vacate the premises may be treated as a wrongful (constructive) eviction for which the tenant may recover damages.

FACTS: Baxter (P) rented premises for a term of one year from Milheim (D). Unknown to her (Baxter [P]) at the time of execution of the lease, the adjoining premises (also owned by Milheim [D]) functioned as "an assignation house, where immoral men and women were constantly meeting for immoral purposes . . ." Because of the vulgar conduct of her neighbors, Baxter (P) vacated the premises. Baxter (P) sued to recover damages and be relieved of further rent responsibilities. From judgment in her favor, Milheim (D) appeals.

ISSUE: May a tenant be relieved of rent responsibility and recover damages on the grounds of being forced to vacate by a wilful act of the landlord which prevents that tenant from using the premises as he wishes?

HOLDING AND DECISION: Yes. All leases carry an implied covenant for the quiet enjoyment of the leased premises; and any act wilfully done by a landlord which breaches this covenant and forces the tenant to vacate the premises may be treated as a wrongful (constructive) eviction for which the tenant may recover damages. Stated another way, a constructive eviction occurs whenever a landlord, by illegal act, materially disturbs the possession of his tenant. Such construction eviction justifies (1) abandonment of the premises with no further rent liability and (2) damages where appropriate for the tenant. Here, though there is no evidence that Milheim (D) had actual knowledge of the use to which his premises were being put, such is not necessary. His knowledge was inferred from the overwhelming circumstances by the jury below. Judgment must be affirmed.

EDITOR'S ANALYSIS: This case points up the generally accepted concept of covenant for the quiet enjoyment of leased premises. Not all conduct by a landlord which interferes with the tenant's enjoyment of leased land will constitute a breach of this covenant, however. The interference must be substantial — must materially impair the tenant's ability to remain in possession of the leased premises. Then and only then will the tenant be relieved of the responsibility to pay rent. There is no single generally accepted criteria for what interferences are substantial enough and what are not. In addition to immoral acts (supra), insect or vermin infestation, major amenity malfunction (flooded out, etc.) and, in some instances, illegality are other criteria that may result in a finding of constructive eviction.

BLACKETT v. OLANOFF
— Mass. — (1977)

NATURE OF CASE: Action for rent due and owing.

FACT SUMMARY: Tenants (D) alleged that Blackett (P), the landlord, had breached his covenant of quiet enjoyment as a defense to an action for rent.

CONCISE RULE OF LAW: Where a landlord permits conduct of third persons which substantially impairs the right of quiet enjoyment of other tenants, it is a constructive eviction.

FACTS: Olanoff (D) and other tenants vacated an apartment building owned by Blackett (P) and others. Blackett (P) sued for rent due and owing. The tenants (D) alleged that their right to quiet enjoyment had been substantially impaired by the landlords (P). Blackett (P) had rented nearby property as a bar. The noise from the bar was often very loud and significantly disturbed the apartment tenants. Blackett (P) periodically warned the bar tenants to keep the noise down as they were obligated to do under the lease. The noise would be abated for a while, but it always became loud again. The tenants (D) finally vacated the apartments and Blackett (P) sued for rent. The court found that the tenants' right to quiet enjoyment had been substantially interfered with and that this constituted a constructive eviction which was a defense to an action for rent. Blackett (P) appealed, alleging that there could be no constructive eviction where the landlord had not, by his actions, caused the breach of the covenant.

ISSUE: Can a constructive eviction be found where the landlord permits a third party to substantially impair the rights of other tenants?

HOLDING AND DECISION: Yes. Normally, there must be some action by the landlord himself which causes the constructive eviction. Intent to deprive the tenants of their rights is not required. Where the landlord permits an activity to continue, which he can control, which causes significant impairment of the rights of other tenants, this constitutes a breach of the landlord's covenants. Here, Blackett (P) permitted a bar next to a residential apartment. Blackett (P) had the power to control the noise in the bar under the terms of its lease. Blackett (P) knew that the noise from the bar was disturbing tenants and failed to correct the matter. Under these circumstances, a constructive eviction may be found. Affirmed.

EDITOR'S ANALYSIS: Other examples of nonconduct by the landlord which have been held to constitute constructive eviction are: failure to supply adequate light, heat, etc. Burt, Inc. v. Seven Grand Corp., 340 Mass. 124 (1959); authorization by the landlord for a tenant to obstruct the view, light and air of another tenant to a substantial extent. Case v. Minot, 158 Mass. 577 (1893); and a defective boiler causing excessive soot and smoke for a long period of time. Westland Housing Corp. v. Scott, 312 Mass. 375 (1942).

JOHNSON v. O'BRIEN
SUPREME COURT OF MINNESOTA, 1960.
258 Minn. 502, 105 N.W. 2d 244

NATURE OF CASE: Action for damages for personal injuries.

FACT SUMMARY: Johnson (P) injured himself when the step in a stairway of premises leased from O'Brien (D) gave way.

CONCISE RULE OF LAW: Where a landlord has knowledge of conditions which would lead a reasonable man exercising due care to believe that danger exists on leased premises at the time that a tenant takes possession; and that such tenant, exercising due care, would not be able to discover the danger by himself, the landlord is under a duty to disclose his knowledge to his tenant.

FACTS: Mrs. Elletson leased an apartment from O'Brien by an oral month-to-month tenancy with no covenant to repair. The outside stairway, which was used to reach her walk-up apartment, was over 30 years old. This fact, however, was evidently never communicated to her by O'Brien. When her son, Johnson (P), came to visit her, one of the steps gave way, causing him to fall and injure his back. He sued for damages. From judgment in his favor, O'Brien (D) appeals, contending that a jury instruction which indicated that he had a duty to inform his tenant of the condition of the stairway was erroneous.

ISSUE: Does a landlord have a duty of due care to inform his tenant of latent defects in the demised premises?

HOLDING AND DECISION: Yes. Where a landlord has knowledge of conditions which would lead a reasonable man exercising due care to believe that (1) danger exists on leased premises at the time that a tenant takes possession, and (2) that such tenant, exercising due care, would not be able to discover the danger by himself, the landlord is under a duty to disclose his knowledge to his tenant. This is a matter of negligence liability. Such liability is clearly not limited to instances where the lessor has actual knowledge of a specific dangerous condition on the premises, but includes instances where his knowledge of general conditions in the premises should cause him to realize potential danger. Here, the 30-year-old condition of the staircase should have made the landlord, O'Brien (D), aware of potential danger to tenants. As such, he had a duty to inform them of such condition.

DISSENT: The dissenting Justice points out that, by the general rule of no implied warranty to repair, the landlord should not be held liable for injuries due to latent defects in the premises absent some express covenant to repair such.

EDITOR'S ANALYSIS: This case points up the general rule that a landlord has a duty to disclose latent defects in leased premises. Liability for failure to disclose is based upon the theory that a landlord, in effect, places his tenant in danger by allowing him to take possession without knowing about dangerous latent defects. Three hurdles must usually be overcome by a tenant in establishing liability in such cases: (1) he must prove the landlord knew of the latent defect; (2) he must prove that the landlord had concealed the existence of the latent defect; and (3) he must prove that he did not know of the latent defect.

BOWLES v. MAHONEY
CIRCUIT COURT OF APPEALS OF DIST. OF COLUMBIA, 1952.
202 F. 2d 320, Cert. Denied, 344 U.S. 935, 1953

NATURE OF CASE: Action for damages for personal injuries.

FACT SUMMARY: Mahoney (P) was injured when a retaining wall collapsed on him on premises his uncle leased from Bowles (D).

CONCISE RULE OF LAW: Absent any contractual or statutory duty, a landlord will not be held liable for an injury to a tenant resulting from a defect in the premises developing during the term of the lease; and the duties owed to an invitee of a tenant are the same as those owed to the tenant himself.

FACTS: Mahoney (P) was living with his Uncle, Gaither. Gaither was leasing a dwelling from Bowles (D). Some years before, Bowles (D) had erected a retaining wall to maintain a passageway between the leased dwelling and the one adjacent to it. This wall ran down across the public parking area, as well. While Mahoney (P) was playing near this wall on the public parking area, it collapsed on him, injuring him. He sues Bowles (D) for damages. At trial, his mother (Mrs. Armstrong) testified that she had notified the real estate agent of Bowles (D) about a crack in the wall, but that nothing was done about it. From a judgment for Mahoney (P), Bowles (D) appeals.

ISSUE: Does a landlord have a duty to repair dangerous conditions which arise during the term of a lease?

HOLDING AND DECISION: No. Absent any contractual or statutory duty, a landlord will not be held liable for an injury to a tenant resulting from a defect in the premises developing during the term of a lease, and the duties owed to an invitee of a tenant are the same as those owed to the tenant himself. Before a landlord can be held liable for injuries incurred by others on his premises, some duty to those others must be established. As an invitee of a tenant stands in the place of that tenant in relation to the landlord, no greater duty than that owed a tenant may be imposed. It is well settled, however, that unless a landlord expressly assumes liability for keeping premises in repair, the tenant, not the landlord, must assume liability for injuries caused by negligently allowed defects in the premises. Here, there was no statutory or contractual duty for Bowles (D) to keep the premises in repair. The duty was Gaither's. As such, neither Bowles (D) nor the District of Columbia (controllers of the public parking area) may be held liable. The judgment must be reversed.

DISSENT: The dissenting Justice Bazelon characterizes the rule that a defect developing during the term of a lease cannot be the basis of landlord liability an anachronism. He points out that the rule was a quasi- "caveat emptor" rule for leases when such were still considered mere sales of an interest (term) in land. The development of contract theory in landlord tenant relations, however, has brought with it implications of mutual responsibilities of parties to a lease, during the running of the term. The social and economic considerations involved lead Bazelon to conclude that the burden of this responsibility (maintenance and repair) should be shifted to the landlord.

EDITOR'S ANALYSIS: This case points up the general rule that there is no implied duty to repair in a lease. As the sale of an interest in land, a lease confers that total interest (a term). For that interest or term, the tenant has total responsibility (including, usually, tort liability to third parties) since he has bought it. This is in contrast, of course, with contract theory in which each party has a set of mutual obligations to one another. As such, each party to a lease has only an obligation to not harm the other's interest. For a landlord, this means not disturbing the tenant's term interest (covenant of quiet enjoyment). For a tenant, this means not disturbing the landlord's remainder interest (not committing waste). Note, however, that these covenants are not mutually dependent (as contract rights are). As such, the disturbing of a landlord's covenant of quiet enjoyment by a tenant does not imply permissible wasting of the landlord's remainder by the tenant.

NOTES:

FABER v. CRESWICK

SUPREME COURT OF NEW JERSEY, 1959.
31 N.J. 234, 156 A. 2d 252

NATURE OF CASE: Action for damages for personal injuries.

FACT SUMMARY: Faber (P) was injured when she fell through a plaster-board floor section in premises leased from Creswick (D).

CONCISE RULE OF LAW: The negligent omission by a landlord to perform a duty to repair will result in tort liability for any proximately caused injuries to tenants or third parties (e.g., family, invitees); and, even in the absence of a covenant to repair, omission by a landlord to disclose defects actually known to him (whether negligently or fraudulently) will result in tort liability for any proximately caused injuries to tenants or third parties as well.

FACTS: Faber (P) had leased a summer house from Creswick (D). Prior to the lease, Creswick (D) had completed a "do-it-yourself" remodeling job in the house, which included the placing of thin plaster board over a portion of the stairwell leading to the attic. The plaster board was so situated that it would appear to be just another part of the floor in the attic. Upon taking possession of the premises, Mrs. Faber (P) who had orally negotiated but not actually executed the lease herself (her husband did the negotiating) fell through the plaster board, suffering injuries. Creswick (D) had never given any indication of the inherently dangerous situation of the plaster board flooring. Mrs. Faber (P) sued for damages, citing a lease clause which stated that the landlord would, "... have the house thoroughly clean and in good order and repair at the beginning of this lease ..." From a dismissal, she appeals.

ISSUE: May a landlord be held liable for injuries caused by a defect in leased premises where the victim is not a party to the lease?

HOLDING AND DECISION: Yes. The negligent omission by a landlord to perform a duty to repair will result in tort liability for any proximately caused injuries to tenants or third parties (e.g., families, invitees); and, even in the absence of a covenant to repair, omission by a landlord to disclose defects actually known to him (whether negligently or fraudulently) will result in tort liability for any proximately caused injuries to tenants or third parties, as well. It is true that Mrs. Faber (P) lacks privity to the lease. This is an outdated concept, however. It is utterly unrealistic to say that a head of a household can bargain for a lease to a house without taking the safety of his family into material consideration. Here, the hazardous condition of the plaster board flooring was known to the landlord, Creswick (D). His failure to disclose this fact was actionable generally, and his failure to correct it was actionable on the lease. Though Mrs. Faber (P) did not execute the lease, she was obviously a contemplated resident. Dismissal must be reversed and remanded for new trial.

EDITOR'S ANALYSIS: This case points up the general rule for negligently failing to repair where there is a duty to do so. Caveat emptor, however, generally precluded such a duty, since absent an express contractual provision by a landlord at common law, there was no reason why he should have anything at all to do with the premises, the possessory interest in which had been sold to another for a term. Generally, covenants to repair may invoke either privileges or duties to repair by one party or another. Traditionally, the most common was the covenant for the tenant to make all repairs as a matter of duty to the landlord. (Under common law he could be held to a duty of due care in tort for invitees entering his land while he was in possession, as well.) The trend of authority, however, is that repairs are the responsibility of the landlord (as is compliance with the housing codes). In California, for example, it is provided by statute that a tenant has a right to deduct from his rent the cost of any necessary repairs which the landlord refuses or neglects to make.

NOTES:

SARGENT v. ROSS

113 N.H. 388 (1973)

NATURE OF CASE: Wrongful death action.

FACT SUMMARY: Sargent's (P) daughter was killed when she fell down a set of stairs leading up to a leased apartment.

CONCISE RULE OF LAW: A landlord will be liable for any unreasonably dangerous conditions which he permits to remain on leased property, even after control over it has been relinquished.

FACTS: Ross (D) had constructed a set of stairs leading up to a second floor apartment which Ross (D) leased to her daughter-in-law. Sargent (P) used the daughter-in-law as a baby sitter for her son. The stairs were very steep and the guard rail was insufficient to prevent a child from falling through it. The child fell to his death while under the care of the daughter-in-law. Sargent (P) brought a wrongful death action against Ross (D) for negligent construction of the stairway and against the daughter-in-law for her negligent care of the child. The jury found for the daughter-in-law, but against Ross (D). Ross (D) appealed alleging that she had no duty of care since this was not a common stairway and it was under the control of her tenant, the daughter-in-law. Sargent (P) relies on the exception to the rule that a landlord is not responsible for injuries occurring on areas over which there is no longer control, i.e., negligent repair of the premises.

ISSUE: Should a landlord be liable for unreasonably dangerous conditions which are permitted to remain on leased premises even after control over them has been relinquished to the lessee?

HOLDING AND DECISION: Yes. The rule protecting landlords from liability for dangerous condtitions on leased property is outmoded. Rather than carve out further exceptions to this rule, we opt to discard the general rule. A landlord will be liable for injury resulting from a dangerous condition which exists on leased property even if control over the condition has passed to the lessee. Rather than a "control" test, the emphasis will be whether the landlord acted reasonably under all of the circumstances. If an unreasonably dangerous condition was permitted to exist, the landlord should be liable since the tenant generally has no authority to remedy structural defects such as herein. The jury could have found that the steps were too steep and the guard rail was inadequate to prevent an injury. The obviousness of the risk to an adult would not apply to a child of very tender years. The judgment is affirmed.

EDITOR'S ANALYSIS: Sargent is a minority result. In Dapkunas v. Cagle, 42 Ill. App. 3d 644 (1976), the court refused to adopt Sargent. The court found that Sargent adopted a rule paralleling strict liability and finding a breach of a warranty of habitability which was breached by an unreasonably dangerous condition. The Dapkunas court found that the exceptions to the caveat emptor rule were sufficient in most cases to meet the expectations of the parties.

LOUISIANA LEASING CO. v. SOKOLOW

CIVIL CT. OF THE CITY OF NEW YORK, QUEENS COUNTY, 1966.
48 Misc. 2d 1014, 266 N.Y.S. 2d 447

NATURE OF CASE: Action to remove tenants as objectionable.

FACT SUMMARY: Sokolow (D) and his family were objected to by the middle-aged tenants below them because of the noise their children made.

CONCISE RULE OF LAW: A landlord has no right to eject a tenant-couple for a breach of a noise covenant in a lease by their children where (1) the complaining tenant moved in after the tenant-couple, and (2) the noise was not, in and of itself, found to be deliberate or excessive.

FACTS: Sokolow (D), his wife, and children leased an apartment from Louisiana Leasing Co. (P) for a term. In that lease there was an express covenant which stated that "No tenant shall make or permit any disturbing noises ... or ... interfere with the rights, comforts of convenience of other tenants." Subsequently, the Levins moved in immediately under Sokolow (D) in the building. They made complaints about the noise made by Sokolow's (D) children. Sokolow (D) admitted that the children did run and play but stated that they always took their shoes off and that the noise was never excessive. Eventually, Louisiana Leasing (P) brought action to have Sokolow (D) removed from the premises for breaching the above covenant.

ISSUE: May a tenant be evicted under a noise covenant in a lease where the noise involved is not at all excessive?

HOLDING AND DECISION: No. A landlord has no right to eject a tenant-couple for a breach of a noise covenant in a lease by their children where (1) the complaining tenant moved in after the tenant couple, (2) the noise was not, in and of itself, found to be deliberate or excessive. Sokolow (D) got there first. There is no evidence of any complaints from prior tenants in Mr. Levin's or any other apartment. Only ordinary noise (walking, playing by children) was produced; it is hardly the fault of Sokolow (D) that the building was made with thin walls. In all, it would be totally inequitable to evict him. The petition must be denied.

EDITOR'S ANALYSIS: This case involved a petition in equity. That is why the equitable considerations controlled. Nevertheless, one important doctrine implicitly determined this case "moving to the nuisance." Generally, a person cannot move into an apartment, etc., knowing it to be subject to some nuisance, then object to it as a nuisance once in possession. This is still another offshoot of the common-law view of a lease as the sale of an interest in land (term). The application of the doctrine of caveat emptor to land leads logically to the rule that the purchase of an interest in land with a nuisance on it gave the tenant only what he bargained for; and that he should not subsequently be allowed to challenge it.

NOTES:

KING v. COONEY-ECKSTEIN CO.
SUPREME COURT OF FLORIDA, 1913.
66 Fla. 246, 63 So. 659

NATURE OF CASE: Suit to recover compensatory damages for personal injuries.

FACT SUMMARY: Defendant, lessee of a wharf, failed to keep it in repair during his occupancy, and, due to this failure, plaintiff was injured.

CONCISE RULE OF LAW: Even though the lessor covenanted to repair the leasehold, the tenant is under a duty to repair and keep the premises in a reasonably safe condition for persons who lawfully enter them.

FACTS: Cooney-Eckstein Co. (D) was the lessee of a dock, which the lessor covenanted "to keep in good repair." More than two years after the lease began, a decayed plank gave way and injured King (P) who was carrying lumber to a ship being loaded at the dock. The lessor had reserved the right to use the dock for loading and unloading. Although the loading in which King (P) was injured may not have been under Cooney-Eckstein's (D) direction, it does not appear that any one other than Cooney (D) was in control of or occupied the dock at the time of the injury. The defect in the plank was not obvious to a casual observer, but could have been seen by a reasonably careful inspection.

ISSUE: Where a lessor has covenanted to keep the premises in repair, is a lessee liable for damages caused by defects in or dangers on the premises to persons lawfully thereon, which could have been avoided by the tenant's taking appropriate care?

HOLDING AND DECISION: Yes. The tenant and occupier of premises is bound to keep the premises in reasonably safe condition for persons who lawfully go upon the premises by express or implied invitation. The tenant is prima facie liable for damages caused by defects in or dangers on the premises that reasonably could have been avoided by the tenant's appropriate care. This is the law, even where the lessor covenanted to keep the premises in repair. In this case, since Cooney (D) occupied the dock at the time of the injury, and the injury was caused by a defect which reasonable inspection would have revealed, Cooney (D) is liable for King's (P) damages.

EDITOR'S ANALYSIS: In general, a landlord is not liable for injuries resulting from a defective condition of the leasehold. The lessee takes responsibility for the damages occurring incident to the defect because, although merely a lessee, he has the right to possession and control of the land. The exceptions to this rule of imposing liability on the lessee for personal injuries caused by a defect in the condition of the leasehold are: (1) those areas under control of the lessor such as buildings wherein the landlord has several tenants; (2) those defective conditions which exist prior to the time the lessee takes possession, of which the lessor has knowledge and of which the lessee is not notified; (3) those leaseholds which are used frequently by the public.

SUYDAM v. JACKSON
COMMISSION OF APPEALS OF N.Y., 1873. 54 N.Y. 450

NATURE OF CASE: Action to recover rent alleged to be due under a lease.

FACT SUMMARY: Jackson (D) leased a store from Suydam (P) for a term of three years. After two years, Jackson (D) notified Suydam (P) that the store had become untenantable due to a leak in the roof.

CONCISE RULE OF LAW: The landlord-tenant relationship imposes a duty upon the lessee to make such ordinary repairs as are necessary to prevent waste and decay of the premises. This burden to repair is not upon the lessor.

FACTS: Jackson (D) entered into a three-year lease for a certain store with Suydam (P). The lease did not contain any covenant to repair on Suydam's (P) part. Its term ran from May 1, 1966. On May 1, 1968, Jackson (D) notified Suydam (P) that the store had become untenantable and unfit for occupancy, and he surrendered possession of it. The alleged untenantability was caused by a roof leak which had been caused by the elements and by age and which rendered the premises damp and wet. Neither Jackson (D) nor his sub-tenants made any repairs. Jackson (D) rests his defense on a statute which relieves a lessee from paying rent where a building has been so destroyed or injured by any cause, other than any fault or neglect by the lessee, so as to be untenantable.

ISSUE: Where the elements and age have caused a roof to decay and leak, can a lessee surrender the premises and cease his rental payments?

HOLDING AND DECISION: No. At common law the lessor was under no obligation to repair. If the premises became wholly untenantable during the term due to destruction by fire, flood, tempest, or otherwise, the lessee still remained liable for the rent. Further, the lessor had an implied duty to return the premises uninjured and undeteriorated by his willful or negligent conduct. The lessee had to make such ordinary repairs as were necessary to prevent waste and decay. The lessee, being present, could with slight effort and expense save a great loss. Hence, the law justly casts this burden upon him. The statute did not shift this burden to the lessor. It refers only to situations in which the premises were injured or destroyed. This means a sudden and total, or near total destruction. It does not include gradual deterioration from the ordinary action of the elements. Since in this case, the destruction was of the latter type, it does not fall within the statute, and Jackson (D) is not relieved of his duty to pay rent on the remaining year of the term of the lease.

NOTES:

(Continued on Next Page)

EDITOR'S ANALYSIS: The longstanding rule has been that in the absence of a statute or agreement to the contrary, a lessor is not required to improve or repair the leased premises, and a covenant to repair on the part of the landlord would not be implied. However, some states have adopted the doctrine of implied warranty of habitability which imposes upon the landlord the duty to keep the premises in a habitable condition. The doctrine of partial eviction has also been used to relieve lessees of their duty to pay rent where part of the premises have become inhabitable.

NOTES:

KENNEDY v. KIDD
557 P. 2d 467 (1976)

NATURE OF CASE: Claim against an estate.

FACT SUMMARY: Kennedy (D) died in an apartment and his body was not discovered for several weeks which required the landlord, Kidd (P), to completely refurbish the apartment.

CONCISE RULE OF LAW: A tenant is liable for injury to the apartment caused only by ordinary acts of negligence absent a specific lease provision to the contrary.

FACTS: Kennedy (D) entered into a month-to-month lease of an apartment from Kidd (P). Unknown to anyone, Kennedy (D) died in his apartment. Kennedy's (D) death was not discovered for several weeks and, by that time, the body had become rather badly decomposed. Kidd (P) filed a claim against the estate for unpaid rent, refurbishing the apartment, and loss of rental income due to the refurbishment. The Administrator of Kennedy's estate (D) allowed only Kidd's (P) claim for unpaid rent. Kidd (P) sued for the balance on the theories that a tenant was obligated to return the apartment in the same general condition as it was in when the lease began and the public policy required that the estate, rather than the landlord, bear such losses as herein. Kidd (P) admitted that there was no action available for acts or omissions committed during Kennedy's (D) lifetime.

ISSUE: Is a tenant liable for any and all damage occurring to the apartment absent a specific lease provision to this effect?

HOLDING AND DECISION: No. Under the common law the tenant is not the landlord's insurer. He need take only reasonable care of the property to prevent damage. Under statutory law, the tenant is liable only for damage caused by simple acts of negligence. While a lease may modify these statutory or common-law duties, in the absence of a specific lease provision, damage of the type herein involved will not support a claim against decedent's estate. Public policy cannot require that decedent's estate bear the loss without a corresponding expansion of our laws on duty and liability. We find that Kidd (P) cannot prevail against Kennedy's estate (D).

EDITOR'S ANALYSIS: A tenant is not the insurer of the property absent a contract clause. Under common law, he is not liable for normal wear and tear to the property. Hill v. McKay, 31 Del. 213. A tenant is not liable for damage caused by acts of nature which he could not have foreseen and which he was powerless to prevent. No common-law duty exists in such cases. Pollard v. Shaeffer, 1 U.S. 210.

POLACK v. PIOCHE

SUP. COURT OF CALIFORNIA, 1868. 35 Calif. 416

NATURE OF CASE: Action to recover damages for nonperformance of a covenant to repair.

FACT SUMMARY: Polack (P) leased certain premises to Pioche (D) who agreed to make repairs, excepting damage by the elements or acts of God. The premises were damaged by a torrent of water from a natural reservoir.

CONCISE RULE OF LAW: If it appears that a given loss has happened in any way through the intervention of a human being, it cannot be held to have been an act of God or damage by the elements.

FACTS: Polack (P) leased certain land and a residence to Pioche (D), who agreed to make repairs with the exception of damage by the elements or acts of providence. During the term of the lease the premises were damaged by a torrent of water sweeping through them. The torrent was produced by the accumulation of water from unusual rains which was collected in a natural reservoir on the land of a third party. Prior to the damages, adjacent land occupiers, including Pioche (D), strengthened the reservoir's embankment. But some unknown person interfered with the embankment and through their interference the embankment was made to give way, thereby causing the torrent and the damage.

ISSUE: If it appears that a given loss has happened in any way through the intervention of a human being, can it be held to have been an act of God or damages by the elements?

HOLDING AND DECISION: No. Acts of God are those which could not happen by the intervention of a human being, such as storms, lightnings, and tempests. "The elements are the means by which God acts." Hence, any loss which has happened in any way through the intervention of a human being cannot be held to be an act of God or damage by the elements. A general covenant to repair is binding upon the tenant under all circumstances, and if the tenant desires to relieve himself from liabilities resulting from any cause, he must except them from the operation of the covenant. In this case, Pioche (D) only excepted acts of God and damage by the elements. Had the water which caused the damages broken through the embankment without interference by a human being, the loss would fall into an exception in Pioche's (D) covenant. But, since the water would not have broken through without the help of a person, the damages were caused by a stranger, and Pioche (D) is liable by the force of his covenant.

EDITOR'S ANALYSIS: Where a lessee covenants to make certain repairs, the covenant will be construed to extend only to the repairs stipulated. Ordinarily, no covenant to make additional repairs will be implied. An express agreement that the tenant will not be liable for certain repairs does not, generally, obligate the landlord to make the repairs. However, there is opposing authority.

NOTES:

MELMS v. PABST BREWING COMPANY

SUP. COURT OF WISCONSIN, 1899. 104 Wis. 7, 79 N.W. 738

NATURE OF CASE: Action for waste.

FACT SUMMARY: Pabst Brewing Co. (D) is the owner of an estate for the life of another of certain land. Melms (P) is the owner of the remainder and claims that Pabst (D) committed waste by destroying a house on the land.

CONCISE RULE OF LAW: In the absence of any contract to use the property for a specified purpose, or to return it in the same condition in which it was received, a radical and permanent change of surrounding conditions must always be an important and sometimes controlling consideration upon the question whether a physical change in the use of the buildings constitutes waste.

FACTS: Pabst Brewing Co. (D) acquired Ms. Melms' life estate in a certain property. The house on the property was a large brick building built by Mr. Melms in 1864 and cost more than $20,000. Pabst (D) acquired the life estate when Mr. Melms died, leaving his estate in financial difficulties. Pabst (D) acquired full title to a brewery on adjacent land. Melms (P) are the owners of the residential property, subject to Pabst's (D) life estate. After Pabst (D) purchased the property, the general character of the surrounding neighborhood rapidly changed. Factories, railway tracks and brewing buildings were built until the property in question became an isolated lot and building, standing twenty to thirty feet above street level. The residence became of no practical value and would not rent for enough to pay the taxes and insurance on it. Pabst (D) removed the house and graded down the property to street level. Melms (P) contends that these acts constituted waste.

ISSUE: Does a change in the nature of a building, though enhancing the value of the property, always constitute waste if the identity of the estate has been changed?

HOLDING AND DECISION: No. The rule that any change in a building upon the premises constitutes waste has been greatly modified. While such a change may constitute technical waste, it will no longer be enjoined when it clearly appears that the change will be a meliorating one which actually improves the property rather than injuring it. Under ordinary circumstances the landlord or revisioner is entitled to receive the property in substantially the same condition as it was when the tenant received it. However, in the absence of any contract to use the property for a specified purpose or to return it in the same condition in which it was received, a radical and permanent change of the surrounding conditions, which deprives the property of its value and its usefulness as previously used, must always be an important, and sometimes controlling consideration upon the question whether a physical change in the use of buildings constitutes waste. Here there was no contract. Pabst's (D) rights may continue for a number of years. The evidence shows that the property became valueless for the purpose of a residence, due to the change of the surrounding neighborhood. In light of these considerations, Pabst's (D) acts did not constitute waste.

(Continued on Next Page)

SIGSBEE HOLDING CORP. v. CANAVAN

CIVIL COURT OF THE CITY OF NEW YORK, BRONX
COUNTY, 1963. 39 Misc. 2d 465, 240 N.Y.S. 2d 900

EDITOR'S ANALYSIS: The purpose of the doctrine of waste is the preservation of the property for the benefit of the owner of the future estate without permanent injury to it. As this case demonstrates, the law of waste is not unchanging. Hence, the same act may be waste in one part of the country while in another part it is considered a legitimate use of the land. The usages and customs of each community are important in the decision of whether a certain act constitutes waste.

NOTES:

NATURE OF CASE: Action to evict.

FACT SUMMARY: While Sigsbee Holding Corp.'s (P) tenant, Canavan (D), replaced old used cabinets with new ones, Sigsbee (P) contends this constituted waste.

CONCISE RULE OF LAW: Where an alteration is essential to the proper use of the premises and increases its value, it may be made by a tenant if a prudent owner of the property would be likely to make it in view of the conditions existing on or in the neighborhood of the affected land.

FACTS: Canavan (D) is a tenant of Sigsbee Holding Corp. (P). As such, he replaced some old used cabinets with new ones. Sigsbee (P) contends that this constituted waste and a violation of a substantial obligation of the tenancy. The old cabinets hung on only two nails, and there was a hole in the ceiling above with an exposed BX cable.

ISSUE: Does a tenant's replacing of old cabinets with new ones constitute waste?

HOLDING AND DECISION: No. The common-law rule which prohibits material and substantial alterations has been changed by the legislature. Now where an alteration is essential to the proper use of the premises and increases its value, it may be made by a tenant if a prudent owner of the property would be likely to make it in view of the conditions existing on or in the neighborhood of the affected land. Where a tenant removes a landlord's sink, stove or refrigerator and replaces them with his own without the landlord's consent, he does not violate a substantial obligation of the tenancy. Likewise, in the absence of a specific covenant in a lease prohibiting the use of washing machines without the landlord's consent, the use of a movable washing machine which is not permanently attached does not constitute a violation of a substantial obligation of the tenancy. The real inquiry in all cases involving alterations made by the tenant is whether there has been damage done which injures the reversion. In this case there was no proof that Canavan's (D) alterations involved an injury to the reversion. The alterations were made in the course of Canavan's (D) proper use and enjoyment of the premises, and enhanced their value. Nor was there any proof that the alterations were a substantial and permanent change in the nature and character of the property.

EDITOR'S ANALYSIS: Likewise, the installation of air-conditioning units which are not attached to the property does not constitute waste. Generally, a tenant may, when it is good husbandry and necessary to the enjoyment of his use, clear off timber and prepare land for cultivation, and sell the timber so cut. But he cannot cut timber merely to sell. Also, a tenant may use mines which have already been opened, but he will commit waste if he opens up new mines or quarries on the demised premises and takes rock, oil, minerals, etc. from them.

MALLORY ASSOCIATES, INC. v. BARVING REALTY CO.

NEW YORK COURT OF APPEALS, 1949.
300 N.Y. 297, 90 N.E. 2d 498

NATURE OF CASE: Action to recover security deposit.

FACT SUMMARY: Mallory Associates (P) alleges that Barving Realty Co. (D) mingled Mallory's (P) security deposit with Barving's (D) personal monies.

CONCISE RULE OF LAW: A statute which forbids the mingling of security deposits with landlord's money is applicable to funds deposited in the state as security under a lease made within the state between corporations created by the state, even though the property of the lease is located outside of the state.

FACTS: In 1946, Mallory Associates, Inc. (P) leased a hotel located in Virginia from Barving Realty Co. (D). The lease provided for a $65,000 security deposit which would be returned to Mallory (P) in full provided Mallory (P) fully carried out all of the terms of the lease. Both Mallory (P) and Barving (D) are New York corporations with offices in New York. Mallory (P) paid Barving (D) the deposit. Mallory (P) alleges that Barving (D) mingled the $65,000 with its own monies, thereby converting it to its use.

ISSUE: Is a statute which forbids the mingling of security deposits with landlord's money applicable to funds deposited in the state as security under a lease made within the state between corporations created by the state where the property of the lease is located outside of the state?

HOLDING AND DECISION: Yes. At common law a deposit of security by a tenant under a lease created a debtor-creditor relationship, and the landlord had the right to use the money until the repayment date. The legislature changed that rule. Now the relationship is one in which the landlord holds the money in trust, and the money cannot be mingled with the landlord's funds. The legislature's purpose was to prevent the depletion of funds deposited with the lessor. The statute was passed to protect security deposits paid in New York by New York residents. The need for protection is no less when the land of the lease is situated outside of New York. Since the legislature did not expressly limit the statute's applicability to property situated within the state, it will apply to property outside of New York. Hence, it is applicable in this case, and Barving's (D) motion to dismiss is denied.

EDITOR'S ANALYSIS: Money paid on the execution of a lease falls into four categories: (1) advance payment of rent; (2) a bonus or consideration for the execution of the lease; (3) liquidated damages; and (4) a deposit to secure faithful performance of the lease's terms. The question as to the purpose of such payment depends on the intent of the parties as determined from the language of the lease, considered in the light of the circumstances surrounding the transaction.

FIFTY STATES MANAGEMENT CORP. v. PIONEER AUTO PARTS, INC.

46 N.Y. 2d 573, 389 N.E. 2d 113 (1979)

NATURE OF CASE: Appeal from dismissal of action to enforce a rent acceleration clause.

FACT SUMMARY: Pioneer (D) contended that a rent acceleration clause in its lease should not be enforced as it constituted a penal forfeiture, and therefore it is disfavored by courts sitting in equity.

CONCISE RULE OF LAW: Rent acceleration clauses are enforceable in the absence of fraud, overreaching, or unconscionability.

FACTS: Pioneer (D) leased commercial property from Fifty States (P) for a period of 20 years. The parties agreed to the inclusion in the lease of a clause which provided that if Pioneer (D) defaulted in its obligation to pay rent, the entire rental amount of the lease would become due and payable. Subsequently, Pioneer (D) failed to make its rent payments. Fifty States (P) called a meeting, yet Pioneer (D) still failed to tender payment. Fifty States (P) sued to enforce the acceleration clause, and Pioneer (D) defended on the basis that enforcement would be an inequitable penal forfeiture. The trial court dismissed the complaint on these equitable grounds, and the appellate court affirmed. Fifty States (P) appealed.

ISSUE: Are rent acceleration clauses enforceable?

HOLDING AND DECISION: (J. Cooke) Yes. Rent acceleration clauses are enforceable in the absence of fraud, overreaching, or unconscionability. In this case the clause was fully bargained for by Fifty States (P) and specifically agreed to by Pioneer (D). It represents the exact amount of damages incurred as a result of the breach and therefore could not be considered a penalty. As a result, the clause was not fraudulently agreed to or unconscionable and was enforceable. Reversed.

EDITOR'S ANALYSIS: The use of rent acceleration clauses aids the landlord in avoiding costly and time consuming litigation. Problems arise concerning the enforcability of such clauses in jurisdiction which require the landlord to mitigate his damages. It is more likely in such jurisdictions that the clause will be held unenforceable as a penalty rather than a valid liquidated damages clause.

NOTES:

JAMAICA BUILDERS SUPPLY CORP. v. BUTTELMAN
MUNICIPAL COURT OF THE CITY OF NEW YORK, QUEENS
COUNTY, 1960. 205 N.Y.S. 2d 303

NATURE OF CASE: Summary proceedings to remove a tenant.

FACT SUMMARY: Buttelman (D), Jamaica Builders Supply Corp.'s (P) lessee failed to pay rent. His lease contained a clause stating that the breach of any covenant or condition by Buttelman (D) would give Jamaica (P) the right to terminate the lease.

CONCISE RULE OF LAW: In deciding whether a provision in a lease creates a conditional limitation or a condition subsequent, the intention of the parties from the language of the entire lease is determinative, and only if there is a clear intention that when an event happens the lease by its terms comes to an end will the provision be considered a limitation.

FACTS: Buttelman (D) occupies an apartment under a written lease running from May 1, 1960 through April 30, 1962. The lease contains a provision whereby if Buttelman (D) breaches any condition or covenant of the lease or is deemed an undesirable tenant by the lessor, Jamaica Builders Supply Corp. (P), Jamaica (P) may terminate the lease by giving Buttelman (D) five days' notice. The lease contains another clause whereby Buttelman (D) agrees to pay attorney fees for a summary proceeding based upon his non-payment of rent, and his failure to pay the fees will result in it being added to his next month's rent. On August 1, 1960, Buttelman (D) failed to pay the rent.

ISSUE: In deciding whether a provision in a lease creates a conditional limitation or condition subsequent, is the provision to be considered standing alone and by itself?

HOLDING AND DECISION: No. In order to terminate a lease in case of a condition, some act must be done upon the happening of the contingent event, such as making an entry. While in the case of a conditional limitation the mere happening of the event is, in itself, the limit beyond which the lease no longer exits, and no entry or other act is necessary to terminate the lease. In order to prevent an immediate forfeiture of a tenancy, conditions tending to defeat a grant are generally strictly construed. The search is for the intention of the parties from the language of the entire lease, and only if there is a clear intention that when an event happens the lease by its terms comes to an end will a provision be considered a limitation. In this case the clause by which Buttelman (D) agreed to pay attorney's fees for a summary proceeding based on his non-payment of rent is typewritten. The clause clearly gives Jamaica (P) an additional remedy by reason of non-payment of rent. It contemplates a situation where rent may not be paid when due and the lease would not come to an end. Searching for the intention of the parties, the typewritten portion of the lease must prevail over printed clauses. The other clause was printed. It appears that the parties did not intend a termination of the lease by reason of non-payment of rent on August 1, 1960.

EDITOR'S ANALYSIS: The decision between a condition and a conditional limitation is procedurally important since the landlord must first regain possession by ejectment in case of condition, but can resort to summary proceedings in case of conditional limitation. An action of ejectment is a relatively slow, fairly complex, and substantially expensive procedure. It is a common-law action which does still exist. In the nineteenth century the summary proceeding was devised. It is a simpler, speedier procedure for obtaining possession.

NOTES:

JORDAN v. TALBOT

SUP. COURT OF CALIFORNIA, 1961.
55 Cal. 2d 597, 12 Cal. Rptr. 488, 361 P. 2d 20

NATURE OF CASE: Action for forcible entry and detainer and conversion.

FACT SUMMARY: When Jordan (P) was behind in her rental payments, Talbot (D), her lessor, entered her apartment, removed her furniture and refused to allow her to re-enter. Her lease gave Talbot (P) the right of re-entry upon the breach of any of its conditions.

CONCISE RULE OF LAW: Ownership or a right of possession to the property is not a defense to an action for forcible entry.

Any unauthorized opening of a closed door is a breaking open of the door sufficient to constitute forcible entry.

A person who obtains possession to property by a forcible entry does not have the right to retain possession.

In the absence of provisions in a lease for enforcement of lien granted by the lease, equitable action would be necessary to make the lien operative.

FACTS: Jordan (P) was a tenant in Talbot's (D) apartment house. Her lease gave Talbot (D) a right of re-entry upon the breach of any of its conditions and a lien upon all personal effects, furniture and baggage in Jordan's (P) premises to secure the rent. When Jordan (P) had become two months behind in her rent, Talbot (D) without her consent, and during her absence, unlocked the door of her apartment, entered and removed her furniture to a warehouse, and refused to allow her to re-occupy the apartment.

ISSUE: Where a lease grants a landlord a right of re-entry upon the breach of any of its conditions and a lien upon the tenant's personal property, has a landlord who enters the tenant's premises by unlocking the door, and removes his/her belongings, committed forcible entry?

HOLDING AND DECISION: Yes. Ownership or a lien upon the tenant's personal property is not a defense to an action for forcible entry. Absent a voluntary surrender of the premises by the tenant, the landlord could enforce his right of re-entry only by judicial process, not by self-help. Since a lessor may summarily obtain possession of real property within three days, he has a sufficient remedy, and self-help is not necessary. Further, a provision in a lease expressly permitting forcible entry would be void as contrary to the public policy.

Any unauthorized opening of a closed door is a breaking open of the door sufficient to constitute forcible entry. It is not necessary that there have been any physical damage to the premises or actual violence. Also, a forcible entry is completed if, after a peaceable entry, the tenant is excluded from possession by force or threats of violence.

A person who obtains possession to property by a forcible entry does not have the right to retain possession. Such detention is unlawful and constitutes forcible detainer.

In the absence of provisions in a lease for enforcement of a lien granted by the lease, equitable action would be necessary to make the lien operative. In this case Talbot (D) entered Jordan's (P) apartment without her consent. His lien and the right of re-entry granted by the lease did not give him the right to enter her apartment. Such unauthorized entry constituted forcible entry, even though there was no actual violence accompanying it. Jordan (P) was refrained from re-entering her apartment by threats of violence (Talbot's [D] employee told her, "Get the hell out of here. You're out."). This constitutes a second basis for the finding of a forcible entry. Lastly, Talbot's (D) detention of the premises by force constituted forcible detainer.

EDITOR'S ANALYSIS: The object of the law of forcible entry and detainer is to prevent the disturbance of the public peace, by the forcible assertion of a private right. Regardless of who has the right to possession, orderly procedure and preservation of the peace require that the actual possession shall not be disturbed except by legal process. Because of the importance of public peace, a tenant's rights under the laws of forcible entry and detainer cannot be contracted away, as demonstrated by this case, where Talbot's (D) right of re-entry and his lien on personal property in Jordan's (P) apartment did not justify his entry, even though not violent, into the apartment. The dissenting Justice believes that where entry is authorized by contract and is made by means of a key only, without any actual force or violence, there has not been a forcible entry. The refusal of the majority to sustain Talbot's (D) contract rights appears, he feels, to constitute state action impairing the obligation of a contract in violation of the United States and California constitutions.

NOTES:

TEODORI v WERNER
490 Pa. 58, 415 A.2d 31 (1980)

NATURE OF CASE: Appeal from a judgment of possession entered for a landlord.

FACT SUMMARY: Werner (D) contended that Teodori's (P) violation of a non-competition clause in a lease precluded Teodori (P) from suing for rent due and in ejectment.

CONCISE RULE OF LAW: A landlord's breach of a lease's non-competition clause is a valid defense to the landlord's actions for rent payments due and in ejectment.

FACTS: Werner (D) leased a store in a shopping center from Teodori (P) for the purpose of operating a jewelry store. The lease included a non-competition clause which prohibited Teodori (P) from leasing space in the shopping center to any other jewelry or gift shop. Subsequently, Teodori (P) obtained a judgment against Werner (D) for unpaid rent and utility payments. Werner (D) petitioned to open the judgments, contending he was released from his obligation to pay by Teodori's (P) violation of the non-competition clause, caused by his renting space to another jewelry business. Teodori (P) contested opening the judgment on the basis that the breach was not a valid defense to the non-payment of rent. The trial court dismissed the petition, and Werner (D) appealed.

ISSUE: Is a landlord's breach of a non-competition clause a valid defense to the landlord's action for rent payments and ejectment?

HOLDING AND DECISION: (J. Roberts) Yes. A landlord's breach of a lease's non-competition clause is a valid defense to his action to recover rent payments and to eject the tenant. In this case the promise not to rent to competing businesses was a significant inducement to Werner's (D) entering into the lease. As a result, the obligation to pay rent and the duty under the non-competition clause cannot be considered independent obligations. The duty to pay rent depended on Teodori's (P) compliance with the non-competition clause and this breach constituted a valid defense to Teodori's (P) action for rents and ejectment. Reversed and remanded.

EDITOR'S ANALYSIS: This case illustrates a self-held remedy available to tenants in some jurisdictions. It allows tenants to cease rental payments upon the landlord's breach of the lease. This approach has been adopted in the Restatement Second of Property. §11.1. Some jurisdictions, however, allow only retroactive abatement of rent.

NOTES:

MARINI v. IRELAND
56 N.J. 130, 265 A.2d 526 (1970)

NATURE OF CASE: Appeal from judgment for default in rent payments.

FACT SUMMARY: Marini (P) contended his tenant, Ireland (D), could not offset the cost of repairing her plumbing against the rent due because he as the landlord had no duty to repair the plumbing.

CONCISE RULE OF LAW: A landlord's failure to repair facilities necessary to maintain the premises in a livable condition, within a reasonable time after being given adequate notice of the need for such repairs, allows the tenant to repair the condition and offset the cost against future rent.

FACTS: Marini (P) leased an apartment for one year to Ireland (D). The lease did not include a specific covenant for repairs and described the premises as four rooms and a bath. The use of the apartment was limited by the lease exclusively for the purpose of a dwelling. Subsequently, Ireland (D) repeatedly attempted to tell Marini (P) that the toilet leaked, yet was unsuccessful in notifying him. She then had a plumber repair the toilet and offset the cost of the repair against her rent payment. Marini (P) sued, contending no offset could be made because he had no duty to repair the toilet. The trial court held for Marini (P), and Ireland (D) appealed.

ISSUE: Can a tenant offset the cost of necessary repairs against future rents?

HOLDING AND DECISION: (J. Haneman) Yes. A landlord's failure to make repairs necessary to maintain the premises in a habitable state allows the tenant to offset the cost of such repairs against future rents after giving the landlord adequate notice of the need for such repairs. In this case, even though no specific covenant to repair was made, the description of the apartment included a bath, and limited the use of the premises to dwelling. The absence of workable toilet facilities rendered the apartment unfit for its intended use, and therefore created a duty in Marini (P) to repair the problem. Upon his failure to do so within a reasonable time permitted Ireland (D) to have the toilet repaired and to offset the cost against future rent. Reversed.

EDITOR'S ANALYSIS: Some jurisdictions, such as California, limit the amount which a tenant may offset against future rents in making necessary repairs. California Civil Code § 1942 provides that such offset may be made but only if the amount of the expenditure does not exceed the amount of one month's rent. The parties may expand this, however, in the rental agreement.

LLOYD v. MURPHY

SUP. COURT OF CALIFORNIA, 1944.
25 Cal. 2d 48, 153 P. 2d 47

NATURE OF CASE: Action for declaratory relief to determine rights under a lease and for unpaid rent.

FACT SUMMARY: Murphy's (D) lease restricted his use of the demised premises to the selling of gasoline and new cars. The federal government ordered the sale of new cars discontinued. Lloyd (P), Murphy's (D) lessor, waived the restriction.

CONCISE RULE OF LAW: The defense of commercial frustration requires that to excuse his non-payment of rent a lessor must prove that the risk of the frustrating event was not reasonably foreseeable and that the purpose for which the property was leased was totally, or nearly totally, destroyed.

FACTS: Lloyd (P) leased certain premises to Murphy (P) for five years beginning September 1941, for the sole purpose of selling new automobiles, selling gasoline and occasionally selling a used automobile. Murphy (D) agreed not to sublet without Lloyd's (P) written consent. In January 1942, the federal government ordered that the sale of automobiles be discontinued. Within the month it modified its order to allow sale to those in the military and to persons with preferential ratings. Lloyd (P) waived the restrictions in the lease in March 1942. But Murphy (D) vacated the premises shortly thereafter. Lloyd (P) re-rented the premises. Murphy (D) continues to sell cars at two other locations.

ISSUE: To rely on the doctrine of commercial frustration, must a lessee prove that the purpose for which the property was leased was totally, or nearly totally, destroyed by an unforeseeable event?

HOLDING AND DECISION: Yes. The doctrine of frustration has been limited to cases of extreme hardship so that business persons can continue to rely with certainty on their contracts. If an event was foreseeable, there should have been a provision for it in the contract, and the absence of such a provision gives rise to the inference that the risk was assumed. Thus, laws or other governmental acts that make performance unprofitable or more difficult or expensive do not excuse the duty to perform. In this case, at the time the lease was executed, the automotive industry was in the process of conversion to supply the needs of the army, and automobile sales were soaring because the public anticipated the restriction of production and sales. It cannot be said that the risk of war and the resulting restriction of the sale of automobiles was so remote that it could not be foreseen by Murphy (D).

Secondly, a lessee seeking to rely on the defense of frustration must prove that the value of the lease has been destroyed. The defense has been allowed in cases involving premises leased as a saloon which were rendered valueless by prohibition. In the present case, the purpose of the lease was not destroyed, but only restricted, and Lloyd (P) proved that it was still of value to Murphy (D). Lloyd (P) waived the restrictions, thus allowing Murphy (D) to use the premises for any legitimate purpose and to sublet them to any responsible tenant. The value is demonstrated by the fact that the premises were rented soon after Murphy (D) vacated them. Hence, the governmental restriction did not destroy the value of the lease. Judgment for Lloyd (P) is affirmed.

EDITOR'S ANALYSIS: As demonstrated by this case the applicability of the doctrine of frustration depends on the total, or nearly total, destruction of the purpose for which the transaction was entered into. The question in such cases is who should bear the risk for such a destruction. The court decided that the consequence of applying the doctrine of frustration to a leasehold involving less than total or near total destruction would be undesirable. Confusion would result from different decisions of the definition of "substantial" frustration, and litigation would be increased as lessees repudiated their leases when they found their businesses less profitable because of regulations accompanying a national emergency.

NOTES:

ALBERT M. GREENFIELD & CO., INC. v. KOLEA
475 Pa. 351, 380 A.2d 758 (1976)

NATURE OF CASE: Appeal from award of damages for breach of lease agreements.

FACT SUMMARY: After a fire had accidentally destroyed the leased premises, Albert M. Greenfield & Co., Inc. (P) ("Greenfield"), the lessor, sought to enforce the lease agreement against Kolea (D), the lessee.

CONCISE RULE OF LAW: The accidental destruction of the leased premises excuses the parties from further performance of their obligations under a lease agreement.

FACTS: On March 20, 1971, Kolea (D) executed two agreements to lease two buildings for a term of two years, beginning May 1, 1971. On May 1, 1972, an accidental fire completely destroyed the building covered by one of the leases. On the following day, barricades were placed around the perimeter of the premises covered by both leases. Kolea (D) then refused to pay rent under either of the leases. Greenfield (P) sued Kolea (D) for breach of the two lease agreements and was granted judgment for $7,200.00

ISSUE: Does the accidental destruction of the leased premises excuse the parties from further performance of their obligations under a lease agreement?

HOLDING AND DECISION: (J. Manderino) Yes. The accidental destruction of a building by fire excuses the parties from further performance of their obligations under a lease agreement. The traditional rule provided that in the absence of a lease agreement to the contrary, a tenant was not relieved from the obligation to pay rent despite the total destruction of the leased premises. Two exceptions to this rule have been widely recognized. Where only a portion of a building is leased, total destruction of the building relieves the tenant of the obligation to pay rent. The second exception provides that impossibility or impracticability of performance arising from the accidental destruction of the leased property ends all contractual obligations relating to the property destroyed. Here, it is more equitable for Greenfield (P), the lessor, to assume the risk of accidental loss of the leased premises.

CONCURRENCE: (J. Roberts) The unexpressed intent of the parties to allocate risks is irrelevant, because the Restatement, Second, Property, allocates the risk of loss in these circumstances to the lessor.

CONCURRENCE: (J. Nix) The common law rule that an accidental fire which totally destroys a building is no defense to a claim for rent is clearly inappropriate in our present society.

EDITOR'S ANALYSIS: As contract law is increasingly applied in the landlord-tenant context, the doctrine of frustration of purpose is being invoked with increasing regularity. This approach recognizes that in situations such as those presented by this case, the parties have bargained for the existence of a building, rather than for the possession of the soil on which the building was located.

NOTES:

LEONARD v. AUTOCAR SALES & SERVICE CO.
SUP. COURT OF ILLINOIS, 1945.
392 Ill. 182, 64 N.E. 2d 477

NATURE OF CASE: Action to recover rent alleged to be due and unpaid under a lease.

FACT SUMMARY: Leonard (P) leased property to Autocar Sales & Service Co. (D) for a term of twenty years ending on November 30, 1946. In March 1943, the government condemned the property until June 30, 1943, with the right to extend for additional yearly periods. Autocar (D) vacated and refused to pay further rent.

CONCISE RULE OF LAW: In order for a tenant to be excused from the payment of rent because of the condemnation of the demised premises, it is essential that the estate of the landlord be extinguished by the condemnation proceeding.

FACTS: Leonard (P) leased certain property to Autocar Sales & Supply Co. (D) for a term of twenty years ending November 30, 1946. On March 11, 1943, the temporary use of the entire property was condemned, for a term ending June 30, 1943, with the right to extend the term for additional yearly periods. Autocar (D) vacated the premises on March 25, 1943, and refused to pay further rent. On May 1, 1943, the temporary use of the premises was condemned for an additional yearly period.

ISSUE: Is the test to apply in determining whether a condemnation excused the tenant from further payment of rent, whether the taking rendered the leased premises incapable of occupation under the lease?

HOLDING AND DECISION: No. The proper test is whether the estate of the landlord has been extinguished. In order for a tenant to be excused from the payment of rent because of the condemnation of the demised premises, it is essential the landlord's estate has been extinguished by the condemnation proceeding. In this case, the condemnation of the leased premises for temporary use merely carved out of Autocar's (D) long-term lease a short-term occupancy. It neither destroyed the property nor Leonard's (P) lease-hold estate in the property. Since Autocar (D) is entitled to receive from the government full compensation for as much of its leasehold estate as is appropriated to public use, there is no hardship or injustice in holding it to its duty to pay rent.

EDITOR'S ANALYSIS: Eminent domain is defined as the right of the nation or state, or those to whom the power has been lawfully delegated, to condemn private property for public use, and to appropriate the ownership and possession of such property for such use, upon paying the owner just compensation, which is to be ascertained according to law. The right of eminent domain is an inherent attribute of sovereignty, and it extends to every kind of property, including not only that which is tangible, but all rights and interests of any kind. In this case the court also considered whether the doctrine of commercial frustration was applicable and decided it was not.

LEFRAK v. LAMBERT
89 Misc. 2d 197, 390 N.Y.S. 2d. 959,
New York City Civ. Ct., Queens Cty. (1976)

NATURE OF CASE: Action for damages for breach of a lease.

FACT SUMMARY: Lefrak (P) sued to recover the balance due on a a three-year lease after Lambert (D) abandoned the premises.

CONCISE RULE OF LAW: A landlord must show he made a reasonable good faith effort to mitigate his damages upon a tenant's abandonment by attempting to rent the premises to a third party for the remainder of the lease period.

FACTS: Lefrak (P) owned a 5,000 unit apartment complex in New York. He leased one unit to Lambert (D) under a three-year lease. Lambert (D) paid a security deposit equalling two-months' rent, and occupied the apartment from September 1973 to November 1974, when he abandoned possession while two months behind in rent. The apartment remained unrented for 17 months. Lefrak (P) sued to recover the balance of the rent due under the lease, $4,552, plus $910 for legal fees. Although denying a duty to mitigate damages, Lefrak (P) presented evidence that a five-member staff worked full time during the period of vacancy screening potential tenants and advertising the availability of units. No evidence was presented showing efforts exclusively aimed at renting Lambert's (D) apartment. Lambert (D) contended he would pay what was fair and did not deny liability.

ISSUE: Does a landlord have a duty to mitigate his damages by asserting a good faith effort to rent abandoned apartments?

HOLDING AND DECISION: (J. Posner) Yes. A landlord must show he made a reasonable good faith effort to mitigate his damages upon a tenant's abandonment by attempting to rent the premises for the remainder of the lease period. The modern trend is to apply contract principles to lease agreements, and the duty to mitigate damages is a long standing precept of contract law. In this case, Lefrak (P) failed to show that a good faith effort had been made to rent Lambert's apartment. The 17 months of vacancy was clearly unreasonable given the size of the complex. As a result, a reasonable period of three months vacancy will be inferred. Therefore, three-months' rent will be added to the two months Lambert (D) was behind, and the security deposit will be subtracted to arrive at damages of $743. Legal fees will be $148.

EDITOR'S ANALYSIS: The preface to the opinion of the Court in this case belies the underlying predisposition of Judge Posner to find for Lambert (D). It is clear that he felt it would be inequitable for an apartment owner with Lefrak's resources to be allowed to recover against a man of simple means like Lambert (D). This led him to abandon the traditional rule that there is no duty to mitigate. On appeal, this case was modified, yet the court did not decide whether a duty to mitigate existed as it found Lefrak (P) had made a good faith effort to rent the apartment.

LEFRAK v. LAMBERT
93 Misc. 2d 632,403 N.Y.S. 2d 397 (Sup. Ct. App. Term) (1978)

NATURE OF CASE: Appeal from award of damages for abandonment of a tenancy.

FACT SUMMARY: The trial court held Lefrak (P) could not recover for the rent due on the full lease after Lambert's (D) abandonment because it found he had not made a good faith effort to mitigate his damages.

CONCISE RULE OF LAW: A landlord may recover the balance of rent payments called for under a lease after the premises are abandoned by the tenant.

FACTS: Lefrak (P) leased an apartment to Lambert (D) for three years. Prior to the termination date of the lease, Lambert (D) abandoned the tenancy while two months behind in rent. Lefrak (P) maintained a full time staff which sought to fill vacancies in the apartment complex through advertising available units and screening applicants. Despite these efforts, the apartment remained vacant for 17 months. Lefrak (P) sued to recover the full rent due under the lease and attorney's fees. The trial court held that Lefrak (P) had failed to make a good faith effort to mitigate his damages by renting the apartment and limited the reovery to three-months' rent. Lefrak (P) appealed.

ISSUE: May a landlord recover for the rent due on the balance of a lease period upon the tenant's abandonment of the tenancy?

HOLDING AND DECISION: (Per Curiam) Yes. A landlord may recover the balance of rent payments due on a lease upon the tenant's abandonment of the tenancy. Whether or not a duty exists in the landlord to mitigate his damages, in this case Lefrak (P) demonstrated he made a good faith effort to rent the apartment, and therefore was entitled to recover the full amount of the lease. Reversed.

EDITOR'S ANALYSIS: The majority rule holds that a landlord has no duty to mitigate damages upon a tenant's abandonment. The rationale for this is that under this rule, a lease is considered a conveyance rather than a contract. The tenant is considered to have purchased the leasehold, and the landlord is under no duty to resell it for him.

NOTES:

WRIGHT v. BAUMANN
SUPREME COURT OF OREGON, 1965.
239 Oreg. 410, 398 P. 2d 119

NATURE OF CASE: Action to recover damages for breach of a contract to make a lease in a building to be erected.

FACT SUMMARY: Baumann (D) agreed to lease an office in a building that Wright (P) agreed to erect.

CONCISE RULE OF LAW: A contract to make a lease is a contract nonetheless; and, unlike with an executed lease, the lessor has an obligation to mitigate damages arising from the breach of contract by the prospective lessee.

FACTS: Baumann (D), a dentist, agreed to lease office space in a building that Wright (P) agreed to erect. Just prior to occupancy, Baumann (D) notified Wright (P) that he did not wish to lease the space after all. Baumann (D) also communicated this fact to two doctors who made an offer to Wright (P) to assume the lease precisely as it was to have been with Baumann (D). Wright (P) refused to accept them, giving no reasons, and commenced this action. From judgment in favor of Wright (P), Baumann (D) appeals, contending that Wright's (P) failure to accept the substitute tenants precluded him from recovering for the underlying breach.

ISSUE: Is the general rule that a landlord need not mitigate damages arising from the breach of a lease applicable to the breach of a contract to make a lease as well?

HOLDING AND DECISION: No. A contract to make a lease is a contract nonetheless; and, unlike with an executed lease, the lessor (landlord) has an obligation to mitigate damages arising from the breach of contract by the prospective lessee. It is the overwhelming majority rule that a lessor need not mitigate damages when the lessee abandons a leasehold. A leasehold is a property interest, his to do with as he wishes, and his conduct in abandoning it is of no import to the landlord. A contract to make a lease, however, brings contract principles into play. It is well settled that a party with whom a contract is breached has a duty to mitigate damage as much as possible. Here, the failure of Baumann (D) to accept the doctors may well have been a failure to mitigate. As such, the judgment must be reversed and remanded for a new trial to determine whether his refusal was justified or a failure to mitigate which would block his recovery. In dictum, the court goes further to point out that the general rule here (no duty to mitigate breach of lease) is based on the outdated notion that a lease is the mere sale of a property interest rather than a contract on which mutual covenants are based.

EDITOR'S ANALYSIS: This case points up a basic difference between contracts and leases regarding recovery of damages. It is elementary contract law that a party against whose interest a contract is breached has a duty to mitigate damages flowing from that breach, to the extent of any reasonable effort. This is because it is felt to be against public policy to allow a party to exploit another's breach beyond its actual scope and profit from it thereby. A lease on the other hand, as the conveyance of an interest in land (rather than a mere set of binding promises), grants to the lessee that interest, in toto, without any interest in his interest being retained by the landlord. (I.e., a landlord has no interest in the lessee's "term of years" interest, only in the remainder interest which is to revert to him, and upon which no "waste can be done.) As such, whatever the lessee does with his interest (abandonment) has no effect whatsoever on the landlord's right, obligations or interest in his interest (remainder) in the property. As such, no duty arises to mitigate the damage from the lessee's abandonment of the property since the landlord has no interest in such abandonment. Since the responsibility to pay rent is independent of the use of the property, the cause of action in recovering it is not affected by the landlord's conduct toward the use of it.

NOTES:

BARASH v. PENNSYLVANIA TERMINAL REAL ESTATE CORP.

26 N.Y. 2d 77, 256 N.E. 707 (1970)

NATURE OF CASE: Appeal from denial of motion to dismiss complaint for partial actual eviction.

FACT SUMMARY: Barash (P) contended he was the subject of an actual eviction, relieving him from rent obligations, by Pennsylvania's (D) failure to provide his office with sufficient fresh air to render occupation of the office practical.

CONCISE RULE OF LAW: Absent an actual physical preclusion from occupation, a tenant is not actually evicted; rather, conditions rendering occupation uncomfortable may only constitute a constructive eviction, and the failure to abandon the premises renders the tenant liable for the rent due during the period of occupation.

FACTS: Barash (P) leased office space in a building under construction which was to have sealed windows and be fully air conditioned. During negotiations with the landlord, Pennsylvania (D), Barash (P) was assured that even when the air conditioning was not in operation, the building would be adequately ventilated to allow occupation of the office at any time. On his first day of occupation, Barash (P) stayed in the office after 6:00 p.m. When the air conditioning was turned off, and the office became hot and stuffy and he found he could not work there. Pennsylvania (D) refused to turn on the air conditioning without added compensation. Barash (P) refused to pay extra and sued, contending the failure to supply adequate ventilation constituted an actual eviction releasing him from rental payments even though he remained in possession of the premises. Pennsylvania (D) appealed from the trial court's denial of its motion to dismiss.

ISSUE: Can a tenant whose tenancy is rendered uncomfortable but not physically impossible avoid rental payments and still remain in possession?

HOLDING AND DECISION: (J. Breitel) No. A tenant whose tenancy is rendered uncomfortable but not physically impossible has been at most constructively rather than actually evicted. The failure to surrender possession of the premises renders him fully liable for rental payments during the period of occupation. In this case, Barash (P) was not physically prevented from occupying the office. Therefore, he was not the subject of an actual eviction. The condition of the office was at most a constructive eviction requiring him to vacate in order to avoid liability for the rental payments. Therefore, the complaint should have been dismissed. Reversed.

DISSENT: (J. Fuld) Barash (P) presented a prima facie case of fraud and mistake which could entitle him to reformation of the contract.

EDITOR'S ANALYSIS: The Restatement Second of Property provides in §6.1 that a tenant under constructive eviction need not abandon the leased premises before suing. However, the majority rule is consistent with the holding in the present case. The defense of constructive eviction is hampered by the common law failure to impose on the landlord a duty to repair the premises.

NOTES:

PINES v. PERSSION

SUP. COURT OF WISCONSIN, 1961.
14 Wis. 2d 590, 111 N.W. 2d 409

NATURE OF CASE: Action to recover deposit made for fulfillment of a lease and for labor done on the leased premises.

FACT SUMMARY: When Pines (P) began to move into a house he had rented from Perssion (D), the premises were in filthy condition and contained code violations. Pines (P) vacated the premises within two weeks.

CONCISE RULE OF LAW: Where leased premises are not in a condition reasonably and decently fit for occupation when the lease term commences, the lessor has breached the implied warranty of habitability, and since the lessee's covenant to pay rent and the lessor's covenant to provide a habitable house are mutually dependent, the lessor's breach of the latter covenant relieves the lessee of any liability under the former covenant.

FACTS: At Pines' (P) request, Perssion (D) showed him a house to rent. Perssion (D) told Pines (P) that he was thinking of buying the house and then renting it out. Actually, he owned the house at the time, but he misstated the facts because he was embarrassed about its condition. Pines (P) found the house to be in filthy condition. Pines (P) testified that Perssion (D) twice said he would clean and fix up the house. Perssion (D) testified that he said he would not do any work on the house until he received a signed lease and deposit. Perssion (D) received a signed lease and the deposit on September 3. On September 6, Pines (P) arrived to move into the house. It was still in filthy condition and lacked the furniture Pines (P) testified Perssion (D) had promised to provide. Pines (P) began doing some of the cleaning and painting. He also called a building inspector, who found that the premises had inadequate wiring, plumbing, handrail on stairs, furnace in disrepair, and windows and doors lacking. On September 11, Pines (P) vacated the house. The lease did state that the house would be furnished.

ISSUE: Where leased premises are not in habitable conditions at the commencement of the lease, is the lessee relieved of any liability for rent under the lease?

HOLDING AND DECISION: Yes. The general rule is that there are no implied warranties of habitability on leased premises. The lessee's remedy is to inspect the premises before leasing them, and he is not entitled to abandon the premises on the ground of inhabitability. Some courts have recognized an exception and have held that there is an implied warranty of habitability on furnished premises. To follow the old rule of no implied warranty of habitability would be inconsistent with the current legislation concerning housing standards. Such legislation has already imposed certain duties on the landlord (i.e., to conform to the building, health, and safety codes). In this case, the house was not in a habitable condition when the lease commenced. Perssion (D) admitted that it was filthy. He lied about owning it, and he testified that it was not cleaned or worked on before Pines (P) moved in. Secondly, the building inspector testified that it was unfit for occupancy. Hence, the implied warranty of habitability was breached. Since Pines' (P) covenant to pay rent and Perssion's (D) covenant to provide a habitable house were mutually dependent, Perssion's (D) breach of the latter relieved Pines (P) of any liability under the former. Pines' (P) only liability is for the reasonable value of the premises during his actual occupancy. Pines (P) will recover his deposit and an amount for his labor minus the rental value.

EDITOR'S ANALYSIS: Under the common law, the landlord did not impliedly covenant to put the premises in a habitable or tenantable condition. The doctrine of caveat emptor applied, and it was up to the tenant to inspect the premises and either exact an express warranty for any repairs or else take the premises as he found them. Likewise, at common law the covenant to pay rent and any covenant to provide habitable premises were considered to be independent of one another. Hence, the breach of one covenant did not justify the breach of the other. As demonstrated here, these rules are changing. Unlike the English farmer who leased property under the common law, the urban dweller is far more interested in the house or apartment than the land which it is on. Hence, courts have begun to hold that there is an implied warranty of habitability in furnished and unfurnished premises, and the breach of this warranty will relieve the lessee's duty to pay rent. In California, the breach of the warranty is a defense to an unlawful detainer action.

NOTES:

JAVINS v. FIRST NATIONAL REALTY CORP.

UNITED STATES COURT OF APPEALS, DISTRICT OF
COLUMBIA CIRCUIT, 1970. 428 F. 2d 1071

NATURE OF CASE: Action to recover rent.

FACT SUMMARY: Javins (D) refused to pay his April rent to First National Realty Corp. (D) because of the approximately 1,500 housing code violations existing in the leased premises.

CONCISE RULE OF LAW: The modern urban tenant seeks more from a lease than the outdated common-law conveyance of an interest in land, rather, he seeks a well-known package of goods and services; and, modern housing regulations imply into every lease a warranty of habitability, the breach of which by the landlord will justify a suspension of the tenant's covenant to pay rent.

FACTS: Javins (D) and others are tenants of First National Realty Corp. (P). First National (P) filed an action to regain possession of the leased premises for failure to pay rent. Javins (D) et all admit not paying rent for April; but, contend that they were relieved from doing so (equitably) by the approximately 1,500 housing code violations which exist in their premises. The trial court, however, refused their offer of proof of the alleged violations and gave judgment for First National (P). Javins (D) appeals, contending that the offer of proof was improperly denied since the housing code violations would relieve him of his duty to pay rent.

ISSUE: Is a tenant precluded from asserting housing code violations as a defense to his rent liability by the common-law concept of a lease as a mere conveyance of an interest in land in which warranties as to habitability exist?

HOLDING AND DECISION: No. The modern urban tenant seeks more from a lease than the outdated common-law conveyance of an interest in land, rather, he seeks a well-known package of goods and services; and, modern housing regulations imply into every lease a warranty of habitability, the breach of which by the landlord will justify a suspension of the tenant's covenant to pay rent. This implied warranty, further, is coextensive with the scope of the housing regulations. The common-law rule that, as a conveyance of an interest in land (not a contract), a lease placed no duty to repair on the landlord. The feudal conditions which gave rise to this rule no longer exist, and it is the duty of the court to reappraise old rules to keep them up to date. Three situations mandate such a change: (1) the old factual assumptions of feudalism are obviously no longer valid; (2) considerable authority in other areas of the law (e.g., consumer protection) have placed implied duties upon sellers that their goods are fit for the purpose sold; and (3) the shortages inherent in the modern housing market give a

NOTES:

landlord too great a bargaining advantage to believe that the market mechanism (competition) can effectively assure quality housing. Modern contract law has long recognized the concept of implied warranties to cover situations in which buyers, relying upon the skill and honesty of their sellers, assume certain facts (such as compliance with housing regulations) not mentioned expressly in their contracts because "they . . . supposed it was unnecessary to speak of (them) because the law provided for them." Such is the case with housing code violations and leases. As a result, the court finds that every lease contains an implied warranty of habitability to the extent of relevant housing regulations. The breach of this warranty relieves a tenant of his duty to pay rent under the lease. As such, the 1,500 violations alleged here must be considered by the court in determining Javins' (D) rent liability. The decision must be reversed. On remand, the trier of fact must determine (1) whether the alleged violations existed during the period for which past-due rent is claimed; and (2) what portion, if any, of the tenant's obligation to pay rent was suspended by the landlord's breach. The action for possession, thereupon, may only be maintained by the landlord if the tenant refuses to pay whatever remaining increment of rent is found to be owed over and above the suspended part.

EDITOR'S ANALYSIS: This case points up the clear trend of authority that every lease contains an implied warranty of habitability (Wisconsin, Hawaii and California have also recently approved such). In Javins, supra, it is found to be coextensive with the housing code of the particular jurisdiction. Other jurisdictions find it to exist independently, with housing code violations mere evidence on the issue of the extent to which a landlord has permitted premises to become uninhabitable. The basis for relief of rent liability comes from the contract concept of mutually dependent covenants. Under this concept, the covenants made by one party are dependent upon the covenants of the other. Breach by one party of a contractual covenant justifies breach by the other. In traditional real property conveyances, however, covenants are not mutually dependent. As a result, only by viewing a lease as a contract may a tenant be relieved of his covenant to pay rent by his landlord's breach of the above-described implied warranty of habitability. Of course, at common law, a lease contained no such warranty. A lease was a mere sale (of an interest in land) and the doctrine of caveat emptor implied that the buyer-tenant take the premises as they were and as they would be for the term of the lease (since that was all he had bargained for or bought). So Javins really establishes two doctrines for leases. (1) That they are contracts with mutually dependent covenants, and (2) that an implied warranty of habitability is one such mutually dependent covenant.

HABIB v. EDWARDS

COURT OF GENERAL SESSION OF DISTRICT
OF COLUMBIA, 1965. Civil Div. No. LT75895

NATURE OF CASE: Action to set aside a default judgment in favor of Habib (P), the landlord, for possession of a dwelling house.

FACT SUMMARY: Edwards (D), Habib's (P) tenant, alleges that she is being evicted by Habib (P) solely because she informed government authorities of housing violations on the premises.

CONCISE RULE OF LAW: A landlord may not evict a tenant for the purpose of depriving the tenant of the right to inform the government of violations of the law.

FACTS: Habib (P) was awarded a default judgment giving him possession of a dwelling house rented from him by Edwards (D) under a month-to-month lease. After Edwards (D) took possession of the premises under her lease in March 1965, she made complaints to housing authorities regarding the conditions of the premises. The premises were inspected. Violations of housing codes were discovered and Habib (P) was directed to make numerous repairs. In August 1965, Habib (P) gave Edwards (D) a thirty-day notice to quit. Edwards (D) alleges that Habib's (D) purpose in giving her such notice was to retaliate for complaints to the housing authority.

ISSUE: In an action for possession of real property, can a tenant rely on the defense that the landlord is evicting the tenant for the purpose of depriving him of the right to inform the government of violations of the law?

HOLDING AND DECISION: Yes. A person has a constitutional right to give information to the government concerning violations of the law, and that right is protected not only against interference by the government but also against interference by private persons. This right does not depend upon any of the amendments to the constitution, but arises out of the creation and establishment by the constitution of a national government. Here, Edwards (D) had the right to inform the housing authority of violations, as well as to the correlative right not to be injured or punished by anyone for having availed herself of that right. The ultimate question in this case is whether the code compels the court to assist Habib (P) in punishing Edwards (D) for having exercised her constitutional right. There is no evidence to indicate such an intention on the part of the legislature. Further, such a construction would raise questions of constitutionality and so must be avoided. Also, the interest at stake is not only that of a person to provide information to the government, but also that of the government in the free and unimpeded access to such information. Intimidation of the sources of information injures the government's interest in the enforcement of its laws. Finally, the fact that the information provided by Edwards (D) concerns housing is an additional important reason for not granting relief in Habib's (P) action for possession. The housing code was enacted to protect tenants against unsafe, unsanitary and other inhuman conditions. To permit landlords to evict tenants who avail themselves of remedies provided in the code, frustrates the public policy expressed in the statutes and impairs their effective enforcement. Edward's (D) motion to set aside the default is granted, and the case is restored to the trial calendar.

EDITOR'S ANALYSIS: Present case law and statutes entitle a landlord to terminate a month-to-month tenancy or a tenancy at will or at sufferance for nearly any (or no) reason. The only requirement is a thirty-day notice. Practically the only defenses to such an eviction are that it was motivated by racial discrimination or by retaliatory eviction, as demonstrated by the above case. In a nonpayment-of-rent case, the tenant may also be able to use substantial housing code violations or breach of the implied warranty of habitability as defenses. This case was returned to the trial court. There, evidence of retaliatory intent was excluded by a judge who did not feel bound by the above opinion. Edwards (D) then appealed to the court of appeals.

NOTES:

EDWARDS v. HABIB

CT. OF APP. OF DIST. OF COLUMBIA, 1967. 227 A. 2d 388

NATURE OF CASE: Action to set aside a default judgment in favor of Habib (P), the landlord, for possession of a dwelling house.

FACT SUMMARY: Edwards (D), Habib's (P) tenant, alleges that she is being evicted solely because she informed government authorities of housing violations on the premises.

CONCISE RULE OF LAW: In the absence of a government body being the landlord, legislation, or racial discrimination, a landlord can terminate a tenancy for any purpose and the tenant cannot question or attack the landlord's motives.

FACTS: Habib (P) was awarded a default judgment giving him possession of a dwelling house rented from him by Edwards (D) under a month-to-month lease. After Edwards (D) took possession of the premises under her lease in March 1965, she complained to the housing authority about the condition of the premises. violations of the housing code were discovered, and Habib (P) was directed to make numerous repairs. In August 1965, Habib (P) gave Edwards (D) a thirty-day notice to quit. Edwards (D) alleges that Habib's (P) purpose in giving her such notice was to retaliate for her complaints to the housing authority.

ISSUE: In an action for possession of real property, is evidence of the landlord's purpose in bringing the action admissible?

HOLDING AND DECISION: No. A month-to-month tenancy may be terminated by either the landlord or tenant by a thirty-day notice. Neither party is required to give any reason for termination. Accordingly, a notice to quit by a landlord does not have to give a reason, and evidence as to the reason for seeking possession is inadmissible. There are three lines of cases which have restricted a landlord's right to terminate a tenancy. These are when the landlord is a governmental body, where rent control legislation has restricted the landlord's contractual rights, and where tenants are evicted in retaliation for registering or voting. The latter both involve specific legislation. Also, a tenant has been permitted to show as a defense that his eviction was sought solely because of his race. In this case, Habib (P) is not a governmental body, there is no specific legislation which is applicable, and Edwards (D) did not make any claim of racial discrimination. Judgment in favor of Habib (P) affirmed.

EDITOR'S ANALYSIS: The court decided that if the rights of landlords are to be restricted and the rights of tenants are to be enlarged, it should be by legislation spelling out the restrictions and rights, with specific provisions as to the manner of enforcement. The landlord's right to terminate a tenancy for any reason, outside of the exceptions named above, was affirmed.

NOTES:

EDWARDS v. HABIB

CIRCUIT COURT OF APPEALS OF DISTRICT OF
COLUMBIA, 1968.   397 F. 2d 687

NATURE OF CASE: Action to set aside a default judgment in favor of Habib (P), the landlord, for possession of a dwelling house.

FACT SUMMARY: Edwards (D), Habib's (P) tenant, alleges that she is being evicted solely because she informed government authorities of housing violations on the premises.

CONCISE RULE OF LAW: While a landlord may evict for any legal reason or for no reason at all, he is not free to evict in retaliation for a tenant's report of housing code violations to the authorities.

FACTS: Habib (P) was awarded a default judgment giving him possession of the dwelling house rented from him by Edwards (D) under a month-to-month lease. After Edwards (D) took possession of the premises under her lease in March 1965, she complained to the housing authority about the condition of the premises. Violations of the housing code were discovered, and Habib (P) was directed to make numerous repairs. In August 1965, Habib (P) gave Edwards (D) a thirty-day notice to quit. Edwards (D) alleges that Habib's (P) purpose in giving such notice was to retaliate for her complaints to the housing authority.

ISSUE: In an action for possession of real property, can a tenant rely on the defense that the landlord is evicting in retaliation for a tenant's report of housing code violations to the authorities?

HOLDING AND DECISION: Yes. In making an affirmative case for eviction, the landlord need only show that the tenant has been given a thirty-day notice. The landlord need not give any reason for evicting a tenant who does not have a lease. However, the landlord is not free to evict in retaliation for a tenant's report of housing code violations to the authorities. The housing and sanitary codes indicate a legislative concern for safe and sanitary housing. Effective enforcement of the codes depends in part on private complaints. Nearly a third of the cases handled by the authorities in 1966 arose from private complaints. To permit retaliatory evictions would frustrate the effectiveness of the code. "In light of the appalling condition and shortage of housing in Washington, the expense of moving, the inequality of bargaining power between landlord and tenant, and the social and the economic importance of assuring at least minimum standards in housing conditions" retaliatory eviction cannot be tolerated. This does not mean that a tenant who can prove a retaliatory eviction is entitled to remain in possession in perpetuity. If this illegal purpose is dissipated, the landlord can evict or raise rents for any legitimate reason or for no reason at all. The question of the landlord's motive will be one for the court or the jury. This case is reversed and remanded to the lower court, where Edwards (D) may rely upon the defense of retaliatory eviction.

DISSENT: A restriction such as this of the landlord's property right should be made by the legislature rather than the court so that appropriate standards could be spelled out and just compensation could be awarded if found to be due.

EDITOR'S ANALYSIS: Other cases have allowed the defense of retaliatory eviction to a tenant who attempted to organize co-tenants to complain to officials about health and building code violations and for a tenant who informed his landlord of his intention to exericse his rights under a repair and deduct statute. Statutes have also been passed which protect tenants from retaliatory eviction for exercising their repair and deduct rights, reporting code violations, and tenant organizing.

NOTES:

O'CALLAGHAN v. WALLER & BECKWITH REALTY CO.

SUP. COURT OF ILLINOIS, 1958. 15 Ill.
2d 436, 155 N.E. 2d 545

NATURE OF CASE: Action to recover damages for negligence.

FACT SUMMARY: O'Callaghan (P) fell in the courtyard of Waller & Beckwith Realty Co.'s (D) building. O'Callaghan (P) is Waller's (D) tenant. Her lease contains an exculpatory clause relieving Waller (D) of liability for negligence.

CONCISE RULE OF LAW: An exculpatory clause which relieves the lessor and its agents from any liability to the lessee for personal injuries or property damage caused by any act or neglect of the lessor or its agents is valid in a lease of residential property.

FACTS: O'Callaghan (P), a tenant in Waller's (D) building, was injured while crossing the paved courtyard on her way from the garage to her apartment. She alleged that her injury was caused by defective pavement. Her lease contained an exculpatory clause which relieves Waller (D) and its agents from any liability to O'Callaghan (P) for personal injuries or property damage caused by any act of Waller (D) or its agents. O'Callaghan (P) concedes that if the clause is valid, it bars her recovery. She contends, however, that such a clause is contrary to public policy, and so is invalid in a lease for residential property.

ISSUE: Is an exculpatory clause which relieves a lessor from liability for his negligence contrary to public policy and therefore invalid in a lease for residential property?

HOLDING AND DECISION: No. Freedom of contract is basic to our law. However, when that freedom expresses itself in a provision designed to absolve a party from the consequences of his own negligence, there is danger that the protections the law has developed may be diluted. The court has refused to enforce contracts limiting liability for negligence between common carriers and shippers or paying customers, between telegraph companies and those sending messages and between masters and servants. The dominant position of the party seeking exculpation and the public interest in these relationships are the basis for this refusal to enforce these contracts. However, the relation between lessor and lessee has been considered a private concern, and leases containing exculpatory clauses have been upheld. Also the relationship of landlord and tenant does not have monopolistic characteristics since there are thousands of landlords in competition with one another. O'Callaghan (P) contends that the housing shortage caused an inequality in bargaining power between lessors and lessees, giving lessors an unconscionable advantage. However, there was no showing that O'Callaghan (P) was concerned with the clause or that she attempted to negotiate with Waller (D) to modify it or that she looked for housing elsewhere. A housing shortage at one time does not indicate the existence of such shortages in the past or future, and judicial determination of public policy cannot be based on transitory circumstances.

DISSENT: According to the undisputed facts of this case, O'Callaghan's (P) lease was executed in 1947 when housing shortages were so great that waiting lists and bonuses to landlords to secure shelter were common. Further negotiation was non-existent. If a person refused to sign the form lease, the apartment would not be rented to him. Also, exculpatory clauses were included in the form leases used by practically all landlords in urban areas. Hence, the competition the majority speaks of was non-existent even on a theoretical level, and the exculpatory clause in this case cannot be seen as an isolated provision in a "private" lease, since it affects thousands of people. In determining whether exculpatory clauses should be held void, the following factors are considered: the importance of the subject to the group agreeing to the clause, their bargaining power, the amount of free choice exercised in agreeing, and competition among the group to be exempted. Here the subject — shelter — is indispensable to the physical well being of tenants. They do not have equality of bargaining power with landlords and no free choice in agreeing, since they will be confronted with the same clause in leases elsewhere. Allowing landlords to immunize themselves against liability for negligence, at a time of critical housing shortages, is inconsistent with much law and public policy.

EDITOR'S ANALYSIS: This case demonstrates the general rule that in the absence of a statute to the contrary, a landlord may, by stipulation in the lease or by other agreement with a tenant, lawfully relieve himself from any responsibility for damages caused by any defect in the leased property. Some courts have held an exculpatory clause to be effective against nonsigners to the lease who were injured on the premises. However, in a number of cases it has been held that such a clause has no effect on nonsigners who sustain in an area which is retained under the landlord's control or is used in common by all of the tenants. Further, an exculpatory clause has been held to have no effect on nonsigners if the defect causing injury was in violation of a statute or ordinance. There is a division of authority as to whether an exculpatory clause is binding upon a member of the tenant's family who did not sign the lease.

NOTES:

SWEENEY GASOLINE & OIL CO. v.
TOLEDO, PEORIA & WESTERN RAILROAD
SUPREME COURT OF ILLINOIS, 1969.
42 Ill. 2d 265, 247 N.E. 2d 603

NATURE OF CASE: Action in tort for damages caused by negligence.

FACT SUMMARY: A train of R.R. (D) derailed, doing damage to the property of Sweeney (P), whose lease for R.R. (D) contains an exculpatory clause as to negligence.

CONCISE RULE OF LAW: In the absence of proof of such disparity of bargaining power between a landlord and tenant that the tenant had no real choice but to accept it, an exculpatory clause in a residential or business lease will ordinarily be enforced, relieving that landlord from tort liability for injuries caused by his negligence.

FACTS: Sweeney (P) leased premises from R.R. (D). In the lease was an exculpatory clause stating that "Lessee shall ... hold harmless Railroad, its agents, servants and employees, from and against any and all claims ... arising out of ... damage ... caused by negligence ... " Sweeney (P) suffered damage to its property when a freight train of R.R. (D) derailed and went through the property leased by Sweeney (P). Sweeney (P) sued for damages. From a judgment for R.R. (D), Sweeney (P) appeals, contending that a statute which exempts railroads from a ban on exculpatory clauses is unconstitutional and such clauses are void as against public policy.

ISSUE: May a landlord shield himself from tort liability through the use of an exculpatory clause in his lease?

HOLDING AND DECISION: Yes. In the absence of proof of such disparity of bargaining power between a landlord and tenant that the tenant had no real choice but to accept it, an exculpatory clause in a residential or business lease will ordinarily be enforced, relieving that landlord fom tort liability for injuries caused by his negligence. It is true that the statutory prohibition against exculpatory clauses which exempts from its provisions agencies of or corporations regulated by any government unit is probably unconstitutional. There is no rational basis for exempting such governmentally sanctioned entities from such a statute. Nevertheless, it is well settled that exculpatory clauses will not be voided by a court unless there is clear evidence that a tenant was coerced into accepting it by virtue of his grossly disproportionate bargaining position with the landlord. No such evidence was produced here. The clause is properly enforceable. Judgment is affirmed.

DISSENT: The dissenting justice sees the attempt by the legislature to prohibit exculpatory clauses as an expression of public policy which the court should follow. He would hold, as a matter of common law, that all exculpatory clauses are void as against public policy.

EDITOR'S ANALYSIS: This case points up the basic contract rationale for voiding exculpatory clauses: disproportionate bargaining power. The trend of authority in leases is for courts to take judicial notice of the national housing shortage. As a result of this shortage, tenants are often forced to accept substandard housing simply because they need a place to live. Under such circumstances, it is felt, enforcing an exculpatory clause, which the tenant had no real bargaining power to oppose, would be "unconscionable." The decision above is not really out of accord with this view. The court above simply feels that the concept of disproportionate bargaining power is inapplicable to two large industrial parties. Note, finally, that the court here (as is the case usually) states in dicta that the problem of exculpatory clauses is really more suited for legislative than judicial consideration.

NOTES:

SAMUELS v. OTTINGER

SUPREME COURT OF CALIFORNIA, 1915. 169Cal. 209, 146 P. 638

NATURE OF CASE: Action to recover monthly rent installments on a lease.

FACT SUMMARY: Ottinger (D) leased a building from Samuels (P), then assigned the lease to Altschular, who paid only one monthly rent installment in two years.

CONCISE RULE OF LAW: The assignment of a leasehold interest does not relieve a lessee of liability for rent payments where such payments have been predicated upon privity of contract by express stipulations of the lease.

FACTS: Ottinger (D) leased a city lot from the D. Samuels Realty Co. (P). Among the provisions of the lease were (1) that rent was "... payable in advance on the twentieth day of the month..."; (2) that any improvements made be considered "... security for rents herein stipulated to be paid...; (3) that insurance on any building erected "...shall be made payable to the lessor... for the purpose of securing... payment of the rents herein stipulated; and (4) that in the case of a holdover, month-to-month tenancy would commence "...at the same monthly rental... payable hereunder." The lease was to last for ten years. After two years, Ottinger (D) sold and assigned his leasehold interest to Altschular. Altschular paid one month's rent to Samuels (P), then defaulted for two years. Samuels (P) thereupon sued Ottinger (D) on the original lease to recover those payments. Upon a judgment in favor of Ottinger (D), Samuels (P) appeals, claiming rental payments are due to him by the express covenants in the original lease.

ISSUE: Does an assignment of the leasehold interest in a piece of property automatically preclude further liability for rent payments under the lease?

HOLDING AND DECISION: No. The assignment of a leasehold interest does not relieve a lessee of liability for rent payments where such payments have been predicated upon privity of contract by express stipulations of the lease. While the general rule for assignment in such cases is that responsibility to pay rent ceases when the leasehold interest ceases, the contractual provisions of the lease here take this case out of the general rule. Essentially, every lease contains two sets of rights and obligations, one arising from its character as a conveyance of an interest in land (privity of estate), the other from its character as a contract (privity of contract). Where no express covenant to pay rent is found in a lease, responsibility to do so arises solely from the fact of occupancy (privity of estate). As such, when occupancy ceases, as by assignment of the leasehold interest, the responsibility to pay rent ceases, as well. Where, however, there is sufficient evidence in the lease of an intention to create an express covenant, the responsibility to pay rent arises from such covenant (privity of contract). As such, assignment of the leasehold interest does not terminate the contractual arrangement to pay rent agreed to in the lease. Here, at least four provisions of the lease indicate the intention of the parties that there was an express covenant to pay rent embodied in it. Ottinger's (D) responsibility to pay rent, therefore, was contractual and was not terminated by the assignment. The decision below is reversed.

The underlying rationale here is that permitting a party to avoid contractual obligations by mere unilateral assignment would be to permit breach of contract. Rather, such assignment in fact leaves the original lessee in the position of being a virtual surety for his assignee.

The court here goes on to point out instances where provisions of a contract will constitute a covenant (e.g., promise to pay rent) and where they merely describe the privity of estate relationship (e.g., "rent payable at," "lessee yielding and paying," or "subject to the payment of" rent.)

EDITOR'S ANALYSIS: This case points up the general rule that an express covenant to pay rent, assumed by a lessee, cannot be assigned. Such express covenant need not be in formal language either. It has been held that an express covenant may be inferred from a lease stipulation which states rent is "payable" at designated times (though a stipulation merely describing his actions as "yielding and paying" rent at designated times has been held not to be an express covenant). Of course, an express covenant will never be found in language which makes the lease subject to the condition that designated rent be paid. (A covenant and a condition are two entirely different things.)

This case also points up the distinctions between and results which follow from privity of estate and privity of contract. Briefly, while assignment terminates privity of estate it cannot terminate privity of contract.

NOTES:

REID v. WEISSNER BREWING COMPANY

COURT OF APPEALS OF MARYLAND, 1898. 88 Md. 234, 40 A. 877

NATURE OF CASE: Action to recover monthly rent installments on a lease.

FACT SUMMARY: Reid (P) leased premises to Miller, who assigned them to Weissner Brewing Co. (D) who assigned them to Jones, who failed to pay rent.

CONCISE RULE OF LAW: The assignment of a lease with all its covenants, terms and conditions, does not impose upon the assignee any rent liability other than that growing out of privity of estate; and that liability ceases when privity of estate ceases.

FACTS: Reid (P) leased certain premises to Miller. Among the provisions of the lease were covenants (1) to pay rent, and (2) not to sublet or assign the premises. On the same day, with the permission of Reid (P), Miller assigned his lease to Weissner Brewing Co. (D) "with all its covenants, terms, and conditions." Two years later, Weissner Brewing Co. (D) assigned the lease to Jones, who failed to pay the next four months' rent. Reid (P) sued Weissner Brewing Co. (D) to recover these four rent installments. Upon judgment for Reid (P), Weissner Brewing Co. (D) appeals contending that its rent responsibility ceased when its privity of estate ceased (by means of the assignment to Jones).

ISSUE: Does a covenant to pay rent, assumed by an assignee, continue for such assignee after the end of his privity of estate?

HOLDING AND DECISION: No. The assignment of a lease "with all its covenants, terms and conditions," still does not impose upon the assignee any rent liability other than that growing out of privity of estate; and, that liability ceases when privity of estate ceases. The liability of an assignee to the original lessor for rent grows out of and is founded upon privity of estate. During the continuance of that privity, the assignee is liable for all covenants which run with the land (e.g., to pay rent), and may be sued for such. After privity of estate ceases, all covenants which run with the land cease as well. Any covenant to pay rent after that must be independently established (privity of contract). Here, the failure of Reid (P) to attach any specific covenant to pay rent to the assignment by Miller to Weissner Brewing Co. (D), constituted a waiver of his rights reserved in the original lease (covenant to pay rent). As such, there was no rent liability based on privity of contract. Since the covenant to pay rent which ran with the land ceased when privity of estate ceased (assignment to Jones), there is no basis for imposing any rent liability on Weissner Brewing Co. (D). Reversed.

EDITOR'S ANALYSIS: This case points out the basic relationship between rent liability and privity of estate and contract. Without express stipulations in a lease, rent liability is only coextensive with privity of estate. As such privity ceases upon assignment, so does rent liability. A different question arises as to the liability of the assignee in such cases, however. The modern rule is that, if the rent liability is a covenant, then it is transferred by assignment; but, if rent liability is a mere condition, then the liability cannot be assigned and no action for damages.

NOTES:

[handwritten notes:]

sued

R → M → WB → Jones

lessor   lessee

M w/permission of R assigned the lease to WB

The covenant between R + M whereby lessee covenanted not to assign or sublet the premises w/o written permission of the lessor was waived when assignment was made by M and is binding on the brewing company

MASURY v. SOUTHWORTH
SUPREME COURT OF OHIO, 1859. 9 Ohio St. 340

NATURE OF CASE: Action to recover cost of insurance premiums covenanted to be paid by original lessee.

FACT SUMMARY: Masury (P) (assignee of original lessor) procured insurance for certain property after Southworth (D) (assignee of original lessee) refused to, despite a covenant by the original lessee to do so.

CONCISE RULE OF LAW: The assignment of a lease includes, as part of privity of estate, the assignment of all covenants which run with the land, and whether any particular covenant is one which runs with the land depends upon the intent of the parties, and the nature of the covenant.

FACTS: Masury (P), as assignee of the reversion interest in certain property of the original lessor of that property, purchased insurance on a building which the original lessee covenanted to build and insure. He then sued Southworth (D), the assignee of the original lessee, for the cost of this insurance. The trial court sustained a demurrer to the complaint on the grounds that as assignee of the lease, Southworth (D) was not bound by contractual covenants such as that of buying insurance for the building. From this order, Masury (P) appeals.

ISSUE: Is the assignee of a lessee's interest in a lease automatically insulated from liability for all covenants which are contractual (promise to do something, in lease) in nature?

HOLDING AND DECISION: No. The assignment of a lease includes, as part of the privity of estate, the assignment of all covenants which run with the land; and, whether any particular covenant is one which runs with the land depends upon the intent of the parties, and the nature of the covenant. The nature of the covenant must be such as "sustains the estate and enjoyment of it," beneficial to both lessor and lessee. Here, the covenant to insure, in order to provide for repairs to the premises, so benefits both parties, and may run with the land as such. While it is usually true that a mere covenant to build in the future is a mere personal contractual covenant which does not run with the land, where it is shown that the improvement is to be of a permanent nature, connected with the enjoyment of the estate and beneficial to both lessor and lessee, the intent that it is to run with the land may be inferred. Here, even though the word "assigns" tends to imply that the covenant involved was contractual, no particular form of words determines whether the original intent of the parties was to create a contractual covenant or one running with the land. The clear intent of the original parties that the covenant to build and insure was to run with the land as a permanent characteristic of the lease, regardless of assignment, must prevail. The judgment must be reversed.

EDITOR'S ANALYSIS: This case points up what is generally accepted as the so-called rule of Spencer's Case. Basically, the assignee of either a reversion or a leasehold estate will not be held for breaching any covenant which either (1) does not "run with the land" or (2) is not in esse (in existence). To run with the land, the covenant must somehow be closely associated with the estate involved. Tests such as in the decision supra are not uncommon, though no universally accepted test has been devised. Covenants in esse (in existence) are those which require some future act (build a wall, etc.), are binding upon an assignee if, but only if, (1) the lease makes it binding on the "lessee and his assigns," or (2) if the act is to be performed upon something in esse (build a wall "on the land," or repair a wall).

NOTES:

DAVIS v. VIDAL

SUPREME COURT OF TEXAS, 1912. 105 Tex. 444, 151 S.W. 290

NATURE OF CASE: Action to recover rent installments.

FACT SUMMARY: Davis (P) leased premises to Dallas Brewery which subsequently made an agreement to "sublet, assign, and transfer" them to Vidal.

CONCISE RULE OF LAW: Where a lessee conveys the entire terms of his lease, parting with any and all reversionary interest, he has made an assignment, and his assignee may be held liable for rent payments by the lessor directly since they are in both privity of estate and privity of contract; but where the lessee retains some reversionary interest, he has made a sublease, and no action by the lessor for rent against the subtenant may be had since they are in neither privity of estate nor privity of contract.

FACTS: Davis (P) leased certain premises to Dallas Brewery. Subsequently, Dallas Brewery executed an agreement whereby it agreed to "sublet, assign, and transfer" its lease to Lou Vidal (D), reserving the rights to (1) charge Vidal interest for any rent that it (Dallas Brewery) might have to pay; (2) declare the agreement null and void upon any such failure by Vidal (D) to pay rent; and (3) to re-enter the premises upon such default by Vidal (D). Davis (P) sued Vidal (D) for unpaid rent. Judgment for Vidal (D).

ISSUE: May a lessor maintain an action for rent against one who has taken over a lease from the original lessee subject to a reversionary interest in that lessee?

HOLDING AND DECISION: No. Where a lessee conveys the entire term of his lease, parting with any and all reversionary interest, he has made an assignment, and his assignee may be held liable for rent installments by the lessor directly since they are in both privity of estate and privity of contract; but where the lessee retains some reversionary interest, he has made a sublease, and no action by the lessor for rent against the subtenant may be had since they are in neither privity of estate nor privity of contract with each other. If an agreement between a lessee and another is such that a reversionary interest is retained by the lessee, he becomes the landlord of the subtenant, and privity of estate and contract exists between them. If the entire estate is transferred, however, the assignee has assumed all the lessee's responsibilities with the lessor, and privity of estate and contract exists between them (assignee and lessor). Here, the retention of a reversionary interest by Dallas Brewing made Vidal (D) a mere subtenant, with whom Davis (P) lacked both privity of estate and privity of contract. Without one of which, no action to recover rent could be had by him. The judgment must be affirmed.

EDITOR'S ANALYSIS: This case points up the basic nature of an assignment. It occurs whenever a lessee conveys the identical estate he acquired under the lease. Any lesser estate conveyed is a sublease. (Note, however, that there is some split of authority as to whether the reservation of a mere right of re-entry reduces a conveyance to the status of a sublease. The majority rule is that it does.)

NOTES:

GRUMAN v. INVESTOR'S DIVERSIFIED SERVICES INC.

SUPREME COURT OF MINNESOTA, 1956.
247 Minn. 502, 78 N.W. 2d 377

NATURE OF CASE: Action to recover rent due on a lease.

FACT SUMMARY: Gruman (P) refused to accept a subtenant chosen by Investor's (D), who had leased the premises from Gruman (P).

CONCISE RULE OF LAW: Where a lease contains a clause that the tenant cannot assign or sublet the premises involved without consent of the landlord, the landlord may refuse any subtenant or assignee, no matter how arbitrarily, without losing his right to recover fully from the tenant all rents owed on the lease.

FACTS: Gruman's (P) predecessor in title leased premises to Investor's Diversified Services Inc. (D) for a term of seven years and one month, at $2075 per month. Almost six years later, Investor's (D) notified Gruman (P) of their intent to vacate; and soon thereafter, their intent to sublet to the postmaster gneral of the United States at $1795 per month with Investor's making up the difference ($2075 -$1795 = $280). Gruman (P) refused to consent to the sublease, consistent with a clause in the lease reserving their right to do so. Investor's, however, merely tendered the difference between the lease rent and the sublease rent ($280), contending that they were entitled to an offset since Gruman (P) had arbitrarily refused to consent to the sublease. Gruman (P) sued. It was conceded for the purpose of determining summary judgment that the postmaster general was a perfectly suitable subtenant. Summary judgment was so entered for Gruman (P), from which Investor's (D) appeals, contending that Gruman (P) lost his rights to full recovery by failing to mitigate damages from Investor's (D) breach of the lease.

ISSUE: Does the contract rule that a party must make a good faith effort to mitigate any damages arising out of another's breach of contract apply to leases in which the landlord reserves the right to refuse permission for the tenant to make any sublease or assignment?

HOLDING AND DECISION: No. Where a lease contains a clause that the tenant cannot assign or sublet the premises involved without consent of the landlord, the landlord may refuse any subtenant or assignee, no matter how arbitrarily, without losing his right to recover fully from the tenant all rents owed on the lease. In short, he has no duty to mitigate damages. Of course, this situation must be distinguished from one in which the landlord by act or statement indicates acceptance of the tenants' abandonment of the premises. Such ratification terminates the lease. Here, however, no such ratification occurred. Gruman (P) was completely within his rights when he arbitrarily refused to accept the postmaster general. He is entitled to fully recover against Investor's (D), since he was under no duty to mitigate damages whatsoever.

EDITOR'S ANALYSIS: This case points up the general rule that a covenant or condition against assignment or subleasing will be recognized, even though it operates as a restraint or alienation (and is frowned upon therefore). This results in the application of the doctrine of strict construction to such covenants or conditions (i.e., a covenant not to assign is not breached by a covenant to sublease, etc.). If such covenant is found, however, it will be absolutely enforced. Even if the refusal by the lessor is totally arbitrary, the court will not "rewrite" the lease in the interests of justice.

NOTES:

DRESS SHIRT SALES INC. v. HOTEL MARTINIQUE ASSOCIATES
COURT OF APPEALS OF NEW YORK, 1963.
12 N.Y. 2d 339, 190 N.E. 2d 10

NATURE OF CASE: Action for damages for arbitrarily and fraudulently refusing to accept a sublessee.

FACT SUMMARY: Hotel Martinique Assoc. (D) refused to accept Benzini as a sublessee of Dress Shirt Sales Inc. (P), forcing Dress Shirt (P) to buy its way out of the lease, then leased to Benzini directly, at a higher price.

CONCISE RULE OF LAW: Unless a lease specifically provides that consent to sublet cannot be arbitrarily withheld, a provision prohibiting subleasing without the lessor's consent permits the lessor to refuse to consent arbitrarily for any reason, or, for no reason at all; and no action in fraud will lie for such refusal unless a direct relationship is shown between a misrepresentation as to the motive for refusal and the damage that results from it.

FACTS: Hotel Martinique Associates (D) leased certain premises to Dress Shirt (P) for a term of 10 years. Contained in the lease were provisions that (1) Hotel Martinique Assoc. (D) reserved the right to consent or refuse to accept any sublessee suggested by Dress Shirt (P); and (2) that no provision of the lease could be waived orally. There was no provision prohibiting the arbitrary withholding of consent by Hotel Martinique Assoc. (D), however. Later, Dress Shirt (P) attempted to sublet to Benzini. Hotel Martinique (D) refused to consent to the sublease on the grounds that the sandwich shop wheich Benzini wished to install was unacceptable to them. In face of this refusal, Dress Shirt (P) decided to buy its way out of the lease, which it did for $30,000 (total lease price was $110,000). Immediately thereafter, Hotel Martinique (D) leased the premises to Benzini at a higher price. Dress Shirt (P) sued to recover the cost of getting out of the lease. From summary judgment for Hotel Martinique (D), they appeal.

ISSUE: May a lessor refuse to consent to the subletting of his premises merely to force his lessee out of the lease and make a better bargain for himself with the prospective subtenant?

HOLDING AND DECISION: Yes. Unless a lease specifically provides that consent to sublet cannot be arbitrarily withheld, a provision prohibiting subleasing without the lessor's consent permits the lessor to refuse to consent arbitrarily for any reason, or, for no reason at all; and no action in fraud will lie for such refusal unless a direct relationship is shown between a misrepresentation as to the motive for refusal and the damage that results from it. There is nothing wrong with the simple exercise of an "unqualified" contractual privilege to refuse to consent to a subletting. Further, it is well settled that damages for fraud will be refused where based on the loss of a contractual bargain since the extent of damage in such cases is totally speculative. Here, Hotel Martinique (D) was fully within its rights when it refused Benzini. Its subsequent deal with him was merely an independent bargain. The misrepresentation as to its motive was similarly independent of the damage done to Dress Shirt. The $30,000 loss was not damage, since it was merely an independent cancellation of the lease. Whatever damage occurred arose from the loss of future profits which Dress Shirt (P) might have made if it had been allowed to conduct its business as it wished. Such loss is too speculative to be allowed. The summary judgment must be affirmed.

EDITOR'S ANALYSIS: This case points up the extreme to which courts recognize restrictive covenants against assignment and subleasing. Courts simply refuse to go into the question of motivation for refusal, regardless of any injustice involved. Perhaps the extremity of this rule is necessary, however, to counteract the extremity of potential consequences to a lessor who does not reserve the right to refuse an assignment or subleasing.

NOTES:

FETTING MANUFACTURING JEWELRY CO. v. WALTZ
COURT OF APPEALS OF MARYLAND, 1930.
160 Md. 50, 152 A. 434

NATURE OF CASE: Action to recover full year's rent from a holdover tenant.

FACT SUMMARY: Fetting Mfg. (D) remained for one month in premises, the lease to which had expired.

CONCISE RULE OF LAW: Where a tenant for a term of years becomes a "holdover" (i.e., retains possession after expiration of the lease), he becomes a trespasser; and a tenancy from year to year, subject to the provisions of the original lease, may be created at the election of the landlord, regardless of the intent or wishes of the tenant.

FACTS: Fetting Mfg. (D) leased premises from Waltz (P) for a term of five years. Approximately six months prior to expiration of the lease, the parties attempted to negotiate a new lease but failed. Approximately three months prior to expiration, Fetting Mfg. (D) notified Waltz (P) of its intent to vacate, but indicated that they might not be able to get out on time. They were directed to contact Waltz's (P) agent to work out some agreement for a temporary extension of the lease. This failed, as well, however, when the agent refused to agree to anything less than a six-month extension. Fetting Mfg. (D) held over approximately one month after the expiration of the lease. They tendered one month's rent to Waltz (P) as payment in full of their additional liability. It was accepted only upon the understanding that Waltz (P) did not accept it as full payment, however. Waltz (P) thereupon sued to recover a full year's rent from Fetting Mfg. (D). Upon judgment for Waltz (P), Fetting Mfg. (D) appeals contending that they should not be held for a full year's rent since they never intended to remain that long.

ISSUE: May a "holdover" tenant be held responsible for an entire term of the original lease by the landlord, even if he knows that the tenant only intends a temporary "holdover"?

HOLDING AND DECISION: Yes. Where a tenant for a term of years becomes a "holdover" (i.e., retains possession after expiration of the lease), he becomes a trespasser; and a tenancy from year to year, subject to the provisions of the original lease, may be created at the election of the landlord, regardless of the intent or wishes of the tenant. The right of the landlord to continue the tenancy is not affected by the tenant's intent, refusal to sign a new lease or give notice of his intent to vacate. While this rule appears to operate a hardship on tenants, it ultimately operates for their benefit, protecting new tenants who have vacated old premises from being shut out by holdover tenants. Here, the repudiation of the tenancy by Fetting Mfg. (D) was not enough to relieve it of further liability. Only if Waltz (P) had resumed possession to the exclusion of Fetting Mfg. (D) could they have been protected from further liability. Since they did not, however, the judgment must be affirmed.

EDITOR'S ANALYSIS: This case points up the general rule for the treatment of a holdover. In short, he is subject to a unilateral renewal of the lease by the original terms by lessor. This is a duty imposed by law upon him for his wrongful act of holding over. Note, however, that a holdover may be permissible if (1) it is brief and consistent with some local custom or usage (e.g., a term falling on a Sunday will be extended to the next Monday); (2) where moving may be shown to pose an immediate threat to some tenant's health; (3) consent of the lessor is obtained; (4) the lessor delays his election unreasonably. Note, finally, that the general rule is that if the original lease was for more than one year, a year-to-year tenancy arises. If the original lease was for less than one year, a lessor (month-to-month) tenancy will arise, until the holdover finally moves out.

NOTES:

MASON v. WIERENGO'S ESTATE
SUPREME COURT OF MICHIGAN, 1897.
113 Mich. 151, 71 N.W. 489

NATURE OF CASE: Action to recover rent from a holdover tenant.

FACT SUMMARY: Wierengo (D) informed Mason (P), his landlord, of his intent to vacate the premises but was taken sick and could not vacate on time.

CONCISE RULE OF LAW: Sickness at the end of the term of a lease does not relieve a holdover of his liability for failing to promptly vacate; and such failure may result in the election by the landlord to renew the lease regardless of the intent of the tenant.

FACTS: Wierengo (D) leased premises from Mason (P) in which he operated a store. Prior to expiration of the lease, he informed Mason (P) of his intent to vacate. During the process of moving out, however, Wierengo (D) was taken seriously ill. His clerks continued to make the move but did not finish until 11 days after expiration of the lease. Wierengo (D) had died six days after expiration of the lease. Electing a renewal for a year upon Wierengo's (D) holdover, Mason (P) sued his estate to recover the year's rent. Upon judgment for Mason (P), Wierengo's Estate (D) appeals, contending that an act of God had rendered performance impossible.

ISSUE: May a tenant be relieved of his liability as a holdover because of incapacitating illness at the time of expiration of the lease?

HOLDING AND DECISION: No. Sickness at the end of the term of a lease does not relieve a holdover of his liability for failing to promptly vacate; and such failure may result in the election by the landlord to renew the lease regardless of the intent of the tenant. Such election creates a tenancy from year to year, subject to the provisions of the original lease. The holding is trespass, wrongful regardless of motive or intent. Here, even the deathly illness of Wierengo (D) does not relieve him of liability. Since there was no evidence of any consent by Mason (P) the judgment must be affirmed.

EDITOR'S ANALYSIS: With one exception, this case still points up the generally accepted rule for holding over of a tenancy because of illness. (The trend of authority is that such liability will not be imposed wherever it can be shown that the moving itself will be injurious to some tenant's health. Above, of course, such was not the case since the moving of the business premises of Wierengo could not be said to have affected his health directly, since he could stay home in bed during it.)

The type of estate created by election of the landlord as above is called a periodic tenancy (as opposed to a mere tenancy by sufferance which involves consent). It begins immediately upon election, for whatever term is appropriate (year for leases greater than a year, month for leases shorter than a year), until either (1) the tenant has vacated at the end of the new period or (2) the landlord gives notice of termination.

NOTES:

MARGOSIAN v. MARKARIAN
SUPREME JUDICIAL COURT OF MASSACHUSETTS, 1934.
288 Mass. 197, 192 N.E. 612

NATURE OF CASE: Action to receive tort damages for personal injuries.

FACT SUMMARY: Margosian (P), a tenant at sufferance at the premises of Markarian (D), slipped and injured herself as a result of a defect in the stairs of the premises.

CONCISE RULE OF LAW: A holdover tenant becomes a tenant at sufference upon notice to quit for non-payment of rent; and as he thereby loses all privity with the landlord, the landlord owes him only the duty to not wantonly or wilfully injure him.

FACTS: Margosian (P) was injured due to a defect in the stairs of premises her husband rented from Markarian (D). However, she had been served with a notice to quit for non-payment (her husband was deceased) before the accident. She sued to recover for her personal injuries. The trial court found for Markarian (D), and ordered a report to the Appellate Division which affirmed. She now appeals.

ISSUE: May a holdover tenant maintain an action for negligence against a landlord who has given notice to quit?

HOLDING AND DECISION: No. A holdover tenant becomes a tenant at sufferance upon notice to quit for non-payment of rent; and as he thereby loses all privity with the landlord, the landlord owes him only the duty to not wantonly or wilfully injure him. A tenant at sufferance has neither estate nor title, only naked wrongful possession. As such, he is a bare licensee, and the landlord has no other duties toward him than any other licensee. Here, the negligence of the landlord Markarian (D) would only be a basis for a cause of action if Margosian (P) was more than a licensee, or if she could revive the tenancy by payment of rent. Since she is only a licensee, and since Massachusetts law says a holdover cannot revive tenancy by payment of rent, no cause of action for negligence may lie. The report must be affirmed.

The court also pointed out, however, that where states allow a holdover tenancy to be revived after notice to quit, such contingency in itself makes the tenant more than a mere licensee to whom a duty of care is owed.

EDITOR'S ANALYSIS: This case points up one example of the operation of the general rule for holdover tenants. That rule is that when a tenant wrongfully holds over after the expiration of a lease, he becomes a tenant at sufferance unless he asserts a claim of ownership that makes him an adverse possessor. Failure to pay rent plus notice to quit for that reason make a tenant such a holdover tenant at sufferance as well. Of course, such status will never make the tenant subject to liability for trespass since his original entry was rightful.

As is also implied in the decision, no notice is necessary to terminate a tenancy at sufferance. This is the universally accepted general rule with the only exceptions occurring in a minority of states which require notice to terminate where the holdover has done so with the implied or express consent of the landlord.

GOWER v. WATERS

SUPREME JUDICIAL COURT OF MAINE, 1926.
125 Me. 223, 132 A. 550

NATURE OF CASE: Action for trespass.

FACT SUMMARY: Waters (D), landlord to Gower (P), broke into and demanded possession of the premises which Gower (P) wrongfully held.

CONCISE RULE OF LAW: A holdover tenant who has become a tenant at sufferance cannot maintain an action for trespass against a landlord for using only necessary reasonable force to expel the tenant (but excessive force would make the landlord subject to criminal indictment).

FACTS: Gower (P) had occupied premises as a tenant of Waters (D). Upon becoming in arrears, he was given a notice to quit by Mrs. Waters (D). When he ignored the notice, Mrs. Waters (D), along with a deputy sheriff, went to the premises for the purpose of evicting him. After being refused permission to enter by Gower's (P) wife, Mrs. Waters (D) went to a side bedroom door and entered that way, followed by the deputy and her two sons. She demanded possession, but agreed instead to accept payment later and allow Gower (P) to remain until he found another place. Gower (P) now sues for damages resulting from Waters' (D) entry. He contends she had no right to use force (entering through a side door, which she had to open), and committed trespass thereby. The case was reported for final determination to the court.

ISSUE: May a landlord use force to reenter and demand premises from a holdover tenant at sufferance?

HOLDING AND DECISION: Yes. A holdover tenant who has become a tenant at sufferance cannot maintain an action for trespass against a landlord for using only necessary reasonable force to expel the tenant (but excessive force would make the landlord subject to criminal indictment). This is a common law right of a landlord and will not be abrogated by the statutory remedy of forcible entry and detainer. Here, service of notice to quit made Gower (P) a holdover tenant at sufferance. Waters (D) was completely within her rights to make a forcible entry into the premises to recover possession. The opening of the door was clearly not excessive. Judgment must be for Waters (D).

EDITOR'S ANALYSIS: This case represents the probable minority rule and is definitely contra the trend of authority for self-help by landlords. It is true that, at common law, a landlord had the right to use reasonable (minimum necessary under the circumstances) force, if necessary, to regain possession of property wrongfully held by another. The majority modern rule, however, is that unlawful detainer statutes provide a substitute, not alternative, legal remedy for landlords. Usually a summary proceeding (landlord merely establishes prima facie case — no affirmative defenses by the tenant, such as implied warranty of habitability, etc. are allowed) unlawful detainer is designed to expedite the legal re-entry by a landlord, while avoiding the dangers of violence involved in self-help.

JONES v. TAYLOR

COURT OF APPEAL OF KENTUCKY, 1909. 136 Ky. 39, 123 S.W. 326

NATURE OF CASE: Action for damages for forcible detainer.

FACT SUMMARY: Jones (D), believing he had rented Bedford's (P) farm for a year beginning March 1, 1906, refused to surrender possession of the farm on that date.

CONCISE RULE OF LAW: A tenant is not liable for double rent for holding over if he did so in good faith with an honest belief that he was justified in holding over.

FACTS: Jones (D) rented a farm from Bedford (P) for the years beginning March 1, 1904, and March 1, 1905. On March 1, 1906, Jones (D), insisting that he had rented the farm for the year beginning on that date, refused to surrender possession. Upon his refusal to surrender, Bedford (P) obtained a writ of forcible detainer against him. Bedford was awarded $1,000 in damages: $500 being the reasonable rental value of the premises for the year beginning March 1, 1906, and $500 additional, as double rent for Jones' (D) wrongful refusal to surrender possession. Jones (D) disputes the award of double rent. He raises as a defense his good faith, belief that he had rented the farm, and the fact that he had consulted attorneys and placed them in full possession of all the facts. They advised him that he could remain in possession during the year beginning March 1, 1906.

ISSUE: Is a defendant who holds over with a good faith belief that he is justified in doing so liable for double rent?

HOLDING AND DECISION: No. The English statute allowed double rent against a tenant who wilfully held over. "Wilfully" holding over applies only when a tenant holds over without a good faith belief that he is justified in doing so. In this case Jones (D) laid his case before a competent attorney, and was advised that he had a right to possession. If Jones (D) in good faith, based upon reasonable grounds, believed that he was entitled to possession and motivated by this belief resisted Bedford's (P) efforts to evict him, he is not liable for double rent. The purpose of allowing recovery of double rent is to punish a tenant from wrongfully withholding property without having in good faith cause to believe he could rightfully do so.

EDITOR'S ANALYSIS: When a tenant for years holds over and becomes a tenant by sufferance, at common law, the landlord may elect either (1) to treat the tenant as a wrongdoer and proceed to eject him, holding him liable for use of the land or (2) to treat him as a tenant from year to year on the same terms as the prior lease. If the landlord chooses to do the latter, the tenant is liable for rent for an entire year. Also, after the tenant holds over, he and the landlord may agree to a continuation on new terms.

NOTES:

SIGROL REALTY CORP. v. VALCICH

SUP. COURT OF NEW YORK, APP. DIV., 1961. 12 A.D. 2d 430, 212 N.Y.S. 2d 224. Aff'd Mem., 11 N.Y. 2d 668, 180 N.E. 2d 904 (1962)

NATURE OF CASE: Action to enjoin defendants and declare plaintiff's title to some bungalows.

FACT SUMMARY: Valcich (D) and others were tenants who had constructed bungalows on a piece of land which Sigrol Realty Corp. (P) purchased.

CONCISE RULE OF LAW: Whether certain chattels will become realty or remain personalty is determined by the agreement between the chattel owner and the landlord. Other chattels remain personalty or become realty regardless of any agreement between the chattel owner and the landlord.

FACTS: Seven bungalows had been built by various tenants on some land owned by Wilmore. The tenants paid rent for the use of the land. They maintained, repaired, and sold the bungalows without let or hindrance from Wilmore. The bungalows were not sunk into or bolted to the ground and were built so they could be removed without injury to them or the land. Valcich (D) and six others assert their ownership of the bungalows. Wilmore sold the land to Sigrol Realty Corp. (P) with the building and improvements thereon, subject to the rights of tenants, if any. When Valcich (D) and the others attempted to remove the bungalows, Sigrol Realty Corp. (P) instituted this action to declare it has title to the bungalows and to restrain Valcich (D) and the others from removing them.

ISSUE: In the case of some chattels, does the agreement between the chattel owner and the landlord determine whether, after attachment, the chattel remains personalty or becomes realty?

HOLDING AND DECISION: Yes. To determine whether chattels annexed to realty remain personalty or become realty, chattels are divided into three classes. The first is chattels, such as gas ranges, which, because of their character as movables, remain personalty regardless of any agreement between the chattel owner and the landlord. The second class consists of chattels, such as brick, stone, and plaster placed in the walls of a building, which become realty. Again this happens regardless of any agreement between the chattel owner and landlord. The third class consists of other chattels which continue to be personalty or become realty in accordance with the agreement between the chattel owner and the landowner. The court decided that the bungalows in this case belong in the third class. Hence, the agreement between Wilmore and Valcich (D) and the other owners will determine whether the bungalows are realty or personalty. The Wilmores never claimed ownership of the bungalows which were erected, maintained, and sold by Valcich (D) and the others without Wilmore's consent or interference. Further, the bungalows were not built with the intention of making them permanent accessions to the realty. They could be easily removed. In light of these facts, the fair inference to be drawn is that the agreement between Wilmore and Valcich (D) and the others was that the bungalows were to remain personalty.

EDITOR'S ANALYSIS: A fixture is a chattel which has become real property. In this case, the bungalows had not become fixtures. For a chattel to become a fixture there must be: (1) an actual or constructive annexation to the land; (2) an adaptation of the chattel to the use to which the land is put; and (3) an objective in intention of the annexer that the chattel become a fixture. This intention is inferred from the circumstances.

NOTES:

IN RE ALLEN STREET AND FIRST AVENUE
COURT OF APPEALS OF NEW YORK, 1931.
256 N.Y. 236, 176 N.E. 377

NATURE OF CASE: Proceedings instituted by a city to acquire title in fee to real property required for widening a street.

FACT SUMMARY: The city acquired title to the real property which a butcher leased to conduct his business.

CONCISE RULE OF LAW: When the city takes property by condemnation, it must pay for fixtures annexed to the property by a tenant, though as between landlord and tenant the annexations remained the tenant's personal property.

FACTS: The city took certain property for the purpose of widening a street. Within the property was a lot which a butcher leased from the owner and on which he conducted his business. The lease between the butcher and his landlord stated that the butcher had the right to remove the fixtures at the termination of the lease. The lease also stated that its term would expire if the premises were taken by the city for any public purpose. An award was made to the owner for the value of the property, and an award was made to the butcher for the value of the fixtures annexed to the property. On appeal the city contends that it does not have to compensate the butcher for the fixtures because his lease provides that it will expire when the property is taken for a public purpose.

ISSUE: Must a city pay for fixtures annexed to property taken by the city, even though as between landlord and tenant the fixtures remained the tenant's personal property?

HOLDING AND DECISION: Yes. The city must compensate a tenant for fixtures annexed to real property, even though these are the personal property of the tenant, whenever the city, by its taking the property, destroys the leasehold interest of the tenant. As between the parties the courts will, at least at times, give effect to an intention by them that annexations should not become part of the realty. However, when the city takes property, it takes the property with all its improvements and extinguishes the title of all who had any interest therein. In this case the clause in the lease providing for termination upon condemnation by the city evidences an agreement between the butcher and his landlord that the butcher would not receive compensation for his leasehold interest. However, the butcher still retains the right to compensation for his interest in any annexations to the property, which but for the fact that the real property has been taken, he would have had the right to remove at the end of his lease.

EDITOR'S ANALYSIS: This case demonstrates the importance of the relation between the parties in determining whether an article is a fixture of not. Trade fixtures are those annexed to the land for the purpose of pecuniary gain in one's business. Due to the policy of wanting to encourage trade and industry, a tenant is permitted to remove trade fixtures from the land, as stated in the butcher's lease in this case.

CAMERON v. OAKLAND COUNTY GAS AND OIL CO.
SUP. CT. OF MICH., 1936. 277 Mich. 442, 269 N.W. 227

NATURE OF CASE: Action to determine title to buildings erected on leased premises by tenant.

FACT SUMMARY: Upon premises it leased from Cameron (P), Oakland County Gas and Oil Co. (D) erected buildings for the purpose of operating an oil and gas station.

CONCISE RULE OF LAW: A structure built by a tenant for the purpose of furthering his business remains the tenant's personal property and may be removed by the tenant regardless of its size or manner of construction.

FACTS: Cameron (P) owned property which Oakland County Gas and Oil Co. (D) leased. Oakland County Gas and Oil Co. (D) erected buildings on the property for the purpose of operating an oil and gas station. The lease contained no provisions as to the ownership of the buildings at the termination of the leasehold.

ISSUE: Does a structure built by a tenant for the purpose of furthering his business remain the tenant's personal property regardless of its size or manner of construction?

HOLDING AND DECISION: Yes. The general rule is whatever is annexed to property becomes part of it and cannot be removed. However, a broad exception to that rule is that fixtures erected for business purposes may be removed by the tenant and remain the tenant's personal property. The law implies an agreement between the landlord and the tenant that such property shall remain personal from the fact that the landlord contributes nothing to the structure and should not be enriched at the tenant's expense. The policy basis for the exception is the interest in encouraging trade. Here Oakland County Gas and Oil Co. (D) erected the buildings for business purposes. Hence the buildings remain its property and may be removed by it.

EDITOR'S ANALYSIS: The trade fixtures exception is a very old one and has been applied to furnaces, dyer's vats, a fire engine set up to work a colliery, a cider mill, and saw mills. However, it is not extended to the destruction of a brick building for the purpose of saving the bricks of which the building is made. The saving of such materials to the tenant is so slight compared with the injury to the land caused by the removal of the building that such destruction constitutes unreasonable economic waste, and will not be permitted.

NOTES:

OLD LINE LIFE INSURANCE CO. OF AMERICA v. HAWN

SUP. CT. OF WIS., 1937. 225 Wis. 627, 275 N.W. 542

NATURE OF CASE: Action to determine title to buildings.

FACT SUMMARY: Shortly before the completion of foreclosure proceedings by Old Line Life Insurance Co. of America (P) on mortgaged land he was leasing, R. Hawn (D) removed several agricultural structures he had erected on the land.

CONCISE RULE OF LAW: A lessee who erects trade fixtures, including agricultural structures, on mortgaged land which may be removed without injury to the land, may remove such fixtures as against the mortgagee.

FACTS: M. Hawn's (D) husband obtained a loan from Old Line Life Insurance Co. of America (P). To secure the loan he mortgaged land owned by him and M. Hawn (D). Thereafter, he conveyed all of his interest in the land to M. Hawn (D). M. Hawn (D) leased the land, which was a farm, to R. Hawn (D). R. Hawn (D) installed on the farm a furnace, steel stanchions, drinking cups for his stock, pipe equipment, hay and manure carriers, a brooder house, hen house, garage, tool shed, and maple sugar shed. Shortly before the completion of foreclosure proceedings, R. Hawn (D) removed from the farm all of the above-mentioned properties.

ISSUE: Can a tenant who has installed agricultural trade structures on mortgaged land remove such structures as against the mortgagee?

HOLDING AND DECISION: Yes. Articles annexed to a farm for agricultural purposes are removable trade fixtures. Where a tenant erects trade fixtures on land which has been mortgaged, and where such fixtures may be removed without material injury to the land, the tenant may remove the fixtures as against the mortgagee. In this case, the relationship between R. Hawn (D) and M. Hawn (D) was that of landlord and tenant. All of the disputed structures belonged to R. Hawn (D), and he had no intention of making them fixtures. He had always asserted his right to remove them at the conclusion of his lease. Hence, he should not be prevented from removing the properties.

EDITOR'S ANALYSIS: The court repeats that the exception as to trade fixtures encourages business. It sees no reason to allow the exception as to one engaged in trade and manufacture, but refuse it to one engaged in agriculture, although some cases have done so. Further it sees no justification for not allowing the exception where the land has been mortgaged. As the court states, "If that were declared law every prospective tenant who intends to install trade fixtures would have to ascertain whether the premises were mortgaged . . . "

NOTES:

SECHREST v. SAFIOL

419 N.E.2d 1384(Mass.-1981)

NATURE OF CASE: Action for return of a deposit.

FACT SUMMARY: Sechrest (D) calimed he was entitled to keep a deposit paid by Safiol (P) when Safiol (P) breached the sales contract.

CONCISE RULE OF LAW: A clause in a sales contract permitting the buyer to terminate if he is unable to procure certain conditions creates an implied obligation on the part of the buyer to attempt to procure those conditions.

FACTS: Sechrest (D) contracted to sell a parcel of property to Safiol (P) and Safiol (P) paid a deposit of $3,800. The contract provided that Safiol's (P) obligation to purchase was conditioned on his obtaining the necessary permits for construction from the proper public authorities. After successfully requesting three separate extenstions for the date of performance, Safiol (P) notified Sechrest (D) that he had not obtained the necessary permits and was thus terminating the contract. He sought the return of his deposit. Sechrest (D) refused, contendinig that Safiol (P) had breached his good faith obligation to attempt to secure the necessary permits, and thus Sechrest (D) was entitled to keep the deposit as damages. The trial court found no such obligation on Safiol's (P) part and ordered Sechrest (D) to return the money. Sechrest (D) appealed.

ISSUE: Does a clause in a sales contract permitting the buyer to terminate if he is unable to procure certain conditions create an implied good faith obligation on the part of the buyer to attempt to procure those conditions?

HOLDING AND DECISION: (Hennessey, C.J.) Yes. Although the contract provision, when read literally, creates no obligation of good faith performance on the part of the buyer, such a literal interpretation must be rejected. Otherwise, the provision would operate to give the buyer an option to purchase without any requirement to act affirmatively. This was clearly not the intent of the parties. Instead, they sought to allow the buyer to terminate only if he was unable to obtain the necessary construction permits from the proper authorities. Accordingly, an implied obligation arose on Safiol's (P) part to make a good faith attempt to secure the permits. Since the evidence shows that he breached his good faith obligation by failing to act, Sechrest (D) is entitled to retain the $3,800 deposit as damages. Reversed.

EDITOR'S ANALYSIS: As the principal case holds, a buyer under such a contract is only obligated to make a good faith effort to procure the contract conditions. He is not required to act unreasonably or spend a disproportionate amount of money in doing so. Thus, in Livoli v. Stoneman, 332 Mass. 473(1955), the buyer was not held to have breached a sales contract where he had failed to secure approval of a subdivision plan due to unanticipated prohibitive costs. The buyer had acted reasonably in that case and was not required to secure approval of his plan "at all costs."

TRISTRAM'S LANDING, INC. v. WAIT
Mass., 327 N.E. 2d 727 (1975)

NATURE OF CASE: Action to recover a brokerage commission.

FACT SUMMARY: Tristram's Landing (P), real estate brokers, located a buyer for Wait's (D) property. When no sale was consumated, Wait (D) refused to pay a commission to Tristram's Landing (P).

CONCISE RULE OF LAW: A seller of real estate has no obligation to pay a commission to his broker unless a sale by the seller to a buyer procured by the broker is actually consummated.

FACTS: Tristram's Landing, Inc. (P), real estate brokers in Nantucket, had previously acted as rental agent for Wait (D). When Wait (D) decided to sell her property Van Der Wolk (P), one of Tristram's Landing's (P) professional brokers, received permission to act as her broker. No mention was made of any commission, although Wait (D) knew that a 5% brokerage commission was standard in Nantucket. Wait (D) did not tell Van Der Wolk (P) that Tristram's Landing (P) could act as exclusive broker for her. The property was offered for sale at $110,000, and Van Der Wold (P) located a prospective buyer, Louise Cashman, who made a written offer of $100,000. Cashman (P) ultimately accepted Wait's (D) counter-offer of "$105,000 with an October 1st closing," which counter-offer had been transmitted through Tristram's Landing (P). On September 22, Wait (D) signed a 15 day extension of the closing date, but Cushman did not sign the extension. Wait (D) eventually appeared for closing on October 1st, but Cashman was not present and later refused to go through with the purchase. Wait (D) took no action against Cashman to compel performance of the sale contract. Van Der Wolk (P) later presented Wait (D) with a bill for $5,250, which sum represented the amount allegedly owed him as a commission. When Wait (D) refused payment Tristram's Landing (P) filed suit, alleging that the purchase and sale agreement had provided for a commission, and that Van Der Wolk (P) had earned it by securing a purchaser who was willing and able to buy Wait's (D) property at the specified price. The trial court agreed but Wait (D) appealed, arguing that no commission was due since Cashman had not actually completed the purchase.

ISSUE: Must a brokerage commission be paid if the broker locates an acceptable buyer for the seller's property but the agreement of sale subsequently entered into between the buyer and seller is never carried out?

HOLDING AND DECISION: No. A seller of real estate has no obligation to pay a commission to his broker unless a sale by the seller to a buyer procured by the broker is actually consummated. Traditionally, a commission is owed once the buyer locates a ready, able and willing buyer, acceptable to the seller, even if a sale to that buyer is never completed. In this case, however, the purchase and sale agreement, stated that the commission would be paid "on the said sale," which must be construed as meaning only if the sale was actually coonsummated. The rule that a sale must actually occur before a commission be-

comes due represents the view of a growing minority of states. It derives from the New Jersey case of Ellsworth Dobbs, Inc. v. Johnson. That case realized that, in practice, both seller and broker expect the latter's commission to be paid out of the proceeds of the sale. If the sale fails to materialize, the seller should not have the burden of paying the commission, especially since he may be without the funds to do so. Thus, the judgment in favor of Tristram's Landing must be reversed.

EDITOR'S ANALYSIS: The rule of Tristram's Landing, Inc. v. Wait represents, as the court acknowledges, the minority view. The rule has the advantage of protecting the seller, presumably the less wealthy of the two, from liability to the broker. However, in many cases it will be the breaching buyer who is legally responsible for the fact that the sale was not consummated. In such a circumstance, the seller would clearly have a right to sue for specific performance of the contract, while the broker would have, at best, a tenuous cause of action against the buyer based on a third party beneficiary theory. Thus, the Wait rule casts the burden of the loss on the party who stands the least chance of forcing it to be borne by the party whose conduct caused it.

NOTES:

LUETTE v. BANK OF ITALY NATIONAL TRUST & SAVINGS ASSN.

CIR. CT. OF APP., NINTH CIR., 1930. 42 F. 2d 9

NATURE OF CASE: Action for rescission of contract.

FACT SUMMARY: Luette (P) and Bank of Italy ~~National Trust & Savings~~ Assn. (D) entered into an installment contract for the sale and purchase of land. Luette (P) learned of an adverse claim against Bank of Italy (D) and sought to have the contract rescinded. *to the outcome of which is uncertain*

CONCISE RULE OF LAW: There can be no rescission by a vendee of an executory contract of sale merely because of lack of title in the vendor prior to the date when performance is due.

FACTS: Luette (P) entered into a contract to purchase land from Bank of Italy National Trust & Savings Assn. (D)'s predecessors in interest. Luette (P) paid a deposit and was to pay monthly installments for seven years. Bank of Italy (D) was to convey the deed upon completion of the payments. Luette (P) made the payments for two years. Luette (P) alleges that an adverse claim has been asserted; the outcome of which is uncertain. Luette (P) asks that Bank of Italy (D) be enjoined from cancelling Luette's (P) contract and that they be relieved of having to make payments pending the outcome of the claim. Luette (P) asks that if the court cannot grant the injunction, the contract be rescinded.

ISSUE: Can there be a rescission by a vendee of an executory contract of sale because of lack of title in the vendor prior to the date when performance is due?

HOLDING AND DECISION: No. The court will not issue an injunction since Luette (P) makes no ~~pleading of any~~ *allegations that D is* relief. Secondly, there can be no rescission by a vendee of an executory contract of sale merely because of lack of title in the vendor prior to the date when performance is due. In this case, there is no showing that Bank of Italy (D) is in default, since under the contract the deed would not be conveyed for three more years. Assuming a defect does exist, Bank of Italy (D) still has three years in which to perfect its title. *+ Fraud* *likely to become insolvent*

EDITOR'S ANALYSIS: An installment land contract is used as an instrumentality for the long-range financing of the purchase of land. As demonstrated in this case, under such an arrangement, the purchaser goes into possession immediately and is obligated to pay specified installments. The vendor will deliver the deed upon completion of the payments. The vendor's security is the right to retake the land if the purchaser defaults in making payments. The more common method of financing the purchase of land is the mortgage.

NOTES:

CLAPP v. TOWER

SUP. CT. OF N.D., 1903. 11 N.D. 556, 93 N.W. 862

NATURE OF CASE: Action to quiet title.

FACT SUMMARY: Clapp (P) alleges that he is the owner of certain property in which Tower (D) claims an interest. Clapp (P) asks that Tower (D) be required to set forth their claims so their validity may be determined.

CONCISE RULE OF LAW: A valid and binding contract of sale of land operates as conversion so that the vendor's property, as viewed by equity, is no longer real estate in the land, but personal estate in the price.

FACTS: Tower (D) allege that they are the heirs of C. Tower, deceased. C. Tower sold certain land to Hadley. When Hadley defaulted in making payments on the land, C. Tower's executors foreclosed Hadley's contract, and the land became part of C. Tower's estate. The executors acted upon the theory that the land was subject to the rule of equitable conversion and treated it as personal property. They sold it to Clapp (P), who has since been in possession of it. Clapp (P) claims ownership by virtue of the deed received from the executors. Tower (D) claim ownership by virtue of their heirship.

ISSUE: Where a binding contract for the sale of land has been entered into, does such contract operate as a conversion so that the land is thereafter treated as the vendor's personal property?

HOLDING AND DECISION: Yes. Once a binding contract for the sale of land has been made, the vendor still holds legal title, but only as a trustee, and he acquires an equitable ownership of the purchase money. His property, as viewed by equity, is no longer real estate in the land, but personal estate in the price. Hence, if the vendor dies before payment, it goes to his executors and not to his heirs. In this case the execution and delivery of the contract of sale to Hadley worked a conversion of the land into personalty. His interest after the execution of the contract, and at the time of his death was the money contracted to be paid by Hadley. Since the real estate had assumed the character of personalty it went to the executors, according to the terms of the will, rather than being distributed as real estate according to the law of succession of the state and so going to Tower (D). Hence the executors could, after the cancellation of Hadley's contract, sell the land to Clapp (P).

EDITOR'S ANALYSIS: This case demonstrates the rule of equitable conversion under which land may be treated as money and money as land. The doctrine has its origin in the maxim that "Equity looks upon that as done, which ought to be done." Equity regards the contracting parties of a binding and valid contract of sale of land as having changed positions, and the original estate of each as having been converted — that of the vendee from personal into real property, and that of the vendor from real into personal property.

MOSES BROTHERS v. JOHNSON
SUP. CT. OF ALA., 1890. 88 Ala. 517, 7 So. 146

NATURE OF CASE: Action to enjoin Johnson (D) from cutting timber on land sold to him by Moses Brothers (P).

FACT SUMMARY: Johnson (D) began to cut down trees on land which he had bought from Moses Brothers (P) and for which he had paid a five dollar deposit and was to pay the remaining fourteen hundred dollars in annual installments.

CONCISE RULE OF LAW: A vendor of real estate who enters into an executory agreement to convey title on the payment of the purchase money may obtain an injunction against the purchaser of the land, if the purchaser is committing waste which impairs the security or renders it insufficient.

FACTS: Moses Brothers (P) sold land to Johnson (D) for fourteen hundred and forty dollars. Johnson (D) only paid five dollars. He was to pay the balance in annual installments for five years. Moses Brothers (P) retained title which they would convey upon final payment. Johnson (D) took possession and began clearing the timber off the land. The land was near a city where firewood was in demand. Johnson (D) did not have assets to cover his debt to Moses Brothers (P).

ISSUE: Can the vendor in an executory contract to sell land, who has retained title, obtain an injunction against the purchaser who is committing waste on the land?

HOLDING AND DECISION: Yes. A vendor who sells on credit, retaining the title as security for the purchase money, sustains the same relation to the vendee, so far as the question of security goes, as does the mortgagee to the mortgagor. If the security of the mortgagor is insufficient, the mortgagor will not be allowed to impair the security by committing waste on it. However, if the security is sufficient, the court will not grant an injunction to restrain the mortgagor from cutting timber, or committing waste, on the mortgaged property. The court will only interfere where the security is not sufficient. In this case Moses Brothers (P) allege that Johnson (D) is insolvent, and that because the land is near a city where firewood is in demand, the land is worth more with the timber on it. Johnson (D) alleges that he is solvent and has assets to cover debts, excepting his debt for the land. Hence, the land is the sole security for the promised purchase money. Since cutting down the timber would diminish the land's value, and the land is the sole security, Johnson (D) will be enjoined from cutting down the timber.

EDITOR'S ANALYSIS: The court states that a vendor of real estate, who enters an executory contract to convey title on the payment of the purchase money, sustains the same relation to the vendee, as a mortgagee does to a mortgagor. Both the vendor and the mortgagee have legal title which, in the absence of stipulations for possession, will maintain an action of ejectment. Both can retain legal title against the other parties, until the purchase money or the mortgage debt is paid. Yet, both are at last but trustees of the legal title for the mortgagor or vendee, if the purchase money or mortgage debt is paid.

NOTES:

SWEENEY, ADMINISTRATRIX v. SWEENEY
SUP. COURT OF ERRORS OF CONNECTICUT, 1940.
126 Conn. 391, 11 A. 2d 806

NATURE OF CASE: Action to cancel a deed.

FACT SUMMARY: Maurice, Sweeney's (P) intestate, deeded property to John Sweeney (D) and recorded the deed. John (D) deeded the property back to Maurice, but that deed was not recorded.

CONCISE RULE OF LAW: Where a deed has been formally executed and delivered, the presumption that the grantee assented to delivery can be overcome only by evidence that no delivery was in fact intended.

FACTS: Sweeney (P) is Maurice Sweeney's widow and administratrix. Maurice deeded property to John Sweeney (D). This deed was recorded. Pursuant to Maurice's request, a second deed was executed which deeded the property back to him. This deed was not recorded. A week or two later, Maurice took John (D) the recorded deed, and a week or two after that he took John (D) the unrecorded deed. John (D) gave the second deed to his attorney. When the latter's office was burned, the deed was destroyed. Maurice's purpose in making the second deed was so that he would be protected if John (D) predeceased him. Maurice continued to live on the deeded property until his death. He made leases in regard to it and exercised full control over it without interference from John (D). The trial court concluded that there was no intention to deliver John's (D) deed to Maurice and there was no delivery or acceptance thereof.

ISSUE: Has a deed been delivered where it was formally executed and manually delivered and where there is no evidence that no delivery was intended?

HOLDING AND DECISION: Yes. It is true that physical possession of a duly executed deed is not conclusive proof that it was legally delivered. Delivery must be made with the intent to pass title if it is to be effective. However, where a deed has been manually delivered. There is a rebuttable presumption that the grantee assented since the deed was beneficial to him where deeds are formally executed and delivered, this presumption can be overcome only by evidence that no delivery was in fact intended. In this case the only purpose in making the deed expressed by either party was Maurice's statement that it was to protect him in case John (D) predeceased him. Since this purpose would have been defeated had there been no delivery with intent to pass title, this conclusively establishes the fact that there was legal delivery. John (D) also contended that the delivery was on the condition that John (D) predecease Maurice. However, a conditional delivery can only be made by placing the deed in the hands of a third person to be kept until the happening of the condition. The court's ruling is reversed.

EDITOR'S ANALYSIS: The delivery must be voluntary and must occur with the mutual intention of the parties to pass title. The term "escrow" is sometimes used as importing any deposit of a deed for delivery upon the performance of a condition. There can be no escrow without conditional delivery of the deed to a third person as depositary. "Conditional delivery to a grantee vests absolute title in the latter."

JOHNSON v. JOHNSON
SUP. CT. OF RHODE ISLAND, 1903.
24 R.I. 571, 54 A. 378

NATURE OF CASE: Action to have deed set aside and declared null and void.

FACT SUMMARY: Mary Johnson executed a deed of property to Mary A. Johnson (P). She deposited the deed with Moies with the direction that it should be given to Mary A. Johnson (P) if anything happened to her. Mary Johnson continued to exercise control over the property until her death.

CONCISE RULE OF LAW: An essential element of a delivery, whether absolute or conditional, is that the grantor part with possession and control over the deed at the time of delivery.

FACTS: Mary Johnson made and executed a deed to certain property to Mary A. Johnson (P). She deposited the deed with Moies, directing him that it should be given to Mary A. Johnson (P) if anything happened to her, Mary Johnson. Moies understood from her directions that Mary Johnson retained the right to recall the deed at any time and the right to sell and dispose of the property. She did continue to exercise dominion over the property until her death. She advertised it for sale, paid taxes on the mortgage and collected the rents.

ISSUE: Is it necessary for a delivery that the grantor intend to divest himself of possession and control of the deed at the time of delivery?

HOLDING AND DECISION: Yes. In order to constitute a delivery, the grantor must absolutely part with the possession and control of the deed. A deed may be effectual to convey title, although delivered to a third person to hold until the grantor's death, and then to deliver it to the grantee. But for such a delivery to be valid, the deed must be left with the depositary without any reservation on the part of the grantor, either express or implied, of the right to recall it or otherwise control its use. In this case there was evidence of a parting with the manual possession of the deed by Mary Johnson, but she did not part with the control of it. Hence an essential element of delivery was lacking, and the deed must be set aside.

EDITOR'S ANALYSIS: This case demonstrates that an instrument cannot be said to be delivered in escrow, and does not constitute an escrow, where possession by the depositary is subject to the control of the depositor. The deposit must be irrevocable. The court, in this case, stated that Mary Johnson's intended disposition of the property was evidently of a testamentary character. However, an instrument which is intended to operate as a will, without being executed in accordance with statutes relating to wills cannot be allowed to have the effect of a will.

STONE v. DUVALL
SUP. CT. OF ILL., 875. 77 Ill. 475

NATURE OF CASE: Action to set aside a deed.

FACT SUMMARY: Duvall (P) executed a deed by which he conveyed property to Mary Stone upon his death. Mary Stone having died, Duvall seeks to set the deed aside.

CONCISE RULE OF LAW: The uncontemplated death of a grantee to a deed in escrow before the performance of the condition or before final delivery does not affect the escrow or allow the setting aside of the deed.

FACTS: Duvall (P) executed a deed conveying all interest in land owned by him to his daughter, Mary Stone. He directed a Justice of the Peace to record the deed and to hold it until his death and then deliver it to Mary Stone. When Mary Stone died, Duvall (P) took the deed executed to her from the Justice. Mary Stone and her husband, W. Stone (D), were in possession of the property when she died. He continued in possession. Duvall (P) claims that the deed was not made pursuant to his instructions, and that it was not delivered to Mary Stone or anyone for her.

ISSUE: If the grantee to a deed in escrow dies before the performance of the condition or before final delivery, is the escrow abrogated?

HOLDING AND DECISION: No. The delivery is good. If either of the parties die before the performance of the condition, but the condition is performed thereafter, the deed is good. By the performance of the condition the deed takes effect by the first delivery without any new or second delivery. In this case the deed was delivered in escrow. It cannot take full effect until the occurrence of the event that was made conditional to its delivery. Since that event was Duvall's (P) death, and he has not yet died, full title has not yet vested in the grantee, Mary Stone. At the time of Duvall's (P) death, the deed will take effect and will vest title in Mary Stone and pass the property to her heirs, William Stone (D). The deed will not be set aside. The court also pointed out that until Duvall's (P) death, he is entitled to use of the property. It is as though he has a life estate and Mary Stone's heirs have the remainder.

EDITOR'S ANALYSIS: This case demonstrates that the uncontemplated death of a party does not affect an escrow where there has been a deposit made. This is true whether the death occurs before the performance of the condition or before final delivery. Here Mary Stone's death was not contemplated, and its happening was not made determinative, as Duvall's (P) was. Hence it had no effect and does not abrogate the escrow.

NOTES:

MAYS v. SHIELDS

SUP. CT. OF GA., 1903. 117 Ga. 814, 45 S.E. 68

NATURE OF CASE: Action to clarify title.

FACT SUMMARY: A deed which Shields (D) deposited in escrow and which was recorded was improperly delivered to the grantee Flunt who sold to Sanders, who sold to Mays (P).

CONCISE RULE OF LAW: Where a grantor delivers a deed in escrow and learns that it has been improperly delivered to the grantee, or that it has been recorded, he must take active measures to prevent innocent persons from acting to their injury.

FACTS: Shields (D) signed a deed and deposited it in escrow with Thompson. Thompson was to deliver it to Flunt, the grantee, when Flunt paid the balance of the purchase money. The deed was recorded. Shields (D) knew of this. It was then improperly delivered to Flunt. Flunt was in possession of the land before the deed was executed. Flunt sold to Sanders, who sold to Mays (P).

ISSUE: Where a grantor delivers a deed in escrow and learns that it had been recorded and does not take steps to prevent injury to third persons who buy on faith of possession of the deed or the record, will the grantor be estopped from disputing the rights of such third persons?

HOLDING AND DECISION: Yes. Generally where there has been an improper delivery by a depositary and a subsequent purchase from the grantee, it is held that no title passed and the purchaser acquires no rights against the grantor. It is an equal hardship to both the grantor and the purchaser, and where the equities are equal the law must prevail. But where they differ, the superior equity must prevail. If the grantor ratifies the delivery or learns that the deed has been recorded, he must attempt to recover possession of the deed or to have the record expunged so as to prevent innocent persons from being injured by reliance on the deed. Failure of the grantor to act will estop him from denying the rights of innocent persons who buy on faith of possession of the deed or the record of it. In this case, Shields (D) admits that he knew that the deed had been recorded. Further, Flunt was in possession of the land. When one is in possession of property and the title is duly recorded, he is clothed with double evidence of ownership. Flunt was so clothed here. Hence, if Sanders or Mays (P) did not know of the improper delivery and record, and bought on the faith of Flunt's possession under a recorded deed of which Shields (D) had notice, they will be protected in their purchase.

EDITOR'S ANALYSIS: As this case states, the general rule is that where an instrument placed in escrow is thereafter delivered by the escrow holder in violation of or without compliance with, the terms or conditions of the escrow agreement, no rights or title pass. The basis of this rule is that there has been no lawful delivery, and lawful delivery is as essential to the validity of a deed as is a genuine signature. However, as this case demonstrates, rights of third persons will be protected where the grantor is so negligent, careless, and inattentive of the rights of others as to estop the grantor from claiming title.

SMITH v. HADDAD

SUP.S.CT.OF MASS.,1974, 314 N.E.2d 435

NATURE OF CASE: Action to determine title to land.

FACT SUMMARY: The parties disputed the boundary line between their lands because it was unclear if the predecessor in title of one of the parties began a measurement described in the deed from the middle or the side of a 66-foot wide public highway.

CONCISE RULE OF LAW: In the absence of a clear showing of a contrary intent, a measurement given from a stream or public or private way shall be presumed to begin at the side line of that stream or way.

FACTS: Nichols, in 1949, owned all of the land in question. In that year, he conveyed a portion to Smith's (P) predecessor in title and reserved a portion for himself. The boundaries followed two streets, one now a public highway (Main Street). Smith's (P) predecessor in title in his grant to Smith (P) reserved a 175-foot wide parcel fronting Main Street. The predecessor later conveyed that parcel to Haddad (D). It was ambiguous whether the 175-foot measurement began at the center or edge of Main Street. As Main Street was 66 feet wide, a 33-foot difference in the boundary between Smith's (P) and Haddad's (D) respective land was possible. The trial court held that measurement began at the side of the way, and this appeal followed.

ISSUE: In the absence of a clear showing of a contrary intent, will a measurement given from a stream or public or private way be presumed to begin at the side line of the stream or way?

HOLDING AND DECISION: Yes. In the absence of a clear showing of a contrary intent, a measurement given from a stream or public or private way shall be presumed to begin at the side line of that stream or way. It is also presumed that even where the specified boundary line is clearly at the side of the way, the deed was intended to transfer the abbreviated rights to the fee of the way as well. This is based on the belief that it is unlikely that the grantor would want to reserve title to the fee of the way. It is also unlikely that a grantor would measure from the center of the way, although he can always indicate otherwise. As the presumption was not rebutted, the decision must be affirmed.

EDITOR'S ANALYSIS: The court gave little reason for the presumptions except that they seem to make sense. Further, the presumptions, which have been applied for well over a century, to be discontinued now "would create chaos in land titles, defeat the reasonable expectations of conveyancers, and cause substantial financial hardship to many innocent landowners." The accuracy of a description of land must be sufficient to locate the land by referring to the deed and admissible extrinsic evidence. Admissible evidence must show from the circumstances that the words could refer to only one piece of land.

NOTES:

HILLIKER v. RUEGER
CT. OF APP. OF N.Y., 1920. 228 N.Y. 11, 126 N.E. 266

NATURE OF CASE: Action to recover damages for breach of covenant of seizin.

FACT SUMMARY: Rueger (D) sold Hilliker (P) land. Hilliker (P) entered into a contract to sell the land to Schaefer. Schaefer refused to complete the contract, claiming that the title was not marketable.

CONCISE RULE OF LAW: A covenant of seizin means that the grantor, at the time of the conveyance, had a good, absolute, and indefeasible estate of inheritance in fee simple and had the power to convey the same.

FACTS: Rueger (D) sold certain land to Hilliker (P). The Ruegers (D) covenanted that they were seized of the property in fee simple. Hilliker (P) then entered a contract to sell the property to Schaefer, who paid Hilliker (P) a deposit. He then refused to complete the contract on the grounds that the title was unmarketable. He sued Hilliker (P) to recover his deposit. It was determined that Hilliker (P) did not have marketable title, and Schaefer recovered his deposit, interest, and expenses.

ISSUE: Can a grantee recover for breach of a covenant of seizin where he was not evicted?

HOLDING AND DECISION: Yes. A covenant of seizin means that the grantor, at the time of the conveyance, was lawfully seized of a good, absolute, and indefeasible estate of inheritance in fee simple and had power to convey it. If the covenant is broken by failure of the title, the grantee can maintain an action at once to recover the damages sustained as the direct result of the breach. It is not necessary that the grantee be evicted, since possession does not satisfy a covenant of seizin. In this case the court found that Rueger (D) did not have title to part of the land conveyed. Hence, there was a breach of Rueger's (D) covenant of seizin which entitles Hilliker (P) to whatever damages he sustained as a result. However, Hilliker (P) cannot recover attorney fees paid in defending in the action brought by Schaefer. This is because such recovery can only be allowed where a direct attack is made upon a title. Schaefer's action was not such an attack since he claimed that the title was not marketable. The fact that it was not marketable did not establish that it was bad.

EDITOR'S ANALYSIS: A grantor who covenants that he is lawfully seized of the land guarantees that he owns the estate, and can convey it. The fact that the land conveyed is subject to a mortgage or is subject to some restriction as to its use does not cause a breach of the covenant of seizin. The covenant of seizin is one of the three standard present covenants for title. A present covenant for title guarantees that a described situation exists at the time the covenant is made.

SCHOFIELD v. THE IOWA HOMESTEAD CO.
SUP. CT. OF IOWA, 1871. 32 Iowa 317

NATURE OF CASE: Action upon the covenants of a deed for lands.

FACT SUMMARY: Schofield (P) brought this action based on the covenant of seizin in the deed for land conveyed to him by the Iowa Homestead Co. (D). Schofield (P) conveyed a portion of the land to another before bringing this action.

CONCISE RULE OF LAW: The covenant of seizin runs with the land and confers upon the last grantee a right of action.

FACTS: Iowa Homestead Co. (D) conveyed certain property to Schofield (P). A covenant of seizin was expressed in the deed. Schofield (P) conveyed a part of the land to another. Schofield (P) brought this action based on the covenant. Iowa Homestead Co. (D) contends that the covenant passed with the land from Schofield (P) to the purchaser, and recovery in this action for the land thereby conveyed is barred.

ISSUE: Does a covenant of seizin run with the land?

HOLDING AND DECISION: Yes. The majority rule is that the covenant does not run with the land and that the right to a cause of action is personal to the grantee and is not conveyed to subsequent grantees. However, a few American jurisdictions follow the English rule that the covenant does run with the land and conveys a right of action to the last grantee. This rule is the more just. The object of all covenants in conveyances of lands, relating to their title or enjoyment, is to secure indemnity to the party entitled to the premises in case he is deprived of them. The last purchaser is the most interested and fit person to claim the indemnity since he will be the greatest (and only) sufferer if he is evicted. In this case, since Schofield (P) had conveyed the land to another, he had no right of action. That right was conveyed with the land to his purchaser. Also, it does not matter that only part of the land was conveyed. Covenants running with the land are divisible, and each purchaser who buys a portion of the land can maintain an action upon the covenant to recover for his land.

EDITOR'S ANALYSIS: This case represents the minority rule in the United States. In some jurisdictions statutes provide that covenants of seizin run with the land. There is also authority to the effect that the covenant of seizin runs with the land only when the covenantor is in possession at the time of the conveyance. When he is not in possession, the covenant is a personal one, under that rule.

NOTES:

SOLBERG v. ROBINSON

SUP. CT. OF S.D., 1914. 34 S.D. 55, 147 N.W. 87

NATURE OF CASE: Action to recover damages on covenants in a deed.

FACT SUMMARY: Robinson (D) conveyed land to Smith, who conveyed it to Solberg (P). Vesey brought an action against Solberg (P) to quiet title, and it turned out that Vesey was the owner of the land.

CONCISE RULE OF LAW: A grantor who conveys property by deed is estopped, as against the grantee, to assert anything in derogation of the deed such as that he had no title at the time of the conveyance or that no title passed by the deed.

FACTS: Robinson (D) delivered a warranty deed purporting to convey certain land to Smith. Smith delivered to Solberg (P) a warranty deed purporting to convey said land to Solberg (P). Neither Robinson (D) nor Smith were ever in actual possession of the land. Then, Vesey brought an action against Solberg (P) to quiet title on the land. Solberg (P) defended this action, but it turned out that Vesey was the owner of the land, and that while Robinson's (D) title appeared to come through Vesey, the deed which purported to divest Vesey of title was forged. The warranty deeds included covenants of seizin and quiet enjoyment. Solberg (P) seeks to recover the amount Robinson (D) received for the land, plus interest, and the expenses in defending the Vesey case.

ISSUE: Will a grantor who assumes to convey property by deed be estopped, as against the grantee, to assert anything in derogation of the deed?

HOLDING AND DECISION: Yes. Where a grantor represents himself as the owner of the fee to a piece of land and agrees that he will protect the grantees, and it later develops that he was not the owner and cannot defend the grantees, and they call upon him to respond in damages, the grantor will be estopped from saying that he did not have and did not convey the constructive possession of the land as he represented he had and for which he received a valuable consideration. It is true that in order for a covenant of quiet enjoyment to run with the land so that a remote grantee may recover, the covenantee must have received some estate in the land to which the covenant could attach. Where the covenantor was without title, it is necessary that possession be delivered in order to carry a covenant with the land. However, constructive possession is sufficient to carry the covenant with the land. In this case, Smith acquired no title to the land by virtue of the deed from Robinson (D). But Smith did have apparent title even as against Vesey. The county record showed that he had a perfect chain of title, and therefore he and his grantees should be held to have had constructive possession. As against Robinson (D), Solberg's (P) constructive possession continued so long as he believed himself to be in actual possession. Hence, it did not terminate until Solberg (P) received notice of Vesey's action. It is from this date that interest on the purchase price should be recovered.

EDITOR'S ANALYSIS: The court also allowed recovery for Solberg's (P) expenses in defending against the Vesey action, even though Robinson (D) was not notified of the action. Some courts hold that a covenantee cannot recover from the covenantor, the expenses of defending title unless the covenantor was notified of the action. But in this jurisdiction there was a statute allowing for recovery for such expenses. The statute does not require notice to the covenantor or make recovery conditional upon such notice. This case demonstrates that in order for a covenant to run with the land, the covenantee must receive some estate in the land, either from a good title or from actual or constructive possession.

NOTES:

EARLE v. FISKE

SUP. JUDICIAL CT. OF MASS., 1870. 103 Mass. 491

NATURE OF CASE: Writ of entry to recover land.

FACT SUMMARY: N. Fiske conveyed land to B. Fiske (D) and E. Fiske for their lives and, subject to their life estate, to M. Fiske. The deeds were not recorded. After N. Fiske died, B. Fiske (D), as her sole heir, conveyed the land to Earle (P). That deed was recorded.

CONCISE RULE OF LAW: Although an unrecorded deed is binding upon the grantor, his heirs and devisees, and also upon all persons having actual notice of it, it is not valid and effectual as against any other persons.

FACTS: N. Fiske conveyed certain property to B. and E. Fiske (D) for their lives, and subject to their life estate, to M. Fiske. The deeds were dated 1864, but were not recorded until 1867. N. Fiske died in 1865, leaving her son B. Fiske (D) as her sole heir. In 1866, he executed and delivered to Earle (P) a deed of the property. This deed was recorded in 1866. B. and E. Fiske (D) contend that since N. Fiske had given the deed dated 1864, nothing passed from her to B. Fiske (D) so as to allow him to convey the land to Earle (P).

ISSUE: Does an unrecorded deed have any force or effect as to a purchaser without notice?

HOLDING AND DECISION: No. An unrecorded deed is sufficient, as between the original parties to it, to transfer the whole title. However, for the protection of creditors and purchasers, the rule has been established that while an unrecorded deed is binding upon the grantor, his heirs and devisees, and all persons having actual notice of it, it is not binding as against any other persons. As to others, the person who appears of record to be the owner is to be taken as the true and actual owner, and his apparent ownership is not divested or affected by an unknown and unrecorded deed that he may have made. The purpose of the recording system is that a purchaser of land has a right to rely upon the information furnished by the registry of deeds, and he is justified in taking that information as true and acting upon it accordingly. As a purchaser without notice, the unrecorded deeds have no effect as to Earle (P). As against his claim, N. Fiske's unrecorded deeds have no binding force or effect.

EDITOR'S ANALYSIS: This case demonstrates the importance of recording in determining conflicting claims to real property. The only instances where recording plays a significant part in the field of personal property is in connection with chattel mortgages and conditional-sales agreements. However, as demonstrated here, recording is quite pertinent to real property. Generally, the various recording acts are the basis of deciding conflicting claims to real property. The extent to which a subsequent purchaser is protected against a prior unrecorded deed depends on the type of statute in the local jurisdiction. There are four distinct types of statutes: notice statutes, race-notice statutes, period-of-grace statutes, and race statutes.

NOTES:

AYER v. PHILADELPHIA & BOSTON FACE BRICK COMPANY

SUP. JUDICIAL COURT OF MASSACHUSETTS, 1893.
159 Mass. 84, 34 N.E. 177

NATURE OF CASE: Writ of entry to foreclose a mortgage.

FACT SUMMARY: Waterman gave a second mortgage containing a covenant of warranty on certain land to Ayer's (P) assignor. The mortgage was subject to a first mortgage. Later, through a foreclosure of the first mortgage, Waterman obtained title and conveyed to Philadelphia & Boston Face Brick Company (D).

CONCISE RULE OF LAW: Under a deed with covenant of warranty, a title later acquired by the grantor inures to the grantee, against both the grantor himself and one claiming title by descent or grant from the grantor after his acquiring new title.

FACTS: On March 1, 1872, Waterman gave a mortgage to Boston Five Cents Savings Bank. On February 21, 1874, Waterman gave a second mortgage to Ayer's (P) assignor. This mortgage contained a covenant of warranty and mentioned the first mortgage. Boston Five Cents Savings Bank foreclosed, and Barstow purchased the land at the foreclosure sale. Waterman then purchased the land from Barstow, and subsequently conveyed to Philadelphia & Boston Face Brick Co. (D). After the conveyance to Philadelphia & Boston Face Brick Co. (D), Ayer (P) brought a writ of entry against the Brick Co. (D) as tenant, to foreclose the 1874 mortgage.

ISSUE: Under a deed with covenants of warranty, does a title later acquired by the grantor inure to the grantee against one claiming title by grant from the grantor?

HOLDING AND DECISION: Yes. The title inures to the grantee by way of estoppel. The covenant of warranty operates by way of estoppel to prevent a grantor from asserting any after-acquired title to property which he purports to convey. In this case, the title to the premises would have inured to Ayer's (P) assignor as against any subsequent purchaser from Waterman. Waterman's covenant of warranty operates by way of estoppel, notwithstanding the mention of the mortgage. A purchaser from the mortgagor without actual notice of a second mortgage takes no better title than the mortgagor. Hence, Philadelphia & Boston Face Brick Co. (D) received no better title than Waterman possessed, and Ayer (P) is entitled to judgment.

EDITOR'S ANALYSIS: As demonstrated by this case, the covenant of warranty estops the grantor from asserting any after-acquired title to property which he purports to convey. Another way of expressing this rule is that the title subsequently acquired by the grantor inures to the benefit of the grantee. The grantor of a conveyance cannot say that the grantee had no authority to purchase or capacity to take. Likewise a grantor is estopped by the deed to assert fraud in its inducement (as distinguished from fraud in the factum) or to claim that an attesting witness selected by him was incompetent.

MORSE v. CURTIS

SUPREME JUDICIAL COURT OF MASSACHUSETTS, 1885.
140 Mass. 112, 2 N.E. 929

NATURE OF CASE: Writ of entry.

FACT SUMMARY: Curtis (D) received a mortgage on certain land from Clark by assignment. Although his assignor had notice of an earlier mortgage on the land to Morse (P), Curtis (D) had no actual notice of that mortgage.

CONCISE RULE OF LAW: If a purchaser, upon examining the registry, finds a conveyance from the owner of the land to his grantor, which gives the grantor a perfect record title, the purchaser is entitled to rely upon such title and is not required to search the records further to see if there has been any prior unrecorded deed of the original owner.

FACTS: On August 8, 1872, Hall mortgaged certain land to Morse (P). On September 7, 1875, Hall mortgaged the land to Clark, who had notice of the earlier mortgage. This mortgage was recorded on January 31, 1876. The earlier mortgage was recorded on September 8, 1876. On October 4, 1881, Clark assigned his mortgage to Curtis (D), who had no actual notice of the mortgage to Morse (P).

ISSUE: If a purchaser examines the registry and finds a conveyance which gives his grantor a perfect record title, is the purchaser required to search further to see if there has been any prior unrecorded deed of the original owner?

HOLDING AND DECISION: No. The earliest registry laws provided that no conveyance of land was good and effectual in law against anyone but the grantor or grantors and their heirs, unless the deed had been properly recorded. An exception to this rule was adopted, and it was held that a prior unrecorded deed would be valid against a second purchaser who took his deed with a knowledge of the prior deed. The basis for this exception was that it was a fraud for a second purchaser to take a deed if he had knowledge of the prior deed. In this case, Curtis (D) had no actual knowledge of Morse's (P) prior mortgage. However, Morse (P) contends that he had constructive notice, because Morse's (P) mortgage was recorded before the assignment. The court feels that the better rule is that where a purchaser has examined the registry and found a conveyance to his grantor which gives him a perfect record title, the purchaser is entitled to rely upon such record title. He is not required to search the records afterwards in order to see if there has been any prior unrecorded deed of the original owner. Hence, in this case once Curtis (D) found record of Hall's mortgage to Clark, he was not required to search further to discover the Morse (P) mortgage which was recorded after the Clark mortgage.

EDITOR'S ANALYSIS: Only recordable documents will give record notice when placed on the land records. Local statutes must be examined to ascertain what documents are recordable. The principal exclusion from the requirement of recording is a short-term lease. An instrument that purports to be a deed but which has not been executed with the formalities required by law, such as a deed which has not been acknowledged, may not be a recordable document. Placing such a deed on record will not provide record notice in regard to it.

THE BUFFALO ACADEMY OF THE SACRED HEART v. BOEHM BROS., INC.

COURT OF APPEALS OF NEW YORK, 1935.
267 N.Y. 242, 196 N.E. 42

NATURE OF CASE: Submission of a controversy pursuant to civil practice act.

FACT SUMMARY: Buffalo Academy of the Sacred Heart (P) agreed to convey certain land to Boehm Bros., Inc. (D) to satisfy a debt. Boehm Bros., Inc. (D) refused to accept on the ground that the title was unmarketable because of building restrictions of the subdivision where the lots were situated.

CONCISE RULE OF LAW: A purchaser of a lot which formed part of a larger tract is not charged with notice of restrictive covenants contained in a prior deed from the same grantor to any other lot or parcel of the same general tract, even though the deed is recorded and by its terms applies to all other lots.

FACTS: Buffalo Academy of the Sacred Heart (P) agreed to discharge a debt to Boehm Bros., Inc. (D) by conveying to Boehm Bros., Inc. (D) good and marketable title to certain realty. Buffalo (P) agreed that if the title proved unmarketable, it would pay Boehm Bros., Inc. (D) $60,000 in cash. Buffalo (P) executed a deed to the property. Boehm Bros., Inc. (D) refused to accept on the ground that the title is unmarketable. Boehm Bros., Inc. (D) contends that the title is unmarketable because the subdivision in which the property is located is subject to a uniform building plan which restricts use of it to residential purposes. Boehm Bros., Inc. (D) contends it is also unmarketable because of Buffalo's (P) convenants in a deed to Kendal. In the deed Buffalo (P) agreed to not sell gasoline or erect filling stations on the remaining lots.

ISSUE: Is there a uniform building plan which restricts the use of the property so as to render the title unmarketable?

Does a covenant to a grantee by a grantor of subdivision lots that he will not sell gasoline or erect filling stations on the remaining lots render title to the remaining lots unmarketable?

HOLDING AND DECISION: No. The court decided that there was no uniform building plan restricting use of the property to residential purposes. It based its decision on the following: No restriction plan was indicated in the maps filed; none of the deeds contained covenants by Buffalo (P) that the remainder of the tract would be subject to restriction; and Buffalo (P) made restrictions only when he thought them necessary, but did not follow a fixed plan of restricting use of the lots.

No. The court decided that Buffalo's (P) covenant not to build filling stations on the remaining lots did not render the title unmarketable. In reaching its decision the court first looked to the deed which contained the covenant. The deed did not expressly make Buffalo's (P) covenant run with the land. Buffalo (P) did not agree that his grantees would not sell gasoline or erect filling stations on the remaining lots. Applying the rules that restrictive covenants must always be

NOTES: (Continued on Next Page)

construed strictly against those seeking to enforce them and that a land owner is only bound by restrictions appearing in his deed, the title is marketable, since no restrictions are mentioned in Boehm Bros., Inc.'s (D) deed. Lastly, a purchaser of a lot which forms part of a larger tract is not charged with notice of restrictive covenants contained in a prior deed from the same grantor to any other lot of the same tract, even though the deed is recorded and by its terms applies to all other lots. In the absence of exceptional circumstances, a purchaser takes notice from the record only of encumbrances in his direct chain of title.

EDITOR'S ANALYSIS: Some states have followed the opposing rule that the recording of a deed containing restriction covenants by a common grantor gives notice of the restrictions to all subsequent grantees. This case demonstrates recording problems that arise in relation to subdivisions which involve multiple transfers out of a common grantor with various covenants in the deeds that are designed to restrict not only the land conveyed, but also the land retained by the common grantor.

NOTES:

GUILLETTE v. DALY DRY WALL, INC.

SUP.S.CT.OF MASS.,1975. 325 N.E.2d 572

NATURE OF CASE: Appeal from issuance of injunction.

FACT SUMMARY: Guillette (P) and Daly (D) each purchased land from a common grantor, but the deed to Daly (D), the later purchaser, did not contain restrictions found in Guillette's (P) deed which limited construction in the subdivision to single-family dwellings.

CONCISE RULE OF LAW: A purchaser of land is bound by a restriction contained in deeds to his neighbors from a common grantor, even when he takes without knowledge of the restrictions and under a deed which did not mention them.

FACTS: Gilmore, the grantor, sold lots in the Cedar Hills subdivision to various people. Two plans, one dated in 1967 and the other in 1968, restricted the use of the land to single-family dwellings. All deeds, other than the one to Daly (D), either set out the restrictions or incorporated them by reference. Only the Guillette (P) deed and one other contained a provision restricting lots retained by the seller, Gilmore. Daly (D) purchased its lots in 1972, and made no inquiry concerning restrictions or a development plan. Daly (D) obtained a permit to build 36 apartment-type units. Guillette (P) sought to enjoin Daly (D) from violating the restrictions. An injunction issued. Daly (D) appealed arguing that it could not be bound when it took without knowledge of the restrictions and under a deed which did not mention them.

ISSUE: Is a purchaser of land bound by a restriction contained in deeds to his neighbors from a common grantor even when he takes without knowledge of the restrictions and under a deed which did not mention them?

HOLDING AND DECISION: Yes. A purchaser of land is bound by a restriction contained in deeds to his neighbors from a common grantor, even when he takes without knowledge of the restrictions and under a deed which did not mention them. Where, as here, the grantor binds his remaining land by writing, reciprocity of restriction between the grantor and grantee can be enforced. "In such cases a subsequent purchaser from the common grantor acquires title subject to the restrictions in the deed to the earlier purchaser." Each grantee who is within the scope of the common scheme is an intended beneficiary of the restrictions and may enforce them against the others. Here, the deed from Gilmore to Guillette (P) conveyed not only a lot but an interest in the remaining land then owned by Gilmore. The deed was properly recorded, and Daly (D) took with notice. Affirmed.

EDITOR'S ANALYSIS: As Massachusetts has a grantor-grantee index, it would not have been a difficult task for Daly (D) when searching title to examine the other grants made by Gilmore. Generally, when a common grantor has not bound his remaining land by writing, the statute of frauds prevents enforcement of restrictions against the grantor or a subsequent purchaser of a lot not expressly restricted. While this case appears to bring attention to record notice, it actually illustrates a reciprocal negative servitude imposed by the common grantor upon the subdivision.

SANBORN v. McLEAN

SUP. COURT OF MICHIGAN, 1925.
233 Mich. 227, 206 N.W. 496

NATURE OF CASE: Action to enjoin erection of gasoline filling station.

FACT SUMMARY: Sanborn (P) and McClean (D) trace the titles to their adjoining lots to the proprietor of the subdivision. Residences are built on all the surrounding lots. Sanborn (P) objected to McClean's (D) erection of a gas station on her lot.

CONCISE RULE OF LAW: If the owner of two or more lots, which are situated so as to bear a relation to each other, sells one with restrictions which are of benefit to the land retained, during the period of restraint, the owner of the lot or lots retained can do nothing forbidden to the owner of the lot sold. This is the doctrine of reciprocal negative easements.

FACTS: On December 28, 1892, McLaughlin, who was then owner of the lots on Collingwood Avenue, deeded four of the lots with the restriction that only residences would be built on the lots. On July 24, 1893, McLaughlin conveyed several more lots with the same restriction. Sanborn (P) traces title to McLaughlin. McClean's (D) title runs back to a deed dated September 7, 1893, which does not contain the restrictions. No buildings other than residences have been erected on any of the lots of the subdivision.

ISSUE: If the owner of two or more lots, which are situated so as to bear a relation to each other, sells one with restrictions which are of benefit to the land retained, during the period of restraint, can the owner of the lot or lots retained do anything forbidden to the owner of the lot sold?

Is a reciprocal negative easement personal to owners?

HOLDING AND DECISION: No. The doctrine of reciprocal negative easements makes restrictions which are of benefit to the land retained mutual so that the owner can do nothing upon the land he has retained that is forbidden to the owner of the lot sold. In this case McLaughlin deeded lots with the restriction that only residences be built on them. Such restrictions were imposed for the benefit of the lands retained by McLaughlin to carry out the scheme of a residential district, and a restrictive negative easement attached to the lots retained. Since his was one of the lots retained in the December 1892 and July 1893 deeds, a reciprocal negative easement attached to the lot which later became McClean's (D).

No. Reciprocal negative easements are not personal to owners but are operative upon use of the land by any owner having actual or constructive notice thereof. In this case the reciprocal negative easement attached to McClean's (D) lot may now be enforced by Sanborn (P) provided McClean (D) had constructive knowledge of the easement at the time of purchase. At the time of purchase McClean (D) had an abstract of title showing the subdivision and that his lot had 97 companion lots. He could not avoid noticing the strictly uniform residence character of the companion lots, and the least inquiry would have revealed the fact that his lot was subject to a reciprocal negative easement. The injunction is granted.

EDITOR'S ANALYSIS: Reciprocal negative easements must start with common owners. They cannot arise and fasten upon one lot by reason of other lot owners conforming to a general plan. Such easements are never retroactive, and as demonstrated here, they pass their benefits and carry their obligations to all purchasers of land provided the purchaser has constructive notice of the easement.

NOTES:

GALLEY v. WARD

SUP. COURT OF NEW HAMPSHIRE, 1880. 60 N.H. 331

NATURE OF CASE: Bill in equity to set aside the levy of an execution.

FACT SUMMARY: Jane Smith sold certain land to Galley (P). By mistake the deed was recorded under her husband's name. Ward (D) assigned a claim he had against Jane Smith to Morris (D) who brought suit against her.

CONCISE RULE OF LAW: Where a third party is in the open, visible and notorious occupation of land, a purchaser or creditor is chargeable with notice of facts he would have learned regarding the party's title, had he made reasonable inquiry, even though he was ignorant of the party's occupation of the land.

FACTS: In 1871, Jane Smith sold Galley (P) certain land. She intended and believed that she conveyed it in fee simple to him. But, by mistake, the deed was executed by her husband, and she merely released power and homestead. It was indexed, "Smith Robert to Galley William" (P) and was recorded in November 1875. In September 1878, Jane and Robert executed and delivered to Galley (P) a deed for the purpose of ratifying and confirming Galley's (P) title. Galley (P) took possession upon receiving the first deed and has remained in open, visible, exclusive and notorious possession of it ever since. In 1876, Ward (D) assigned a claim against Jane Smith to Morris (D). Morris (D) inquired as to whether Jane Smith had conveyed the lot and was informed that she hadn't. He brought suit on the claim and obtained an execution which was levied on the property.

ISSUE: Can an attached creditor be charged with constructive notice of the title of a third party who is in possession of land under an unrecorded deed, even where the creditor was not aware of the third party's possession?

HOLDING AND DECISION: Yes. A purchaser of land, knowing that a third person is in the open, visible and notorious occupation of it, is chargeable with notice of such facts in reference to the latter's title as he would have learned upon reasonable inquiry. In this case, the nature of Galley's (P) possession was sufficient to put a purchaser knowing of his possession on inquiry. And when there is such a possession as would charge a purchaser who knew of that possession with knowledge of an adverse title, a purchaser ignorant of that possession without excuse is equally chargeable. "If a purchaser neglects to make inquiry as to the possession, he is not entitled to any greater consideration than if he had made it and ascertained the actual facts of the case." There is no reason to distinguish between a purchaser and a creditor. In this case, Morris (D) had no knowledge of Galley's (P) possession, but he was free to examine the apparent condition of the premises. He must be charged with what he would have learned upon reasonable inquiry as to Galley's (P) right of possession. Had he inquired he would have learned of Galley's (P) equitable title.

EDITOR'S ANALYSIS: The court states that when a grantee records his deed, a subsequent purchaser is chargeable with constructive notice of its contents whether he has ever seen the deed or has any knowledge of its existence. Likewise, an open, notorious, exclusive, and visible possession charges a purchaser or creditor with knowledge of an adverse title whether he is aware of the possession or not. The doctrine in both situations is based on fraud or culpable negligence. Just as a purchaser's failure to examine the record constitutes negligence, so would his wilful ignorance of such facts of notorious possession by a third party as would put a purchaser cognizant of these facts on his guard against some unrecorded deed or equitable claim, constitute negligence.

NOTES:

TOUPIN v. PEABODY
SUP. JUDICIAL COURT OF MASSACHUSETTS, 1895.
162 Mass. 473, 39 N.E. 280

NATURE OF CASE: Bill in equity for specific performance.

FACT SUMMARY: Toupin (P) had an unrecorded five-year lease containing an option to renew it. Toupin's (P) landlord conveyed the land to Peabody (D), informing him that the tenants did not have written leases.

CONCISE RULE OF LAW: Where a statute makes unrecorded leases for more than seven years invalid against persons other than the lessor and his heirs and others having actual notice of it, any agreement for renewal which will give the lessee possession, for more than seven years falls within the statute, and, if unrecorded, is invalid against a purchaser.

FACTS: Driscoll, being the owner of certain land, executed and delivered to Toupin (P) a lease for five years with the right to renew it for five more years. The date of the lease was September 1888, and it was not recorded. In December 1891, Driscoll conveyed the property to Peabody (D). Peabody (D) knew that Toupin (P) occupied the property as a tenant, but Driscoll informed him that none of the tenants had written leases. Toupin (P) did not inform Peabody (D) of the lease, and Peabody (D) did not inquire as to the terms of Toupin's (P) tenancy. Peabody (D) did cause a search of title to be made, and the title was pronounced to be good. Toupin (P) seeks to renew the lease, according to its terms. Peabody (D) refuses to renew it.

ISSUE: Does a lease for five years with the right to renew it for five more years fall within a statute which makes unrecorded leases for more than seven years invalid against persons other than the lessor and his heirs and others having actual notice of it?

HOLDING AND DECISION: Yes. The purpose of the statute is to enable a purchaser of land to rely upon the information furnished by the registry of deeds, if he has no actual notice of some different facts concerning the property's title. The intention of the statute is that a bona fide purchaser, without actual notice, may rely with certainty upon the fact that no instrument which does not appear on the record can give a tenant the right to any term longer than seven years. A lease, such as the one in this case, for five years with the right to have a renewal for five more is as much within the mischief which the statute seeks to remedy as a lease for ten years. The reason for requiring the ten-year lease to be recorded apply equally to the five-year lease with the renewal term. Hence, Toupin's (P) lease is not valid against Peabody (D), since it was not recorded and since Peabody (D) had no actual notice of it.

EDITOR'S ANALYSIS: The court also had to decide that Peabody (D) had no actual notice of Toupin's (P) lease. Peabody (D) was aware that Toupin (P) was a tenant, but he was informed that there was no written lease. The lease was unrecorded, so was not revealed by the title search. Hence, Peabody (D) had no actual notice.

NOTES:

BRINKMAN v. JONES
SUP. COURT OF WISCONSIN, 1878. 44 Wis. 498

NATURE OF CASE: Action of ejectment to recover possession of certain property.

FACT SUMMARY: Jones conveyed property to Shove. In an unrecorded contract, Shove agreed to reconvey the property to Jones for a certain sum. Shove conveyed the property to Brinkman (P). Jones conveyed the property to his son, Jones (D).

CONCISE RULE OF LAW: Where a purchaser had knowledge of facts which would put a prudent person upon inquiry and which, if prosecuted with ordinary diligence, would lead to actual notice of a title conflict, it is his duty to make inquiry and he will be guilty of bad faith if he neglects to do so, and will be charged with the actual notice he would have received from inquiry.

FACTS: In August 1870, Jones conveyed his property to Shove. On the same day Shove delivered to Jones a contract in which he agreed to reconvey the land to Jones or his heirs if a certain sum was paid within a certain time. The court held that the deed and contract together created a mortgagor-mortgagee relationship between Jones and Shove. The deed was recorded, but the contract was not. In 1876, Shove conveyed the property to Brinkman (P). Jones occupied the land continuously from 1857 to 1877. In 1877, he conveyed the land by quitclaim deed to his son, Jones (D).

ISSUE: Where a purchaser has notice of facts which would put a prudent person upon inquiry and which if prosecuted with ordinary diligence would lead to actual notice of a title conflict, will he be charged with actual notice?

HOLDING AND DECISION: Yes. Notice must be held to be actual when the subsequent purchaser has actual knowledge of such facts as would put a person upon inquiry, and which, if prosecuted with ordinary diligence, would lead to actual notice of a conflict in title. Where the purchaser has notice of such facts, it is his duty to make inquiry, and he is guilty of bad faith if he neglects to do so. Consequently, he will be charged with the actual notice he would have received from inquiry. In this case, Jones had occupied the land for years prior to the 1870 deed and continued to do so after the deed. Further, the farm continued to be known as the Jones farm and Brinkman (P) spoke to Jones (D) about purchasing it. For the purposes of this appeal it must be held that he was then informed of Jones' (D) claim to an interest in the land. It was clearly a question for the jury whether Brinkman (P) had notice that Jones (D) claimed an interest in the land and whether a person of ordinary prudence, with that knowledge could then, in good faith, purchase the land from Shove upon Shove's mere declaration that he owned the land. Judgment for Brinkman (P) is reversed and a new trial is granted.

(Continued on Next Page)

TOLAND v. COREY

SUP. COURT OF THE TERRITORY OF UTAH, 1890.
6 Utah 392, 24 P. 190

EDITOR'S ANALYSIS: Generally, except as varied by statute, actual possession of land is such notice to all of the world. the presumption is that inquiry of the possessor will disclose how and under what right he holds possession. In the absence of such inquiry, the presumption is that had such inquiry been made, the right, title or interest under which the possessor held would have been discovered. In this case, the court also decided that a grantor's possession is presumed adverse to his grantee where it has continued for a long time after the grant, and is inconsistent on its nature with the grantee's rights by the terms of the deed.

NOTES:

NATURE OF CASE: Action to have a deed cancelled.

FACT SUMMARY: Corey (P), a tenant for life, purchased the remainder, but did not record the deed. She was in continuous possession of the property. Her son, the previous owner of the remainder, gave two mortgages on the premises after she had purchased the remainder.

CONCISE RULE OF LAW: Actual possession is actual notice of title, and all persons with notice of such possession are put upon inquiry, even though such possession may be consistent with record title.

FACTS: Corey (P) owned a life estate in certain property, and her son owned the remainder. He conveyed his interest to Toland (D), who conveyed it to Corey (P). These deeds were not recorded at the time Corey's (P) son gave two mortgages on the premises to Doon. Before Corey's (P) son had conveyed his remainder he and Corey (P) had given Doon a previous mortgage. Doon brought suit to foreclose on the mortgages. Corey (P) knew nothing about the second two mortgages which her son conveyed after she owned the remainder. Before judgment, Corey (P), to pay off the mortgages and for no additional consideration, made the deed which this action seeks to have set aside.

ISSUE: Is actual possession actual notice of title which puts all person with notice of such possession upon inquiry where such possession is consistent with record title?

HOLDING AND DECISION: Yes. Actual occupancy is enough to put parties dealing with premises upon notice. In this case, Doon contends that Corey's (P) possession was consistent with the title shown by the record, and so he, as mortgagee, was under no obligation to look beyond the record, but could consider Corey's (P) possession as her life estate only. The court feels that the better rule is that all persons with notice of an occupant's possession must take notice of his full title in the premises even though the possession may be consistent with record title. It is easy to find out the real situation by inquiry of the occupant, and it is the purchaser or mortgagee's duty to so inquire. Hence, in this case the two latter mortgages given by Corey's (P) son after he had conveyed the remainder were not valid liens upon the property.

EDITOR'S ANALYSIS: Possession is notice not only of whatever title the occupant has but also of whatever right he may have in the property. As this case demonstrates, the knowledge chargeable to a person after he is put on inquiry by possession is not limited to such knowledge as would be gained by examining the public records. In order to constitute notice, possession must be actual, open, visible, exclusive and unequivocal or unambiguous.

STRONG v. WHYBARK

SUP. COURT OF MISSOURI, 1907.
204 Mo. 341, 102 S.W. 968

NATURE OF CASE: Bill in equity to have title quieted in certain property.

FACT SUMMARY: Both Strong (P) and Boyden (D) claim an interest in certain property. Strong's (P) title is derived through the vendee of a recorded deed who paid five dollars for the property. Boyden's (D) title is derived through the vendee of a prior unrecorded deed who paid $640.

CONCISE RULE OF LAW: A quitclaim deed made in consideration of five dollars paid by the grantee to the grantor was based on a valuable consideration sufficient to entitle the grantee to the rights of a bona fide purchaser for value.

FACTS: S. Hayden by warranty deed and for a consideration of $640 conveyed certain land to Moore on March 6, 1861. On August 26, 1863, S. Hayden conveyed the same land by quitclaim deed for a recited consideration of "natural love and affection and five dollars" to J. Hayden. That deed was recorded in 1868. The Moore deed was recorded in 1874. Strong's (P) title is derived through conveyances by J. Hayden. Boyden's (D) title is derived through conveyances by Moore.

ISSUE: Is a quitclaim deed made in consideration of five dollars based on a valuable consideration sufficient to entitle the grantee to the rights of a bona fide purchaser?

HOLDING AND DECISION: Yes. A valuable consideration is defined as money or something that is worth money. It is not necessary that the consideration should be adequate in point of value. Five dollars or any other sum in excess of one cent, or dime, or dollar, which are the technical words used to express nominal considerations, is a valuable consideration within the meaning of the law of conveyancing. The courts upon principles of equity and justice have repeatedly held that if the subsequent purchaser either had notice of the unrecorded deed, or was a purchaser without having paid a good and valuable consideration for the land, then he would take nothing by his purchase. In this case there is no evidence that J. Hayden knew of the prior unrecorded deed to Moore. Since she paid a valuable consideration, she is entitled to the right of bona fide purchaser. Judgment for Boyden (D) is reversed and a new trial is granted.

EDITOR'S ANALYSIS: Without the consideration question in this case, there would have been no question as to J. Hayden's title since her deed had been recorded and Moore's had not, and there was no evidence that she had knowledge of the prior deed. Technically speaking, a purchaser is one who acquires real property in any other manner than by descent. "Purchase" has been said to mean to obtain property by paying an equivalent in money; the acquisition of property by one's own act or agreement as distinguished from the act or mere operation of law; the transmission of property from one person to another by their voluntary agreement (valuable consideration).

NOTES:

McDONALD & CO. v. JOHNS

SUP. COURT OF WASHINGTON, 1911.
62 Wash. 521, 114 P. 175

NATURE OF CASE: Action to foreclose a mortgage.

FACT SUMMARY: On May 4, 1908, Johns (D) gave Bechtol a mortgage to secure the payment of a pre-existing debt. On May 5, 1908, he gave McDonald & Co. (P) a mortgage on the same land also as security for a pre-existing debt. The second mortgage was recorded first.

CONCISE RULE OF LAW: The conveyance of land as security for a pre-existing debt, without any new consideration being given, will not operate as a purchase of value, or render the transferee a bona fide purchaser, or defeat any existing equities.

FACTS: Prior to May 4, 1908, Johns (D) was indebted to Bechtol. On that date he executed and delivered to Bechtol a mortgage. He was also indebted to McDonald & Co. (P), and on May 5, 1908, he executed and delivered a mortgage on the same land to McDonald & Co. (P). Both mortgages were given to secure the payment of the pre-existing debts, and no new or additional consideration or extension of time of payment was given as inducement to the making of either mortgage. The McDonald & Co. (P) mortgage was recorded first.

ISSUE: Is a creditor who takes a mortgage as security for the payment of a pre-existing debt, without giving any new consideration, a bona fide purchaser?

HOLDING AND DECISION: No. The conveyance of land as security for a pre-existing debt, without any new consideration being given, does not operate as a purchase of value or render the transferee a bona fide purchaser. Nor will such a conveyance defeat any prior liens or equities. The basis for this rule is that in such a conveyance the creditor parts with no value, surrenders no right, and does not worsen his legal position. Because such a conveyance involves no parting with money or an actual change in the creditor's legal position, it is not for valuable consideration, and does not make the creditor a bona fide purchaser. Hence, he is not given the protections the recording acts accord to bona fide purchasers. In this case the fact that the McDonald's (P) mortgage was recorded first does not cause it to defeat the unrecorded Bechtol mortgage, since that mortgage was executed and delivered first. The equitable mortgage, the mortgage first given, will prevail over the subsequent mortgage recorded prior to it.

EDITOR'S ANALYSIS: This case demonstrates the rule that in order to entitle a mortgagee to the protection accorded to a bona fide purchaser, his mortgage must be supported by a valid consideration. It also demonstrates the general rule that a creditor who takes a mortgage on realty merely as security for the payment of a pre-existing debt, without giving any new consideration, is not entitled to the protection accorded to a bona fide purchaser, as against prior liens or equities. In the absence of special equities growing out of notice, good or bad faith, or want of consideration, the mortgage first recorded will take priority over other mortgages on the same property.

ELIASON v. WILBORN
SUPREME COURT OF THE UNITED STATES.
281 U.S. 457, 50 S. Ct. 382

NATURE OF CASE: Action to compel county registrar to cancel deeds and certificates of title and to issure certificates.

FACT SUMMARY: The Eliasons (P), who had entrusted their certificate of title to Napletone, unsuccessfully sought the county registrar to cancel deeds and certificates issued to the Wilborns (D).

CONCISE RULE OF LAW: One acquiring title to registered land and knowing that transfer of ownership depends upon the provisions of the Torrens Act (which require the production of the outstanding certificate before a new certificate is issued), assumes any risk involved in the issuance of a new certificate if he entrusts his certificate to another.

FACTS: The Eliasons (P), who held a registered certificate of title under the State Torrens Act entrusted keeping of the certificate to Napletone with whom he was negotiating. Napletone, together with a forged conveyance in his own name, turned the certificate into the county registrar. In return, Napletone received a title certificate with himself as the registered owner on its face. Napletone conveyed to the Wilborns (D) who paid in value and were unknowing of Napletone's maneuvers. Before the certificate could be issued to the Wilborns (D), the Wilborns (D) learned of the Eliasons' (P) claim. The Eliasons (P) notified the registrar of the forgery which had occurred, but the registrar refused to cancel the deeds and certificates issued to Napletone and the Wilborns.

ISSUE: Is one who acquires title to registered land, knowing that transfer of ownership depends upon the Torrens Act, proceeding at his own risk if he entrusts his certificate to another?

HOLDING AND DECISION: Yes. The Eliasons (P) bought and got what they paid for, and assumed the risk of losing their title without having parted with it and without being heard. There is also the same kind of risk involved in enclosing blank checks, entrusting goods to a bailee under some conditions, or conveying one's property by a deed not yet recorded and executing a second deed to another person who takes and records the later deed without notice of the former. As between two innocent persons one of whom must suffer the consequences of a breach of trust the one who made it possible by his act of confidence must bear the loss.

EDITOR'S ANALYSIS: Entirely distinct from the recording system, the "Torrens title system" exists in some fifteen states (but not in California where it was repealed in 1955). The procedure involved here is as follows: (1) in a proceeding in rem, the court appoints a title searcher to investigate the records; (2) all interested parties are afforded notice; (3) the court gives its approval to the searcher's report; (4) a certificate of title is issued good against almost the whole world; (5) the county recorder of titles keeps one duplicate, the other goes to the owner.

NOTES:

ABRAHAMSON v. SUNDMAN

SUPREME COURT OF MINNESOTA, 1928.
174 Minn. 22, 218 N.W. 246

NATURE OF CASE: Appeal from judgment decreeing ownership of real property.

FACTUAL SUMMARY: Tuxedo Park Company conveyed registered title to Johnson, who in turn conveyed to Abrahamson (P), but neither deed was ever filed with registrar, so that Glass-Melane Lumber Company who foreclosed a lien against Johnson, had a new title certificate issued in its own name.

CONCISE RULE OF LAW: Under the Torrens Title Land System an owner of property, who takes possession after title is registered, receives no protection from subsequent registrants if his claim does not appear on the certificate of title.

FACTS: Tuxedo Park Company conveyed a lot by deed to Johnson who built a house and then conveyed to Abrahamson (P). Neither deed was filed with the registrar, and no indication of Abrahamson's (P) possession was ever noted on the registration certificate. Meanwhile, Glass-Melane Lumber Company foreclosed a lien against Johnson for lumber provided. The lot was sold, there was no redemption, and a new certificate of title was issued to Glass-Melane who then conveyed to Sundman (D). Sundman (D) had a new certificate issued in his name. Abrahamson was not made a party to the lien foreclosure and had no notice of the proceedings, and so had no chance to redeem the sale of the house they possessed. Abrahamson (P) sought a new certificate of title in his name, and cancellation of title to Sundman (D).

ISSUE: Does Abrahamson (P) have a superior claim of title over Sundman (D)?

HOLDING AND DECISION: No. All proceedings under the Torrens Act were flawless. Title is created by the decree and certificate of registration only. The Act indicates that Abrahamson (P) was entitled to no more than a three-year leasehold interest because of his possession. Although the state statute did not directly deal with those instances where possession is taken after certificate of title is registered, knowledge of an unregistered claim cannot be considered fraud, if conveyance is made to an innocent purchasor who paid value for the property. Follette v. Pacific L & P Corp., supra, can be distinguished since it related to occupants who, at the time the original registration was decreed, were not made parties thereto. Here, Abrahamson (P) came into possession after the original registration was made.

EDITOR'S ANALYSIS: In those jurisdictions which permit title registration, the prohibitive cost of the registration proceeding has deterred many title holders from voluntarily complying. However, where there exists a defect in the title, where the owner seeks to thrwart adverse possession of his property, or where a subdivider can pass the cost of the proceedings on to purchasers by registering the entire tract so as to save each buyer the expense of an individual title search, the Torrens Land Title System appears to be a sought-after convenience.

NOTES:

KILLAM v. MARCH

SUP. JUD. COURT OF MASSACHUSETTS, 1944.
316 Mass. 646, 55 N.E. 2d 945

NATURE OF CASE: Bill in equity brought to remove Cloud from title.

FACT SUMMARY: March (D) leased a garage and driveway from Killam's (P) predecessor in title for a 25-year period in 1938. The lease was recorded but not registered. In 1941, Killam (P) bought the property and acquired a certificate of title which did not mention the lease. March (D) had been using the garage and driveway since Killam (P) acquired their title.

CONCISE RULE OF LAW: A purchaser of registered land who has actual notice of an unregistered lease for more than seven years takes subject to the lease.

FACTS: In 1941, Killam (P) purchased a parcel of registered land and became holder of a certificate of title. The certificate noted that the land was subject to a mortgage and to sewer assessments. On Killam's (P) land there is a driveway leading to a garage, which March (D) has been using since Killam's (P) acquired title. March (D) claims the right to use these premises by virtue of a deed dated 1938, given to them by Killam's (P) predecessor in title for a 25-year term. The lease was recorded but not registered. The lower court found that Killam (P) had actual notice of the lease prior to their purchasing the property.

ISSUE: Does one purchasing registered land take subject to an unregistered lease if he has actual notice of it?

HOLDING AND DECISION: Yes. General Laws C. 185 provide a system for the registration of land titles and contains provisions relative to transfers of land. Section 46 of the act states that subsequent purchasers of registered land taking a certificate of title for value and in good faith shall hold the land free from all encumbrances except those noted in the certificate. Section 51 states that no deed, mortgage or other voluntary instrument, except a will and a lease for a term not exceeding seven years shall be an effective conveyance unless it is registered. Section 57 does not mention good faith. Section 71 requires that leases for more than seven years be registered. This seems to point to the conclusion that no one can claim a leasehold interest for more than seven years in registered land where the lease has not been registered. However, in construing C. 185, well-settled principles of statutory construction must be kept in mind. Various sections of a statute must, if reasonably possible, be interpreted so as to be harmonious and not contradictory, and the legislative intention must be ascertained in light of the common law and previous statutes. The recording acts prior to C. 185 reveal that a purchaser acquiring title with actual notice of a prior deed takes subject to it. The basis of this rule is that a party with such notice could not take a deed without fraud. The same provision as to leases is found in the early statutes and has been retained in General Law C. 183. The court decides that C. 185 construed against this background does not give certificate holders an indefeasible title as against interests of which they had actual notice. Any other construction would ignore the provision of Section 46 that one acquires registered land free from unregistered encumbrances if he is a purchaser in good faith. In this case, since it was found that Killam (P) did have actual notice of March's (D) unregistered lease for 25 years, Killam took subject to March's (D) lease.

EDITOR'S ANALYSIS: A transfer of registered land to a bona fide purchaser conveys an indefeasible title, but the acts protect only the bona fide purchaser. A transferee who takes with knowledge that his transferor acquired title by fraud or a purchaser who buys registered land with notice of the fact that it is in litigation is not a purchaser in good faith. Likewise, as demonstrated here, a purchaser of registered land takes subject to an unregistered lease which he had actual notice of. However, the rights of a subsequent purchaser or lessee whose lease is duly registered and who does not know of a prior unregistered lease will prevail over the former lessee's.

NOTES:

STATE STREET BANK & TRUST CO. v. BEALE
SUP. JUD. COURT OF MASSACHUSETTS, 1967.
Mass. 227 N.E. 2d 924

NATURE OF CASE: Bill in equity to impose a constructive trust on certain property.

FACT SUMMARY: State Street Bank & Trust Co. (P) alleges that Beale (D) fraudulently caused certain property belonging to State (P) to be registered in his name.

CONCISE RULE OF LAW: "Petition for Review," as used in a statute covering review of land registration proceedings, does not include proceedings to impose a constructive trust so that such proceedings need not be brought within the time the statute requires that petitions for review be filed.

FACTS: State Street Bank & Trust Co. (P) was the owner of a parcel of land. Beale (D), knowing of their ownership, petitioned for a degree of registration fraudulently representing that he did not know any other person having an interest in the property. Hence, State (P) did not receive notice afforded parties to registration proceedings. Beale (D) also filed two false affidavits in support of his claim. He made one of the affidavits either with intent to defraud the court or with such willful disregard of the facts as to be tantamount to fraud. He also knew of the falsity of the second affidavit. In reliance on these affidavits the land court entered a decree registering the parcel in his name on October 31, 1960. State (P) brought this action on March 20, 1962. Beale (D) demurred on the basis of General Laws C. 185, Section 45. Section 45 provides that any person deprived of land by a decree of registration obtained by fraud may file a petition for review within one year of the entry of the decree.

ISSUE: Does "Petition for Review" as used in the statute covering review of land registration proceedings include proceedings to impose a constructive trust?

HOLDING AND DECISION: No. It is well settled that a traditional remedy for a person who has been deprived of land by fraud is restitution, and the duty to make such restitution is often enforced by imposing a constructive trust. Three sections of C. 185 preserve the remedies of a person deprived of land by fraud. One of the sections specifically mentions constructive trusts. In this case, State's (P) bill does not challenge the registration decree or ask that the decree be declared void. Rather, State (P) acknowledges that legal title is now vested in Beale (D) and claims title by constructive trust. If "Petition for Review" as used in Section 45 is interpreted so broadly as to include a bill for the imposition of a constructive trust, the above-mentioned provisions which appear to preserve the remedy would be severely weakened. The purpose of General Law C. 185 is to provide a means by which title to land may be readily and reliably ascertained. It is not to reduce the availability of the traditional remedy of restitution. Hence, the court holds that "Petition of Review," as used in Section 45, does not include a proceeding to impose a constructive trust. Judgment for Beale (D) is reversed.

EDITOR'S ANALYSIS: Subject to general rules, in order to maintain an action for damages for the wrongful deprivation of land, a plaintiff must establish that he is wrongfully deprived of his land by its registration in the name of another, either by actual or constructive fraud, that there was no negligence on the part of the plaintiff, that he is not precluded in any way from bringing an action for the recovery of the land, and that the action itself is not barred by limitations. The plaintiff can recover not only the value of the land, but also the value of buildings and other improvements on the land. The plaintiff may successfully maintain an action against the person in whose name the land has been fraudulently or wrongfully registered, notwithstanding the absence of actual fraud in obtaining the decree, and notwithstanding a petition for review on the ground of fraud has been denied.

NOTES:

BOTHIN v. THE CALIFORNIA TITLE INSURANCE AND TRUST CO.

SUPR. CT. OF CALIF., 1908. 153 Calif. 718, 96 P. 500

NATURE OF CASE: Action to recover damages for breach of a covenant in a title insurance policy.

FACT SUMMARY: Bothin (P) discovered that certain of his property, which was insured against title defects by California Title (D), was adversely possessed by Partridge, and that there was a recorded deed of trust by which Partridge had conveyed such property.

CONCISE RULE OF LAW: If a title insurance policy excepts: (1) the tenure of present occupants, and (2) incumbrances not shown by public record, such policy guarantees the record title; but, neither the occupancy of such property by adverse possession nor the recorded deed of trust by such adverse possessor constitutes a defect insured against.

FACTS: California Title (D) issued to Bothin (P) a policy guaranteeing his title to lots 71 and 72 in San Francisco. The terms of the policy excepted from coverage any defects in title due to "1. Tenure of the present occupants...; 4. Instruments, liens, encumbrances... not shown by any public record..." After purchasing the property, Bothin (P) discovered (1) that Partridge adversely possessed 14 feet of lot 71; and (2) that there was on record in the San Francisco recorder's office a prior deed of trust by which Partridge had conveyed that property to the trustees of a San Francisco bank. Partridge brought an action against Bothin (P) to quiet title to the disputed property and judgment was for Partridge. Bothin (P) then sued California Title (D) for damages sustained in defending his title and for depreciation of his property due to the defect in title. Bothin (P) appealed from a judgment in favor of California Title (D) and from an order denying his motion for a new trial. Although it is conceded that Bothin (P) had record title to lot 71, Bothin (P) insists that there was a breach of covenant by reason of Partridge's recorded trust deed.

ISSUE: Did the adverse possession of part of Bothin's (P) property or the recorded deed of trust by such adverse possessor constitute a defect in title insured against?

HOLDING AND DECISION: No. The policy expressly denied insuring against tenure of the present occupant. Since it is admitted that the record title to the disputed property was in Bothin (P), Partridge's claim to the property was through his adverse possession, i.e., his tenure as a present occupant, a defect which was expressly not covered. Bothin (P) also argues that the policy excepted defects not shown by any public record and, therefore, implicitly insured against those defects shown by the public record, e.g., the recorded trust deed from Partridge. However, the policy guaranteed only the record title to be in Bothin (P). A trust deed is not a record title. A deed by one not connected by any conveyance with the record title to land does not create any defect in the record title of the record owner nor constitute a cloud on the record title. Bothin's (P) loss of part of his property did not arise out of any defect in title created by the trust-deed from Partridge but from Partridge's adverse possession. This defect was expressly not insured against. Judgment and order denying motion for a new trial were affirmed.

EDITOR'S ANALYSIS: It is common practice for title insurance policies to contain an exception to rights or claims of any parties in possession of the insured premises. The court in the instant case held in accordance with this practice by construing the words, "tenure of the present occupants" to include holding by adverse possession. In another case "tenancy of present occupants" was construed to mean occupation or temporary possession and did not include holding by adverse possession.

The court in this case stated that, "...the record title is all that a title company can safely or judiciously insure." However, the court did not say why safety dictates this limitation of coverage. It can be argued that a policy of insuring only record title is justified by the fact that many purchasers will inspect property before buying it and therefore discover an apparent defect, such as adverse possession. However, few purchasers are qualified to conduct a title search.

NOTES:

METROPOLITAN LIFE INS. CO. v.
UNION TRUST CO. OF ROCHESTER

CT. OF APPLS. OF NEW YORK, 1940. 283 N.Y. 33, 27 N.E. 2d 225

NATURE OF CASE: Action for breach of provisions in title insurance policies.

FACT SUMMARY: After street improvements to property were made by local government, but before assessments to pay for such improvements were levied, Union Trust Co. (D) issued to Metropolitan Life (P) title insurance policies insuring title to such property against liens or charges existing at the date policies were issued.

CONCISE RULE OF LAW: Assessments levied after the issuance of title insurance policies to pay for property improvements completed before issuance of such policies are not statutory liens and therefore are not a charge or incumbrance within the meaning of the policies as the terms lien, charge and incumbrance are synonymous in this context.

FACTS: Union Trust Co. (D) issued to Metropolitan Life (P) policies insuring against "defects in, incumbrances upon or liens or charges against the title of the mortgagors or grantors to premises described in the mortgage or trust deed existing at or prior to the date of policies." Prior to the issuance of the policies street improvements were made to Metropolitan Life's (P) premises and were to be paid for by assessments levied after the issuance of the policies. Metropolitan Life (P) contends that Union Trust Co. (D) did not state that future assessments when made would become prior liens and that it was Union Trust Co.'s (D) duty under the contract to do so. Metropolitan Life (P) further contends that these assessments were charges and incumbrances within the meaning of the terms as used in the policies and were therefore insured against. Metropolitan Life (P) appeals from judgments granting Union Trust Co.'s (D) motion to dismiss the complaint on the merits.

ISSUE: Are property assessments levied after issuance of a title insurance policy to pay for street improvements completed before issuance of the policy, charges or incumbrances which are insured against?

HOLDING AND DECISION: No. In this case a statute enabled local government to levy assessments to pay for the street improvements and this statute provided that such assessments would be prior liens. However, there could be no levy and no lien until an annual determination was made as to the amount of such assessments. Since there was no determination and assessment until after policies were issued, there was no lien at the time of issuance. Likewise, since the term charge is used synonymously with liens and incumbrances, there were no charges nor incumbrances within the meaning of the policy. Title insurance operates to protect a purchaser or a mortgagee against defects in or encumbrances upon a title existing at the date of such insurance. It is not prospective in its operation and has no relation to liens or requirements arising thereafter. Judgment was affirmed with costs.

EDITOR'S ANALYSIS: This case illustrates the extent to which coverage is a major issue in title insurance. An owner who insures his property may think that he has purchased total protection. A closer reading of the policy and the law will reveal that this is often not true. Policies must be carefully read as technicalities may constitute the realities of the protection purchased.

Title insurance, unlike most other forms of insurance, does not protect against future disasters. Fire insurance will protect the insured from any future fires. Title insurance will only protect against loss arising from defects, liens, or encumbrances which exist as of the date the policy is issued. In a case similar to the instant one, an assessment was levied and became a lien only two days after issuance of the title policy. However, the court held the insuror not liable for such assessment.

NOTES:

GLYN v. TITLE GUARANTEE & TRUST CO.

APPELLATE DIVISION OF THE SUPREME COURT OF
NEW YORK, 1909. 132 App. Div. 859, 117 N.Y.S. 424

NATURE OF CASE: Action for damages for breach of provisions of a title insurance policy and for negligence.

FACT SUMMARY: Title Guarantee (D) conducted a title search for Glyn (P) and then issued title insurance on Glyn's (P) property without advising Glyn (P) of the exact nature of existing encroachments.

CONCISE RULE OF LAW: A company which conducts a title search for a purchaser and then issues title insurance on purchaser's property is held to the standard of duty of an attorney as regards the title search and is held to have breached the provisions of the insurance policy if encroachments which subsequently interfered with purchaser's free use of property existed at the date of policy issuance.

FACTS: Glyn (P) retained Title Guarantee (D) to conduct a title search of No. 49 East 65th Street. Title Guarantee (D) did so and advised Glyn (P) that the survey showed variations between the locations of the fences, stoops, and record lines. However, Title Guarantee (D) did not specify the variations but stated that the variations would not affect the marketability of title and that there were no other defects in title. Relying upon Title Guarantee's (D) advice Glyn (P) purchased property and Title Guarnatee (D) issued a title insurance policy guaranteeing title but exempting the above-mentioned variations. Sometime later Glyn (P) discovered that the stoop, newel post, door cap, and pilaster of adjoining property encroached upon the premises. Glyn (P) claimed that the later discovered encroachments rendered her title unmarketable. Glyn (P) sued for damages resulting from Title Guarantee's (D) negligent title search and for breach of the policy of title insurance. Glyn (P) appealed from a judgment for Title Guarantee (D) in which complaint was dismissed at trial before any evidence was heard.

ISSUE: (1) Did Title Guarantee (D) breach the duty of care when it conducted the title search and (2) did the title insurance policy which Title Guarantee (D) issued insure against defects such as the encroachments which Glyn (P) discovered?

HOLDING AND DECISION: Yes. In its title search Title Guarantee (D) assumed the responsibility of an attorney or conveyancer to Glyn (P). Since Title Guarantee (D) is chargeable with knowledge of any encroachments patent upon inspection and since Title Guarantee (D) did not advise Glyn (P) of the exact character of such encroachments upon the property, Glyn's (P) complaint sufficiently alleges negligence and a failure of duty. The policy of title insurance issued by Title Guarantee (D) insured Glyn (P) against any incumbrances as of the date of the policy. The above-described encroachments constituted such an incumbrance as might interfere with free use of the property. Since Glyn (P) sufficiently alleged in her complaint negligence and breach of contract as an insurer, Glyn (P) was entitled to recover the difference between the value of property when purchased with the encroachments and its value had there been no encroachments. The judgment appealed from was reversed and a new trial granted.

EDITOR'S ANALYSIS: In this case, the court seems sympathetic with the plaintiff. It may be due to the different standards of duty which apply to agreements to conduct a title search and those which simply relate to the insurance contract. A title insurance company which undertakes to search a title for a prospective buyer assumes the responsibilities of an attorney as regards the title search. Therefore, the company may be held liable for any damages which result to the purchaser as a result of a negligent search. Although a title insurance company may be liable for a breach of a provision of an insurance policy, negligence has very little application to the insurance contract.

NOTES:

BEAULLIEU v. ATLANTA TITLE & TRUST CO.

CT. OF APP. OF GA., 1939. 60 Ga. App. 400, 4 S.E. 2d 78

NATURE OF CASE: Action for damages for breach of contract.

FACT SUMMARY: Beaullieu (P) purchased a title guaranty policy from Atlanta Title & Trust Co. (D) for certain land. After entering into possession, he discovered that Padgett had an easement in and over the property.

CONCISE RULE OF LAW: The measure of damages for a breach by an insurer under a policy insuring the title to certain property against encumbrances or encroachments is the difference between the value of the property when purchased with the encumbrance or encroachment upon it, and the value of the property as it would have been without the encumbrance or encroachment upon it.

FACTS: Beaullieu (P) bought certain land for $8,000. He also purchased from Atlanta Title & Trust Co. (D) a title guaranty policy by which it insured Beaullieu (P) against all loss or damage, not exceeding $7,000, which Beaullieu (P) should sustain by reason of any defect of title affecting this property. After he entered into possession of the land, and began building a house on it, Beaullieu (P) learned that Padgett had an easement in and over the property. Atlanta (D) admitted the validity of the easement. The true market value of the land without the easement on the date that Beaullieu (P) bought his policy was $15,000. On that date, the value of the land encumbered by the easement was $5,000. Beaullieu (P) contends that the measure of damages is the difference between the value of the land without the easement ($15,000) and its value encumbered with the easement ($5,000). Atlanta (D) contends that the measure of damages is the difference between the purchase price of the land ($8,000) and its value with the easement upon it ($5,000).

ISSUE: Is the measure of damages for the breach of a contract of title insurance the difference between the market value of the land when purchased with the encumbrance upon it and the market value of the land on that date without the encumbrance?

HOLDING AND DECISION: Yes. The law aims to place the injured party, so far as money can do it, in the position he would have occupied if the contract had been fulfilled. Where an encumbrance is a servitude or easement which cannot be removed at the option of either the grantor or grantee, damages will be awarded for the injury proximately caused by the existence and continuance of the encumbrance. The decrease in the market value of the land may usually be taken as a proper criterion by which to measure damages caused by an easement. In this case, Beaullieu (P) alleges the existence of an easement which cannot be removed either at his option or at the option of the grantor or Atlanta (D). Hence, the measure of damages will be the difference in the value of the land as it would have been on the date of Beaullieu's (P) purchase without the easement and the value on that date with the easement upon it.

EDITOR'S ANALYSIS: An Insured under a title policy is entitled to be reimbursed for all losses actually sustained, not to exceed the amount of his insurance, by reason of the defects of title or liens or encumbrances insured against. The insurer's liability is dependent on the terms of the policy construed according to the same rules of construction as are applicable to other insurance policies. This case demonstrates the general rule that the measure is the difference between the value of the property with the defect and its value without it. The insurer is not liable for damages resulting from title defects or encumbrances excepted from the operation of the policy.

NOTES:

SHELLEY v. KRAEMER
McGHEE v. SIPES

SUPREME COURT OF THE UNITED STATES, 1948.
334 U.S. 1, 68 S. Ct. 836

NATURE OF CASE: Action to enforce restrictive covenant.

FACT SUMMARY: Kraemer (P) successfully brought an action in state court to enforce a restrictive covenant (private agreement) in Shelley's (D) deed which prohibited Shelley (D) from selling his property to any Negro.

CONCISE RULE OF LAW: While a restrictive covenant is not in itself illegal, it simply cannot be enforced by a state court. Since the state court's involvement is tantamount to state action, the government, in effect, becomes a party to the discriminatory act in violation of the equal protection clause of the Fourteenth Amendment.

FACTS: When Shelley (D) moved into his neighborhood, he accepted a condition in his deed which forbid him, upon his moving out, from ever selling to, or permitting Negroes to occupy his land. All deeds signed in the neighborhood contained this restriction, it being the desire of the people in the community to mutually enforce upon themselves and newcomers this agreement. Shelley (D) sold his property to a Negro, whereupon Kraemer (P), a neighbor, successfully sued in state court to have the restrictive covenant enforced, and the sale of the property rescinded. The Supreme Court of Missouri affirmed, and the United States Supreme Court heard the case on a writ of certiorari.

ISSUE: Does the equal protection clause of the Fourteenth Amendment inhibit judicial enforcement by state courts of restrictive covenants based on race or color which seek to restrict the ownership or occupancy of real property?

HOLDING AND DECISION: Yes. If restrictive covenants were imposed by state statute or local ordinance, they would clearly be violative of the Equal Protection clause. Here, however, no action by any state legislative body is involved; rather, the restrictions operate at two levels — among private individuals, and in state courts. Standing alone, the private agreements, as long as they are effected by voluntary adherence, are not unconstitutional. Here, there is more. The courts are being used as a tool by private individuals to deny the full enjoyment of property rights to others. The court rejected the argument that there is no denial of equal protection since the state judiciary is also ready to enforce restrictive covenants made among Negroes to exclude whites. Apart from the fact that the court was aware of no case where this was involved, the rights established are personal rights; indiscriminate imposition of inequalities is no answer. Furthermore, the property owners themselves are not denied equal protection in having access to state courts — no individual has the right to demand state action which results in others being denied equal protection.

EDITOR'S ANALYSIS: Much confusion existed after the Supreme Court's seemingly broad holding in Shelley as to what amounted to unconstitutional state action. Is any private action which is brought and enforced in state court state action? Read to its fullest impact, any private act of discrimination is illegal if state officers are enlisted, in any way, to carry it out. Limited to its facts, Shelley v. Kraemer will only apply to any situation where a third party is attempting to interfere in the contractual relationship between two others. Subsequent decisions have vacillated between these two extreme interpretations.

NOTES:

BARROWS v. JACKSON
SUPREME COURT OF THE UNITED STATES, 1953.
346 U.S. 249, 73 S. Ct. 1031

NATURE OF CASE: Action at law for breach of restrictive covenant.

FACT SUMMARY: Barrows (P) sued Jackson (D) for damages arising from Jackson's (D) breach of a restrictive covenant in a deed which prohibited Jackson (D) from selling his property to any Negro.

CONCISE RULE OF LAW: The decision in Shelley v. Kraemer, which held that restrictive covenants could not be enforced in equity against Negroes because such enforcement would constitute state action denying equal protection of the law, extends to actions seeking damages against a co-covenantor for breach of the restrictive covenant. Damages, as well as suits in equity, would constitute impermissible state action if awarded by a state court.

FACTS: Upon moving into her neighborhood in Los Angeles, Jackson (D), a white, signed a deed prohibiting her from either selling to Negroes, or to permit Negroes from staying on her property except when they act as employees. Barrows (P), a neighbor, brought a complaint in state court alleging that Jackson (D) failed to incorporate a similar restrictive covenant in her deed when she sold the property, and permitted non-Caucasians to move in and occupy her premises. The trial court, citing Shelley v. Kraemer, sustained a demurrer to the complaint, and Barrows (P) appealed.

ISSUE: Can a restrictive covenant which seeks to restrict the ownership or occupancy of real property based on a standard of race or color be enforced at law by a suit for damages against a co-covenantor who allegedly broke the covenant?

HOLDING AND DECISION: No. As announced in Shelley v. Kraemer, private parties to a restrictive covenant may not use state courts or officers to enforce, in equity (requiring the co-covenantor, the defendant, to pass on a restrictive covenant, or ordering the sale rescinded, or divesting the defendant of title in his property), the terms of the agreement. Similarly, were state courts to award damages to a party seeking to vindicate his right in such a covenant, the state would be encouraging the use of restrictive covenants and denying to any defendant a personal right to dispose of his property as he saw fit. In addition, the seller of land bearing a restrictive covenant will either not sell to non-Caucasians or pass on the cost of the anticipated damages. A Negro's right to property will then be on a reduced scale to that of a white's. Although there is a problem with-standing here — a party to the covenant is asserting the rights of prospective buyers — the relationship of the parties here calls for a relaxation of the rule. The defendant in this action is the only effective party to challenge the covenant since she stands to suffer a pecuniary loss. Article I, §10 of the U.S. Constitution, guarding against impairment of contracts by state action, the court concludes, is directed against legislative, and not judicial, intervention.

EDITOR'S ANALYSIS: This case is a logical, and predictable, extension of the rule enunciated in Shelley v. Kraemer so it provides little insight into how far Shelley will be extended. Federal Civil Rights legislation probably provides more mileage in invalidating racial discrimination in real estate transactions than does the Equal Protection clause. The Civil Rights Act of 1866 states that all citizens have the same right to sell, hold and convey property. The Civil Rights Act of 1968, with but a few minor exceptions, suggests that all discrimination based on race in the sale or leasing of property is illegal.

NOTES:

PENTHOUSE PROPERTIES, INC. v. 1158 FIFTH AVENUE, INC.

256 APP. DIV. 685, 11 N.Y.S. 2d 417 (1939)

NATURE OF CASE: Action for a declaratory judgment concerning a restrictive covenant in a proprietary lease agreement.

FACT SUMMARY: 1158 Fifth Avenue, Inc. (D) refused to recognize a transfer of stock and assignment of lease to Penthouse Properties (P).

CONCISE RULE OF LAW: Restrictive covenants under which cooperative apartment houses have been constructed and stock sold are valid.

FACTS: Mrs. Harriss (Co-D) acquired stock and lease interests in 1158 Fifth Avenue, Inc. (D) with full knowledge of provisions restricting her right to assign lease and stock without written consent to the Board of Directors of 1158 Fifth Avenue, Inc. (D) or 2/3 approval by the stockholders. Despite this, Harris (Co-D) transferred interests to Penthouse Properties, Inc. (P), which then demanded stock transfer by 1158 Fifth Avenue (D). 1158 Fifth Avenue, Inc. (D) refused to recognize the transfer due to the Harriss (Co-D) non-compliance with the restrictive covenant. Penthouse Properties (P) then brought this request for court-ordered recognition of the sale.

ISSUE: Are restrictive covenants found in the lease and stock of cooperative apartment houses a violation of the rule against restraint on alienation?

HOLDING & DECISION: (Untermeyer, Justice) No. The court recognizes the special nature of the ownership of cooperative apartment houses by tenant owners and requires that they not be included in the general rule against restraint on the sale of stock in profit-making corporations. Cooperative apartment houses must be distinguished from the usual corporate situation. The primary goal is not profit but the establishment of a community. Every stock holder has an interest in the long-term proprietary lease, alienation of which the corporation has the power to restrain. This is a reasonable restraint, appropriate for the attainment of lawful purposes. Restrictive covenants under which 1158 Fifth Avenue, Inc. (D) has been organized is valid.

EDITOR'S ANALYSIS: This New York court distinguishes between the apartment house coop and the usual trans-actions involving the sale of stock. There is a balance between a desire for free alienation and covenants reasonably intended to promote social utility. The coop apartment situation tips the balance towards upholding specified, reasonable restrictions. Note that this decision is termed in corporate property language. Note also that this case involves no allegations of bad faith or racial discrimination. Compare to Northwest Real Estate Co. v. Serio, 156 Md. 229, 144 A. 245 (1919), in which a restrictive covenant involving a housing development was declared void.

WEISNER v. 791 PARK AVENUE CORP.

6 N.Y. 2d 426, 160 N.E. 2d 720 (1959)

NATURE OF CASE: Appeal from injunction precluding assignment of an interest in realty.

FACT SUMMARY: Weisner (P) contended Gilbert (D) had a duty to act on his behalf to persuade the Board of Directors of Park Avenue Corp. (D) to approve the assignment of her lease to him.

CONCISE RULE OF LAW: An assignment of a lease does not imply a duty on the assignor to act on behalf of the assignee for the approval of the landlord who holds a power to veto the assignment.

FACTS: Gilbert (D) owned a lease on an apartment owned by the 791 Park Avenue Corp. (D). The lease required that assignments had to be approved by a majority of the Board of the Corporation (D). Gilbert (D) entered into a contract to assign her lease to Weisner (P), subject to the approval of the Board. Weisner (P) acted to convince the directors individually to approve the assignments, yet his petition was rejected. He sued, contending Gilbert (D) had an implied duty to act on his behalf to attempt to convince the Board to approve the assignment, and that she had breached the duty. The trial court denied an injunction to preclude assignment of the lease to anyone else, yet the appellate court granted it. Gilbert (D) appealed.

ISSUE: Does an assignment contract imply a duty on the assignor to act on behalf of the assignee to gain approval of the assignment from the landlord?

HOLDING AND DECISION: (J. Burke) No. A contract to assign a lease does not imply a duty on the assignor to act to persuade the landlord to approve the assignment. Weisner (P) recognized this rule in this case by acting on his own to convince the board to approve the assignment. As a result, he had no cause of action or basis for an injunction to preclude Gilbert (D) from assigning the lease upon approval by the board. Reversed.

EDITOR'S ANALYSIS: The court in this case specifically declared that statutes prohibiting discrimination in allowing assignments of property interests on the basis of race, color, religion, or ancestry, did not apply to this case. It was felt that the members of the cooperative could choose who they wished to share their common areas with.

NOTES:

LAUDERBAUGH v. WILLIAMS
SUP. CT. OF PA., 1962. 409 Pa. St. 351, 186 A. 2d 39

NATURE OF CASE: Consolidated actions (1) at law to quiet title and (2) in equity to set aside a grant deed conveying land.

FACT SUMMARY: Lauderbaugh (P at law; D in equity, hereinafter referred to as "P") transferred land by grant deed to one who was not a member of an ownership association in violation of a covenant prohibiting transfers to non-members.

CONCISE RULE OF LAW: Where a restrictive covenant either limits transfers of land to a specified association whose membership standards are vague or purports to be perpetual, it is unreasonable, thus, unenforceable.

FACTS: Lauderbaugh (P) purchased land along Lake Watagwa for an exclusive subdivision. Purchasers of lots were required by restrictive covenant in the deed restricting alienation of the land to be approved as members of the Lake Watagwa (Owners') Association. When the membership was less than ten, only one member was needed to block a prospective member. When membership was greater than ten, three members were needed to block an applicant. Nine years after the first subdivided lots were sold, Lauderbaugh (P) sought to quiet title to remove a cloud on her title, the restrictive covenant. Williams (D) sought to have Lauderbaugh's (P) grant deed to a non-member set aside. The trial court set aside the deed and upheld the covenant's application to the west side of the lake only.

ISSUE: Is a restrictive covenant, which is either vague or purports to be perpetual, unreasonable and unenforceable?

HOLDING AND DECISION: Yes. While a limited and reasonable restraint on the alienation of the land may be upheld, one that is unreasonable will not be enforced. Here, the restraint was unreasonable as control over an owner's right to convey was in the membership of the owners' association and not in the grantor. In addition, the smallest minority of the association could block a conveyance for no defined reason and could object on mere whimsy. While the motive may have been totally pure — to protect a substantial investment — no standards were set to guide the members. Additionally, as the restriction is unlimited in time and purports to be perpetual, this lends greatly to its unreasonableness.

EDITOR'S ANALYSIS: Restrictive covenants are always viewed with suspicion, and generally are not favored in law. The more restrictive a covenant is the closer the court will scrutinize it. Restraints on alienation are disfavored not only because of their often suspicious motives and bad faith, but because they limit commerce and tend to concentrate wealth. A well-defined restraint with clear standards of application has a better chance of being upheld as reasonable, but often the decision will be greatly influenced by the view to such restraints within the jurisdiction in question.

NOTES:

GALE v. YORK CENTER COMMUNITY COOPERATIVE, INC.
SUP. CT. OF ILL., 1960. 21 Ill. 2d 86, 171 N.E. 2d 30

NATURE OF CASE: Action to quiet title to real property.

FACT SUMMARY: Gale (P) and six other plaintiffs sued to quiet title to land that they occupied in perpetual use, but to which legal title was held by York (D), a cooperative housing community in which Gale (P) and others were members.

CONCISE RULE OF LAW: A restraint against alienation of land may be sustained when it is reasonably designed to attain or encourage accepted social or economic ends.

FACTS: Gale (P) and six other plaintiff families belonged to York (D), a cooperating housing community of 72 families. When a member wished to withdraw, he was required to give notice to the Board of Directors, which then had 12 months to purchase the property. Generally, York (D) could levy assessments, redeem memberships, pass on approval of membership transfers of heirs and legatees in case of a member's death, pass on new member admission, expel members for detrimental conduct, approve all building plans, correct nuisances, and order repairs on dwellings. Members were given perpetual use of their assigned lots and otherwise conducted themselves as private owners. Gale (P) alleged that York (D) had too great a power to restrict alienation, and that the restriction must be held invalid.

ISSUE: May a cooperative housing association partially restrain the alienability of its members' property interests in order to maintain its existence as a cooperative enterprise?

HOLDING AND DECISION: Yes. While restraints on alienation are generally void, they may be sustained when reasonably designed to attain or encourage accepted social or economic ends. It is a matter of public policy. Here, the membership agreement was a "studied effort" to give York (D) its necessary power to operate, while giving its members as much freedom as possible. The court must balance the utility of the restraint as compared with the injurious consequences that will flow from its enforcement. It must be decided on a case-by-case basis considering the restraint's length of time, the class of persons excluded, and the prohibited modes of alienation.

EDITOR'S ANALYSIS: Generally, restraints on alienation are held void because they restrict commerce, tend to concentrate wealth, and may prevent creditors from satisfying their claims. These bad points may be overcome on a case-by-case basis by balancing these factors against the social and economic benefits. Those reasonable restraints necessary to the continued existence of a cooperative association will be upheld. Here, the restraints did not tend to concentrate wealth, did not prevent creditors from satisfying claims, and encouraged members to improve their homes.

JUSTICE COURT MUTUAL HOUSING COOPERATIVE, INC. v. SANDOW

SUPREME COURT OF QUEEN'S COUNTY, 1966.
50 Misc. 2d 541, 270 N.Y.S. 2d. 829

NATURE OF CASE: Action for declaratory judgment and permanent injunction.

FACT SUMMARY: Justice Court Mutual (P), a cooperative housing corporation, adapted regulations restricting the playing of musical instruments in its building, where the Sandows (D) resided with their two daughters who were musical artists.

CONCISE RULE OF LAW: New regulations imposed upon shareholder-tenants by a cooperative housing corporation must be reasonable.

FACTS: The Sandows (D) became shareholder-tenants of Justice Court Mutual Housing Cooperative, Inc. (P) after being assured by Justice Court Mutual's (P) sponsor that their daughters would be allowed to practice their musical art. The Sandow's (D) daughters were allowed to practice their music for six years. Then, following tenant complaints, Justice Court Mutual's (P) Board of Directors adopted regulations which: (1) prohibited the playing of a musical instrument by any one person in excess of one and one-half hours per day, and (2) prohibited the playing of musical instruments after 8:00 P.M. The Sandows (D) refused to comply with these regulations and Justice Court Mutual (P) then commenced a summary proceeding which ultimately was dismissed without prejudice.

ISSUE: May a cooperative housing corporation impose new regulations upon a shareholder tenant?

HOLDING AND DECISION: Only if such regulations are reasonable. In the instant case, the corporate by-laws of Justice Court Mutual (P) gave its Board of Directors the power to promulgate such rules and regulations pertaining to the use and occupancy of the premises as might be deemed proper. However, such a power is not absolute. A new regulation may not be arbitrary and unreasonable. The arbitrariness of the one and one-half hour limitation in the instant regulations is evidenced by the fact that such limit would not eliminate the possibility of six hours of constant music in the Sandow (D) apartment, i.e., all four inhabitants could play musical instruments for the allotted one and one-half hours. The limitation would, however, prevent Sandow's (D) daughters from engaging in the extensive practice necessary to acquire expertise. That portion of the regulation prohibiting playing of musical instruments after 8:00 P.M. is in effect tantamount to banning such music completely since after 8:00 P.M. is the only time of day when many people have an opportunity to engage in avocational pursuits. A regulation which mandates a ban upon the exercise of musical art, or the enjoyment of music is arbitrary and unreasonable. Therefore, Justice Court Mutual's (P) complaint in so far as it sought a permanent injunction was dismissed and the regulations restricting playing of a musical instrument was declared to be of no force and effect.

EDITOR'S ANALYSIS: Although in Justice Court, supra, the tenants were successful in resisting new restrictions upon their life style, more litigation may be expected in this area. In an attempt to protect the cooperative's physical plant and to insure harmonious relations among tenants, cooperative housing instruments are frequently filled with various prohibitions. The purchaser should examine the fine print of his contract carefully so that he will be aware of the machinery for future enlargement of these prohibitions. For example, there is no guarantee that such normal incidents of daily living as possession of washers, dryers, or household pets will not be banned at a future date.

This case also highlights another disadvantage of the cooperative type of housing, i.e., the involvement, both personal and financial, with co-owners. Although all neighbors need to get along with one another, co-owners need to achieve the degree of harmony required of business associates. The success of their shared investment may depend to some extent upon that harmony.

NOTES:

GREEN v. GREENBELT HOMES, INC.

COURT OF APPEALS OF MARYLAND, 1963.

273 Md. 496, 194 A. 2d 273

NATURE OF CASE: Action for declaratory relief.

FACT SUMMARY: Greenbelt Homes (D), a cooperative housing development, terminated the mutual ownership contract of Green (P), a member of the corporation, on grounds of Green's (P) misconduct.

CONCISE RULE OF LAW: A member of a cooperative housing development is the holder of a leasehold interest rather than an owner of realty; and the cooperative housing corporation can terminate the contract of a member in accordance with terms of the contract on the grounds of misconduct.

FACTS: Green (P) purchased a dwelling unit and the lot on which it was situated from Greenbelt Homes (D) and occupied that dwelling unit for about two years. Then as a result of complaints by other occupants regarding Green's (P) misconduct, Greenbelt Homes (D) followed the procedures prescribed in the mutual ownership contract and terminated for misconduct such contract with Green (P). Green (P) refused to vacate the premises and this action followed. Green (P) claimed: (1) that according to her contract she was an owner of real property rather than the holder of a leasehold interest and (2) the provisions of the contract relating to termination for misconduct were invalid. Judgment in the lower court was for Greenbelt Homes (D). Green (P) appealed.

ISSUE: (1) Is the purchaser of a dwelling unit in a cooperative housing development the owner of real property? (2) May the mutual ownership contract validly provide for termination due to purchaser's misconduct?

HOLDING AND DECISION: (1) No. The purchaser of a dwelling unit in a cooperative housing development is the owner of a leasehold interest. The corporation, in the instant case, Greenbelt Homes (D), is distinct from its members, no one of whom has a right to receive legal title to any specific property of the corporation. When considering the purposes of rent control acts or other statutes some courts have held that members of a cooperative corporation were owners. However, this cannot be interpreted to mean that the rights of the purchaser-lessee in the cooperative apartment are equivalent to a fee simple interest.

(2) Yes. Courts have recognized that the relationship between a member of the cooperative corporation and the corporation is that of a landlord and tenant and have therefore allowed the corporation the usual remedies of a landlord against a tenant. In accordance with this view, the mutual ownership contract between the corporation and member may impose certain restrictions on the use of the cooperative dwelling unit and those restrictions are considered covenants between the member and the corporation. The breach of such covenant may give the corporation the right to terminate the contract. In the instant case, Green's (P)

contract prohibited objectionable conduct. Greenbelt Homes (D) determined in accordance with the procedures in the contract that Green (P) had violated that prohibition and therefore validly terminated such contract.

EDITOR'S ANALYSIS: Although, as pointed out in Green, supra, the cooperative purchaser has no absolute ownership, such purchaser does have the attributes or indicia of ownership. The court in Hicks v. Bigelow, 55 A. 2d 924 (D.C. Munic. Ct. App. 1947) describes those attributes as follows, "Such purchaser is more than a mere tenant or lessee. She has certain proprietary rights which a mere tenant does not have. She has most of the attributes of an owner. She has a voice in the selection or approval of other tenant-owners. She has a voice, too, in the important matter of any proposed sale or mortgage of the property. More important, she has the exclusive, personal right to occupy her particular apartment."

NOTES:

NEPONSIT PROPERTY OWNERS' ASSN., INC. v. EMIGRANT INDUSTRIAL SAVINGS BANK

COURT OF APPEALS OF NEW YORK, 1938.
278 N.Y. 248, 15 N.E. 2d 793

NATURE OF CASE: Action to foreclose a lien upon land.

FACT SUMMARY: Neponsit Property Owners (P) claim that Emigrant Bank's (D) deed to certain property conveyed such property subject to a covenant contained in the original deed which provided for the payment by all subsequent purchasers of an annual improvements charge.

CONCISE RULE OF LAW: A covenant in deed subjecting land to an annual charge for improvements to the surrounding residential tract is enforceable by the property owners' association against subsequent purchasers if: (1) grantor and grantee so intended; (2) it appears that the covenant is one touching or concerning the land; and (3) privity of estate is shown between the party claiming benefit of the covenant and the party under the burden of such covenant.

FACTS: Neponsit Property Owners' (P) assignor, Neponsit Realty Company, conveyed the land now owned by Emigrant Bank (D) to R. Deyer and wife by deed. That original deed contained a covenant providing: (1) that the conveyed land should be subject to an annual charge for improvements upon the entire residential tract then being developed; (2) that such charge should be a lien; (3) such charge should be payable by all subsequent purchasers to the company or its assigns, including a property owners' association which might thereafter be organized; and (4) such covenant runs with the land. Neponsit Property Owners (P) brought action based upon the above covenant to foreclose a lien upon the land which Emigrant Bank (D) now owns, having purchased it at a judicial sale. Emigrant Bank (D) appealed from an order denying their motion for judgment on the pleadings.

ISSUE: Does a covenant in the original deed subjecting land to an annual charge for improvements run with the land and create a lien which is enforceable against subsequent owners by Neponsit Property Owners (P)?

HOLDING AND DECISION: Yes. A covenant will run with the land and will be enforceable against a subsequent purchaser if: (1) the grantor and grantee intend that the covenant run with the land; (2) the covenant touches or concerns the land with which it runs; (3) there is privity of estate between the party claiming benefit of the covenant and the party who rests under the burden of the covenant. In the instant case the grantor and grantee manifested their intent that the covenant run with the land by so stating in the original deed. The covenant touches or concerns the land in substance if not in form, i.e., the covenant alters the legal rights of ownership of the land, by providing that the burden of paying the cost of maintaining public improvements is inseparably attached to the land which enjoys the benefits of such improvements. The concept of privity of estate between parties usually requires that the party claiming benefit from the enforcement of a covenant own the property which benefits from such enforcement. Although Neponsit Property Owners (P), the corporation, does not own the property which would benefit from enforcement, the corporation is acting as the agent of property owners and should therefore be considered in privity in substance if not in form. Since the covenant complies with the legal requirements for one which runs with the land and is enforceable against subsequent purchasers, the order which denied Emigrant Bank's (D) motion for judgment on the pleadings is affirmed.

EDITOR'S ANALYSIS: It has been suggested that the technical requirements which determine the enforceability of covenants as to future parties, e.g., Neponsit, supra, might well be abandoned and that the the the intention of the covenanting parties be the sole criterion. This suggestion is supported by the following developments: (1) the benefit of a contract may now be assigned, or even created initially for the benefit of a third person; (2) recording systems, though imperfect, afford much protection to the purchaser of land against outstanding burdens of which he may be unaware. It should be noted, however, that the unrestricted enforcement of covenants may seriously impair the usefulness of land.

A student reading this case should keep in mind that Neponsit, supra, is not concerned with the enforcement of covenants between original covenanting parties. That question of enforceability is left to the contracts course.

NOTES:

DICK v. SEARS-ROEBUCK & CO.

SUP. COURT OF ERRORS OF CONNECTICUT, 1932.
115 Conn. 122, 160 A. 432

NATURE OF CASE: Action to enjoin Sears-Roebuck & Co. (D) from engaging in the retail or wholesale furniture business upon the premises.

FACT SUMMARY: Dick (P) ran a furniture business. He conveyed a lot across the street by a deed containing a covenant not to compete or rent to one who would compete with Dick's (P) business. The covenant was binding on his grantee and their heirs and assgins. Dick's (P) business was thereafter incorporated, but Dick (P) continued to have a large financial interest in it. The grantee conveyed the lot to a corporation who leased it to Sears-Roebuck & Co. (D), who sells furniture on the premises.

CONCISE RULE OF LAW: A restriction upon the conduct of a certain business upon a particular piece of land for a reasonable purpose and covering a reasonable period does not violate public policy and is enforceable.

FACTS: Dick (P) owned certain property upon which he conducted a retail furniture business. He conveyed a lot across the street from his business to certain grantees by a deed in which the grantees covenanted that the premises would not be rented for the purpose of conducting a furniture business and that the grantees would not permit it to be so used for fifteen years. Subsequently, Dick's (P) business was incorporated, but he continued to manage it and to have the largest financial interest in it. His grantees conveyed the lot to a corporation by a deed containing a covenant similar to the one mentioned above. The corporation leased the property to Sears-Roebuck & Co. (D). The lease contains no reference to the covenants in the deeds. Sears (D) conducts a department store on the premises in which furniture is sold. It has sold furniture in a substantial amount in direct competition to Dick's (P) business and to the substantial injury of Dick's (P) business and property.

ISSUE: Can a covenant restricting the conduct of a certain business upon a particular piece of land be enforced?

HOLDING AND DECISION: Yes. A restriction upon the conduct of a certain business upon a particular piece of land for a reasonable purpose and covering a reasonable period does not violate public policy. Sears' (D) maintenance of a furniture department in its store on the premises falls within the fair intent of the restriction in the covenant. Also, it is clear that both Dick (P) and his grantee intended the restrictive covenant to be binding on subsequent grantees from the language of the covenant binding the grantees' heirs and assigns. The language of the covenant and the surrounding circumstances make it one which was intended to run with the land. Since the deeds were recorded Sears (D) was bound with notice of the covenants contained in them, even though its lease did not mention them. If Dick (P) still owned his furniture business there would be no question of his right to enforce the covenant against Sears (D). It is necessary to consider whether he still has an interest which should be protected by an injunction. A breach of the covenant gives him, as covenantee, the right to at least nominal damages. But the trial court also found him to have the largest financial interest in the business. Hence the substantial damage to the business, caused by Sears' (d) breach of the covenant gave Dick (P) such an interest to justify the granting of an injunction.

EDITOR'S ANALYSIS: There is a great divergence of opinion on the nature, extent, and construction of covenants restricting building and the use of land. Such restrictions are not favored in law since they are repugnant to trade and commerce, and they will be strictly construed. However, where the intention of the parties is clear, the restriction is reasonable, and it is not against public policy, it will be upheld. For example, restrictions as to the value, location and character of building improvements, building lines, or the nature of the occupancy of the premises.

NOTES:

SHELL OIL COMPANY v. HENRY OVELLETTE & SONS CO., INC.

SUPREME JUDICIAL COURT OF MASSACHUSETTS.
352 Mass. 725, 227 N.E. 2d 509

NATURE OF CASE: Action to enforce a restriction in a deed.

FACT SUMMARY: Shell Oil Company (P), successor in title of the original grantee of the dominant parcel of land, wants to enforce a restriction barring competitive use of adjacent land against Socony Mobil Oil Company (D), which had an option to purchase a servient parcel from the original grantor, Henry Ovelette & Sons Co., Inc. (D).

CONCISE RULE OF LAW: (1) A restriction of the use of land for the competitive benefit of adjacent land does not directly concern the use of the dominant parcel and operate to its advantage, and so, since the restriction will not pass by deed of the dominant parcel, it may not be enforced against a successor in title of the owner of the servient parcel, who imposed the original restriction, by a successor in title of the original grantee of the dominant parcel.

FACTS: Henry Ovellette & Sons Co., Inc. (D) conveyed land by deed to Bloom and some trustees. A restriction in the deed purported to prohibit Ovelette (D) and its successors from using any adjacent property it owned to the competitive disadvantage of the property deeded away. The trustees conveyed to Shell Oil Company (P) some of the land originally acquired by them from Ovellette (D). Ovellette, in turn, granted to Socony Mobil Oil Company (D) an option to buy part of Ovellette's adjacent land for the purpose of building a gas station. Since Shell (P) had already, by this time, built a gas station on its land, it sought to enforce the restriction in the original deed against competitive use on Ovellette (D) and Mobil (D).

ISSUE: Does the benefit of a restriction on competitive use of adjacent land pass by deed to the successor in title of the original grantees?

HOLDING AND DECISION: No. The court considered itself bound by an earlier opinion of Justice Holmes. There, it was held that, in order for a negative covenant to pass by deed to successors in title, (1) a restriction of the use of land for the competitive advantage of adjacent land does not directly concern the use of the dominant parcel and operate to its advantage; and (2) the restriction will not "run" (pass by deed of the dominant parcel to a successor in title, so as to enable him to enforce the restriction against the successor in title of the servient parcel who originally imposed it). In deference to contrary opinions and critical authorities in other jurisdictions, the court notes that it is not unreasonable to prtoect and uphold competitive use covenants which affect only a limited geographic area and do not severely restrain trade. However, because of the special reliance on settled law involved in real estate transactions, the court will not frustrate the expectations of the parties involved here.

EDITOR'S ANALYSIS: Because "running," particularly in instances of negative covenants, restricts the free alienability of property, courts tend to restrict the legal effect of the covenant, and so disfavor a restriction passing through deed. However, many modern business leases and grants use non-competitive use clauses which reach adjacent property. Courts will commonly permit their enforcement in equity (but not law) so long as the intent of the original contractors are clear. The Massachusetts rule, propounded here, is in the minority among the jurisdictions which have considered competitive use covenants.

NOTES:

TULK v. MOXHAY
COURT OF CHANCERY, ENGLAND, 1848.
2 Phillips 774, 41 Eng. Rep. 1143

NATURE OF CASE: Bill for injunction to enforce covenant in deed.

FACT SUMMARY: Moxhay (D) indicated an intention to build upon an open ground, even though he was aware of an original, prohibitive covenant passed on by Tulk (P), forty years earlier, which forbade any construction on the ground.

CONCISE RULE OF LAW: Privity of estate notwithstanding, a person who acquires real property with notice of a restriction placed upon it will not be allowed, in equity, to violate its terms.

FACTS: Tulk (P), owner in fee of a piece of ground, as well as adjacent houses, sold the property to Elms. A covenant in the deed of conveyance prohibited Elms and his assigns from ever constructing upon the ground. The piece of land eventually came into the hands of Moxhay (D), whose purchase deed contained no similar covenant, yet Moxhay (D) admitted he knew of the original covenant. When Moxhay (D) indicated he wanted to build on the piece of ground, Tulk (P) successfully obtained an injunction.

ISSUE: Can the purchasor of a deed of conveyance containing a restriction violate the restriction if he has notice of the original covenant?

HOLDING AND DECISION: No. To hold otherwise would make it impossible for an owner of land to sell part of it without running the risk of seeing the part he retained rendered worthless. At issue is not whether the covenant "runs" with the land, but whether a party may violate a contract entered into by his vendor by using the land in an inconsistent manner. If there was a mere agreement and no covenant, a court would enforce it against a party purchasing with notice; so long as an equity is attached by an owner, no one purchasing with notice can stand in a different situation than the original purchaser.

EDITOR'S ANALYSIS: Notice is the key element of the principle, commonly referred to as "the doctrine of Tulk v. Moxhay," enunciated in this case. Notice of the restriction may be either actual, inquiry or record. The rights and obligations recognized here are variously named, but are generally known as "equitable servitudes." The restriction in the transfer of land need not be embodied in a covenant — an informal contract or agreement is sufficient. A party intended to receive the benefit, as well as the original covenantor, can bring the suit in equity. However, proof of notice is essential to the doctrine.

NOTES:

WERNER v. GRAHAM
SUPREME COURT OF CALIFORNIA, 1919.
181 Cal. 174, 183 P. 945

NATURE OF CASE: Action to quiet title to real property.

FACTUAL SUMMARY: Neighbors in a subdivision, whose deeds contained certain building restrictions passed on by the original grantor, wanted to prevent Werner (P) from non-compliance, even though Werner's (P) deed contained no restrictions since the original grantor had quitclaimed to the then owner of Werner's (P) lot any interest in it.

CONCISE RULE OF LAW: Where a deed does not expressly indicate who receives the benefit of a restriction, only the grantor can seek enforcement, unless he specifically gives neighbors in a subdivision the right. If so given, it must be embodied in the same deed as imposes the restrictions.

FACTS: Marshall subdivided a tract of land into a number of lots which he offered for sale. Marshall, in the deeds to those lots, provided for common restrictions on building specifications. Unquestionably, Marshall had in mind a general and common plan to have some uniformity within the subdivision. After selling 116 out of 132 lots, Marshall quitclaimed (gave up his right to sue for anything arising out of the transaction, and surrendered his claim and title) to the prior owner of Werner's (P) lot thereby releasing the effect of the restrictions so far as it was in his power to do so. In selling all of his lots, Marshall told the respective purchasers that he was exacting the same restrictive provisions from all purchasers. Since Werner's (P) deed contained no restrictions, he brought an action in quiet title, anticipating that his neighbors would sue him for failing to comply with any restrictions.

ISSUE: Can neighbors enforce subdivision restrictions, uniformly imposed according to a general scheme, against a purchasor who acquired title through a quitclaim deed which contains no restrictions?

HOLDING AND DECISION: No. It's immaterial whether Werner (P) had or had not actual notice. The restrictions are cast in the form of conditions, and not covenants (a matter of language). Assuming the restrictive provisions to be covenants, there is yet no privity of contract, the defendants not being original parties to the contracts. Nor is there privity of estate — Werner (P) does not hold under or through any of the defendants, nor any of the defendants through him. The covenants here involved are not for the estate's benefit, but for its detriment. The only way the restrictions are to have force is to cast them as a servitude. (a) The burden imposed is upon the land and incident to its ownership, and (b) the benefit of the covenants was passed as an incident of ownership. Marshall, however, was no longer interested in those lots he conveyed prior to his conveyance of the lot Werner (P)

eventually acquired. As the owner, Marshall had a right to quitclaim his interest. The only remaining question is as to the existence of a servitude in favor of those lots which Marshall still owned when he sold Werner's (P) lot and with which he parted before he gave his quitclaim deed. Servitudes running with the land cannot be created in an uncertain and indefinite fashion. The fact that Marshall apparently followed a general, uniform plan of restrictions is of little weight. It is not his intent that governs, but the joint intent of himself and his grantees. Each deed must be construed as of the time it is given. His apparent understanding with the respective purchasers was not embodied in the deed and so should be given no force.

EDITOR'S ANALYSIS: The California approach to the question of a third party beneficiary theory is a minority one. Most courts would have recognized the neighbors in this case as third party beneficiaries or, on the basis of implied servitude, found that the neighbors were enforcing an implied servitude and not the express covenant later included by the subdivider. See Snow v. Van Dam, which gives the right to both subsequent and prior purchasers.

NOTES:

SNOW v. VAN DAM

SUPREME JUDICIAL COURT OF MASSACHUSETTS, 1935
291 Mass. 477, 197 N.E. 224

NATURE OF CASE: Suit for injunction to enforce restrictions against later purchasor of land.

FACTUAL SUMMARY: Snow (P), who had purchased a subdivision lot south of a division line, secured an injunction against Van Dam (D), a later purchasor of a subdivision lot north of the division line to prohibit him from violating a building restriction in his deed, a restriction present in Snow's (P) deed as well.

CONCISE RULE OF LAW: If a deed does not indicate who receives the benefit of a restriction, owners of appurtenant land in the subdivision — including both earlier and later purchasors — can enjoin any violation of the restriction if they can prove that the original developer, intending to benefit everyone in the subdivision, had a scheme of substantial uniformity in building and use.

FACTS: Shackleford subdivided a tract he owned into lots at two different points in time. In 1907, he subdivided into lots some land lying south of a public highway which ran through the tract. In June 1923, Snow (P) purchased one of these lots subject to a restriction in his deed which prohibited him from erecting other than "one dwelling house." Land lying north of the highway was subdivided in 1919 and sold in January 1923, subject to a similar restriction as those in the southern lots. Van Dam (D), purchasor of a northern lot in 1933, erected a commercial building on the lot. Snow (P) and his neighbors secured a permanent injunction against Van Dam (D).

ISSUE: May neighbors in a subdivision secure an injunction to enjoin violations of a restriction similar to ones in their own deeds, even if the deeds do not indicate who receives the benefit, and the party against whom the restriction is to be imposed is a later purchasor?

HOLDING AND DECISION: Yes. In an earlier decision, the court had held that a benefit favoring subdivision owners, because of the Statute of Frauds, must be created by deed. Here, the court first observes that a restriction, in order to be attached to a piece of real property, and act as a benefit to someone, must (1) tend to benefit the land itself, and (2) must be appurtenant (necessary to the use and enjoyment of some other more principal land). Unless a scheme on the part of the original subdivider to effect some benefit for the whole subdivision can be shown here, the restrictions on Van Dam's (D) lot were not appurtenant to Snow's (P). A "scheme" must be readily apparent to purchasers when the sale of subdivision lots began. Since only the intent of the original grantor, or subdivider, is controlling, neither absolute identity of restrictions upon different lots, nor restrictions placed upon every lot within the subdivision, is essential to proving a scheme. On the other hand, variations among restrictions (or omissions) among the various lots involved, tend to show the absence of a scheme. If there is a scheme, and it can be determined, an earlier purchasor can enforce common, or substantially similar, restrictions against a later purchasor of a lot within the subdivision. An enforceable agreement which runs back to the common grantor can be inferred. Here, the subdivider's failure to develop the northern area of the tract was due to a belief, at the time, that it could not be sold, and apparently not to any intent on his part to reserve it for other than residential purposes.

EDITOR'S ANALYSIS: The prevailing rule is that statements of intent to establish equitable servitudes (restrictions on land use enforceable in equity by property owners who have land in the restricted area) do not have to be expressly written in the deed (one of the few exceptions to the Statute of Frauds). However, to avoid the difficulty of establishing the existence of a scheme which was apparent to a subdivision's purchasors when he first bought into the area, the most reliable way to create equitable servitudes is through express language in a deed. In some jurisdictions, this is the only way to create equitable servitudes; the nature of the restrictions, the parties' intent, the binding effect of the restriction on land retained by the grantor, and a specific description of all land conveyed, must be laid out.

NOTES:

MERRIONETTE MANOR HOMES IMPROVEMENT ASSOCIATION v. HEDA

APPELLATE COURT OF ILLINOIS, 1956.
11 Ill. App. 2d 186, 136 N.E. 2d 556

NATURE OF CASE: Action to enforce restrictive covenants.

FACT SUMMARY: Merrionette Manor Homes Improvement Association (P), sued to enjoin alleged violations of restrictive covenants in Heda's (D) and others' deeds of which the defendants had notice.

CONCISE RULE OF LAW: A property owner's association, consisting of the owners of real property within an area subjected to planned and uniform restrictive covenants, has sufficient interest to bring suit to enjoin alleged violations.

FACTS: Merrionette Manor Corporation, original subdivider of the property involved, recorded covenants which sought to preserve the plan of the subdivision, the character of the homes and the arrangement for land usage. One of these covenants prohibited the construction of a vestibule (a small entrance hall or room) without the joint and simultaneous construction of a like vestibule by the owner of the adjacent dwelling unit and without obtaining permission by Merrionette. Merrionette then caused to be incorporated the Merrionette Manor Homes Improvement Association (P), a group of affected homeowners, for the purposes of enforcing, preserving, and maintaining the protective covenants. In so doing, Merrionette Manor Corporation assigned its control of the covenants to the Association (P). Heda (D) purchased property within the original subdivision. Despite the covenants, which were specified in Heda's (D) deed, Heda (D) built a vestibule. Thereupon, the Association sought an injunction.

ISSUE: May an association of homeowners organized as a nonprofit corporation, whose membership consists of the owners of real property within an area subject to planned and uniform restrictive covenants, bring suit to enjoin alleged violations?

HOLDING AND DECISION: Yes. The court looked to an earlier decision, Neponset Property Owners' Association v. Emigrant Industrial Savings Bank, 278 N.Y. 248, 15 N.E. 2d 793, 118 A.L.R. 982, as controlling, since the question here was one of first impression in Illinois. In Neponsit, the New York court, citing Tulk v. Moxhay, pointed out that the enforcement of these covenants rests upon equitable principles. Hence, privity of estate should not be an obstacle. The court there considered that the solution was to look at the real character of the association. If the association was formed to look after common rights embodied in the covenants, in substance, if not form, there is privity of estate. In Illinois, the law is not so strictly defined as to require in all cases that the one seeking enforcement must show some right or beneficial interest in the land affected by the covenant or in adjoining lands. However, cautions the court, each case must be decided on its own circumstances.

EDITOR'S ANALYSIS: This case represents the minority position in America. Most courts, and Restatement Section 537, hold that since there exists a strong policy against the "running" of the burden of a covenant at law unless there is also a benefit to land. As a result, the burden will not run at law when the benefit is in gross (the benefit is personal to the covenantee, and touches or concerns land of the covenantor). Restatement Section 539 suggests that the burden of a covenant in gross will run in equity. Once again, most courts will not permit this.

NOTES:

PRATTE v. BALATSOS
SUP. CT. OF NEW HAMPSHIRE, 1955.
99 N.H. 430, 113 A. 2d 492

NATURE OF CASE: Bill in equity, seeking a permanent injunction and a temporary restraining order.

FACT SUMMARY: Pratte (P) made an agreement with a restaurant owner, who sold his business to Balatsos (D), who refused to honor the agreement.

CONCISE RULE OF LAW: Restrictive covenants, regarded as equitable easements, may be binding upon the purchaser of the burdened land, if he takes with notice.

FACTS: Pratte (P) made an agreement with Larochelle to install Pratte's (P) juke box in Larochelle's restaurant. The agreement was to last fourteen and one-half years, and be binding on the "heirs, successors, and assigns" of the parties. Larochelle then sold the restaurant to Balatsos (D) who, although he knew of the terms of the agreement, refused to be bound by it. Balatsos (D) contends that the contract between Pratte (P) and Larochelle does not run with the land. Pratte (P) contends that the contract created an easement, which is binding on successors in interest who take with notice of same.

ISSUE: May equitable restrictions be enforced against subsequent purchasers with notice?

HOLDING AND DECISION: Yes. The purchaser of property, who has notice of a covenant concerning the use of that land, takes subject to that covenant. Even though the covenant does not technically "run with the land," it can be regarded as an equitable easement, which will continue to run against subsequent purchasers with notice.

EDITOR'S ANALYSIS: It was clearly the intention of the original parties, Pratte (P) and Larochelle, to bind all successors in interest. Moreover, public policy favors the enforcement of agreements which "run with the business" even if they don't technically "touch and concern" the land. The court reached its result by defining the covenant as an easement, enforceable in equity upon those taking interest with notice thereof.

NOTES:

JONES v. NORTHWEST REAL ESTATE CO.
CT. OF APPEALS OF MARYLAND, 1925.
1949 Md. 271, 131 A. 446

NATURE OF CASE: Bill in equity.

FACT SUMMARY: Northwest Real Estate Co. (P) claimed Jones (D) violated a restrictive covenant by putting an addition on Jones' (D) house without the developer's permission.

CONCISE RULE OF LAW: Covenants purporting to restrict land use will be upheld, where the intention of the parties is clear, and the restrictions within reasonable bounds.

FACTS: Jones (D) built a second story porch on his house. Covenants in his deed and in all deeds in the subdivision required the prior approval of the developer for all alterations. Northwest Real Estate Co. (P) contended that the addition gives the house the appearance of a two-family dwelling, which is not in harmony with the rest of the development (single-family homes).

ISSUE: Can a party empowered by a restrictive covenant to approve construction withhold that approval on the basis of aesthetics?

HOLDING AND DECISION: Yes. Covenants will be enforced according to the expressed intention of the parties, provided the restrictions do not violate public policy. Here, restrictions in the deed clearly gave the developer the right to veto any alterations "for aesthetic or other reasons," and such provisions do not offend public policy.

EDITOR'S ANALYSIS: The court, in the above decision, took judicial notice of the public's constantly increasing demand for homes in restricted residential districts, where "all the houses are to be a certain distance back from the street, are to cost not less than a certain sum of money, are to conform in size and appearance with the surrounding houses, are not to have structures other than a residence on the lot, and so on." Without expressing approval or disapproval of this trend, the court notes that where the parties have voluntarily agreed to so restrict their land, the restrictions will generally be upheld.

RICK v. WEST

SUP. CT. OF N.Y., WESTCHESTER COUNTY, 1962.
34 Misc. 2d 1002, 228 N.Y.S. 2d 195

NATURE OF CASE: Action for declaratory judgment to permit violation of restrictive covenants.

FACT SUMMARY: West (D) refused to permit Rick (P) to sell residential land to a hospital, in violation of restrictive covenants.

CONCISE RULE OF LAW: Restrictive covenants may not be removed on the application of the developer, where purchasers have relied on the restrictions, and where there is no change in the character of the neighborhood.

FACTS: Rick (P), the developer of a residential community, voluntarily imposed upon his 62 acres covenants which restricted them to residential use. West (D), relying upon these restrictions, bought a lot. Later, Rick (P) attempted to sell 15 acres of the subdivision to a hospital, and West (D) refused to consent to this violation of the restrictions. Rick contended that the sale should be allowed, because (1) the original covenants contained a clause providing for "exceptions in certain cases," and (2) substantial changes have occurred in the neighborhood, making the covenants unenforceable.

ISSUE: Can the developer violate restrictive covenants which he voluntarily imposed on his property?

HOLDING AND DECISION: No. Even though Rick (P) voluntarily imposed the restrictions on the lots in his subdivision, West (D) bought her lot lot in reliance on those restrictions. The character of the neighborhood had not changed significantly enough to warrant a violation of the covenant, and while certain exceptions may be allowed, the non-residential use of 15 acres does not constitute a permissible exception.

EDITOR'S ANALYSIS: The retention by a developer of the right to modify the restrictions as to any properties in the development has generally been held to negate the idea of a uniform plan or scheme in the subdivision. In such a case, even if the developer does not exercise this reserved right, one owner will be precluded from enforcing the restrictions against another owner.

NOTES:

MARANTHA SETTLEMENT ASSN. v. EVANS

SUPREME COURT OF PENNSYLVANIA, 1956.
385 Pa. St. 208, 122 A. 2d 679

NATURE OF CASE: Action for a decree for property rights.

FACT SUMMARY: Marantha Settlement Assn. (P) sold lots in a development, one going to Evans (D), with a provision that "The Grantee and his immediate family only shall enjoy the free use of the swimming pool."

CONCISE RULE OF LAW: The extent of any grant of a property interest depends entirely upon the intent of the parties involved as determined by (1) a fair interpretation of the language employed, and (2) consideration of all the attendant circumstances.

FACTS: The Evans-Yale Realty Corp., of which the Marantha Settlement Assn. is successor in title, sold a number of lots in a development. The corporation had constructed a swimming pool on the tract and all of the original purchasers of lots had the following provision in their deeds: "The grantee and his immediate family only shall enjoy the free use of the swimming pool." Evans (P) subsequently purchased some lots from original purchasers. He seeks to use the swimming pool, but Marantha (P) refuses. Marantha filed an action seeking a decree that the provision above-stated set forth is either an easement in gross (to the person only) or a license (revocable) to use the swimming pool. From judgment for Evans (D) that the grant was of an easement appurtenant (to the land), Marantha (P) appeals.

ISSUE: Is the grant of a use of property limited to "The grantee and his immediate family only" necessarily a personal use not transferable with title to the land?

HOLDING AND DECISION: No. The extent of any grant of a property interest depends entirely upon the intent of the parties involved as determined by (1) a fair interpretation of the language employed, and (2) consideration of all the attendant circumstances; and, where a common grantor which had constructed a swimming pool, inserted in its deeds to purchasers a provision that only the grantee and his immediate family should enjoy free use of it, and that the "grantee, his heirs and assigns" had a duty to comply with reasonable regulations which the grantor might make as to the pool, the obvious intention of the parties was to make the right to the pool an easement appurtenant to the land, transferable with title to the land. Viewing the subsequent clause which so refers to "the grantee, his heirs and assigns," the word "only" in the granting clause must be interpreted as limiting "immediate family," not "grantee." As such, there is no limit on the grantee. A fee simple title was granted to the original purchasers here and Evans (D) took that fee with the easement appurtenant to it. The judgment below is affirmed.

EDITOR'S ANALYSIS: This case points up the general standard for interpreting a deed: the intent of the draftsman. As for easements, the extent of a profit or easement is determined by the intention of the drafters as manifested in the terms of the grant. The easement may only be used for the purpose stated in the grant, but the owner always has a right to do those things that are reasonably necessary for a proper enjoyment of the grant. A change of use, however, can never be justified even if it can be established that it would not increase the burden on the servient estate. An easement appurtenant may be used for the general benefit of the dominant estate, and use for non-dominant property is not authorized and may be enjoined.

NOTES:

VAN SANDT v. ROYSTER

SUPERIOR COURT OF KANSAS, 1938.
148 Kan. 495, 83 P. 2d 698

NATURE OF CASE: Action to enjoin Royster (D) and Gray (D) from using an underground sewer drain across Van Sandt's (P) property.

FACT SUMMARY: Van Sandt (P) found his cellar flooded with sewage and discovered for the first time the existence of a sewer drain across his property. Royster (D) and Gray (D) refuse to stop using the drain.

CONCISE RULE OF LAW: Whether there is an implied easement on certain property will be inferred from the intentions of the parties, and such inference will be drawn from the circumstances under which the conveyance was made.

Parties to a conveyance will be assumed to know and to contemplate the continuance of reasonably necessary uses which have so altered the premises as to make them apparent upon reasonably prudent investigation.

FACTS: Bailey owned three adjoining lots numbered 4, 20, and 19. In 1904, a private lateral drain was built running from the house on Lot 4 across Lots 20 and 19. Bailey conveyed Lot 20 to Murphy by a general warranty deed without exceptions or reservations in 1904. Title passed to Royster (D). In 1904, Bailey also conveyed Lot 19 to Jones by a general warranty deed without exceptions or reservations. Jones conveyed part of Lot 19 to Reynolds, who in 1924 conveyed to Van Sandt (P). Gray (D) succeeded title to Lot 4. In 1936, Van Sandt (P) discovered his basement flooded with sewage and filth. Upon investigation, he discovered for the first time the existence of a sewer drain running on, across, and through his property. Royster (D) and Gray (D) refuse to stop using the sewer. Van Sandt (P) argues that no easement has been created on his land, and even assuming there was an easement created, he took the land free from the burden of the easement because he was a bona fide purchaser, without notice.

ISSUE: Can a purchaser be charged with notice of a prior necessary use so as to create an implied easement where the use was not visible, but a reasonable inspection would have made the use apparent?

HOLDING AND DECISION: Yes. When one utilizes part of his land for the benefit of another, a quasi easement exists. The part of the land being benefited is referred to as the quasi dominant tenement, and the part being utilized is referred to as the quasi servient tenement. If the owner of land, one part of which is subject to a quasi easement, conveys the quasi dominant tenement, an easement corresponding to such quasi easement is vested in the grantee, provided such quasi easement is apparent and continuous. An implied easement, in favor of either the grantor or the grantee arises as an inference of the intentions of the parties. This inference is drawn from the circumstances under which the conveyance is made. Factors to consider include whether the claimant is the grantee or grantor, the terms of the conveyance, the consideration given, the extent of necessity of the easement and the extent to which the use, which is the subject of the easement, was or might have been known to the parties. Parties to a conveyance will be assumed to know and to contemplate the continuance of reasonably necessary uses which have so altered the premises as to make them apparent upon reasonably prudent investigation. The degree of necessity required to imply an easement in favor of the grantor is greater than that required in the case of the grantee. But where land may be used without an easement, but cannot be used without disproportionate effort and expense, an easement may be implied in favor of either the grantor or grantee on the basis of necessity alone. In this case, the trial court found that Jones was aware of the sewer at the time he purchased Lot 19. It further found that the easement was necessary to the comfortable enjoyment of the grantor's, Bailey, land. Van Sandt (P) cannot claim that he purchased without notice. He inspected the property at the time of purchase, and knew the house was equipped with modern plumbing which had to drain into a sewer. The majority view is that appearance and visibility of easements is not synonymous, and the fact that the pipe, sewer or drain is hidden underground does not make it non-apparent. Here the easement was apparent within this meaning, and Van Sandt (P) is charged with notice of its existence.

EDITOR'S ANALYSIS: The law does not favor implied easements since they are in derogation of the rule that written instruments speak for themselves. They also retard building and improvements, and violate the policy of recording acts. The implication of easements is based on the theory that when one conveys property he includes or intends to include in the conveyance whatever is necessary for its beneficial use and enjoyment and to retain whatever is necessary for the use and enjoyment of the land retained. In view of the rule that a conveyance is to be construed most strongly against the grantor, an easement in favor of the grantee will be implied more readily than one in favor of the grantor.

NOTES:

MAIORIELLO v. ARLOTTA

SUP. CT. OF PA., 1950. 364 Pa. St. 557, 73 A. 2d 374

NATURE OF CASE: Action in equity to restrain Arlotta (D) from obstructing light and air into Maioriello's (P) kitchen.

FACT SUMMARY: Arlotta (D) built a ten-foot wall on her land which prevents the passage of air and light into Maioriello's (P) kitchen.

CONCISE RULE OF LAW: An easement to light and air will not be implied in the absence of absolute necessity.

FACTS: Maioriello (P) and Arlotta (D) are adjoining property owners. Arlotta (D) erected a ten-foot-high concrete wall, entirely upon her own land, three inches from the property line and Maioriello's (P) kitchen. The wall prevents the passage of any but a small amount of light and air into the kitchen. There was testimony that a skylight could be put in the kitchen ceiling.

ISSUE: In the absence of a showing of absolute necessity, can an easement to light and air be implied?

HOLDING AND DECISION: No. Easements to light and air will be implied only in circumstances showing absolute necessity. Generally, an owner has the privilege of building upon his own land a structure which obstructs the light, air and view of an adjoining owner, even though such structure serves no useful purpose and is erected solely to annoy the adjoining owner. Further, it has been decided that when a wall is on the property line, windows in the wall do not give an easement of light and air. In this case, the lower court ordered the height of the wall to be decreased. In doing so it relied on the fact that little to both Maioriello's (P) and Arlotta's (D) premises had become vested in the same person who subsequently conveyed the two properties separately. The court decided that that grantor thereby created an easement of light and air by implication because of necessity. However, absolute necessity is not shown here. First of all, a small amount of light and air did still reach Maioriello's (P) kitchen. Secondly, there was testimony that a skylight could be built which would supply an ample amount of light and air.

EDITOR'S ANALYSIS: Easements of light and air are not favored as they are said to unduly burden property and prevent its adequate development. Hence, they will not be implied where an intention to create them does not clearly appear and where it is not necessary, as where a substitute source of light and air can be obtained at reasonable expense. The establishment of a building line restriction creates easements of light, air and vision for the benefit of the owners of the property in the restricted area.

NOTES:

PARKER & EDGARTON v. FOOTE
SUP. COURT OF JUDICATURE OF N.Y., 1838. 19 Wend. 309

NATURE OF CASE: Action to recover damages for obstruction of light.

FACT SUMMARY: Foote (D) built a store near the property line on his lot adjoining Parker & Edgarton's (P) lot. The store blocked the windows in Parker's (P) house.

CONCISE RULE OF LAW: Since in the case of light there is no adverse user, nor any use of another's property, to support a presumption against the rightful owner, an easement for light cannot be acquired by prescription.

FACTS: In 1808, Foote (D) owned two adjoining lots. He sold one to Sebbins who built a house on the property line adjoining the two lots. The house had windows which overlooked Foote's (D) lot. Also in 1808, Foote (D) built an addition to the house on his lot leaving sixteen feet between Sebbins' house and his addition. He used that space as an alley until 1832, when he built a store which filled up the whole space between the two lots and blocked the windows in the house built by Sebbins. In 1832, Parker & Edgarton (P) had become the owners of the lot previously owned by Sebbins. Sebbins testified that he had no written agreement, deed, or writing granting permission to have his windows overlook Foote's (D) lot, and that nothing was ever said on the subject.

ISSUE: Can an easement for light be acquired by prescription?

HOLDING AND DECISION: No. to authorize a presumption against a rightful owner, the enjoyment of an easement mut be uninterrupted for a period of twenty years, it must be adverse, not by leave or favor, but under a claim or assertion of right, and it must be with the knowledge and acquiescence of the owner. The presumption is not conclusive. The inference arising from twenty years of use might be explained and repelled. Most of the cases involving this presumption relate to ways, commons, markets, water-courses, and the like, where the user or enjoyment, if not rightful, has been an immediate and continuing injury to the person against whom the presumption is made. But in the case of windows overlooking the land of another, the injury, if any, is merely ideal or imaginary. No one has trespassed on the owner's land or done him a legal injury of any kind. He has acquiesced to nothing. In the case of light, there is no adverse user, nor any use whatever of another's property. Hence, no foundation is laid for any presumption against the rightful owner. The English rule allowing a presumption in cases involving light is inapplicable in the growing cities and villages of this country. In this case it was proved that the light was never enjoyed under a claim of right, but only as a matter of favor. The judgment granting Parker (P) damages was incorrect. A new trial is granted.

EDITOR'S ANALYSIS: Historically, the claim of an easement by prescription rested upon the fiction of a lost grant, that is, the courts presumed, from the long possession and exercise of right by the claimant with the owner's acquiescence, that there must have been originally a grant by the owner to the claimant which had become lost. Some courts hold that an adverse user for the required period creates a conclusive presumption of a lost grant. There is also authority, as demonstrated by this case, that the presumption is rebuttable. Some courts consider the fiction of the lost grant to be outworn and the right to an easement by prescription is declared to be substantially the same as that required to acquire title by adverse possession. The distinctions between prescription and adverse possession are that in the latter title must be through possession, and the possession must be exclusive. In the former title must be through use and the use may be in common with the owner or the public.

NOTES:

DARTNELL v. BIDWELL
SUP. JUDICIAL COURT OF MAINE, 1916.
115 Me. 227, 98 A. 743

NATURE OF CASE: Action to recover damages for trespass.

FACT SUMMARY: Bidwell (D) claimed to have a right of way over Dartnell's (P) property, part of which was acquired by grant, the remainder claimed by prescription. Dartnell (P) contested the prescriptive right.

CONCISE RULE OF LAW: Acquiescence is an essential element in creating a prescriptive easement, and anything which disproves acquiescence rebuts the presumption of a grant.

FACTS: Dartnell (P) brought this action for trespass. As a defense, Bidwell (D) contested that she had a right of way over Dartnell's (P) property. Part of the way was acquired by grant. The remainder was claimed by prescription. Dartnell (P) contested the prescriptive right. She claims to have written Bidwell (D) a letter in which she stated: "You are hereby notified that that portion of my land which you made into a road recently is across my private property. I hereby notify you to at once go back to the original location and width as given in deed." Dartnell (P) requested, but the judge refused to give, an instruction that acquiescence is essential to a prescriptive easement.

ISSUE: Is acquiescence of the owner an essential element in the creation of a prescriptive easement?

HOLDING AND DECISION: Yes. A prescriptive easement is created only by a continuous use for at least twenty years under a claim of right adverse to the owner, with his/her knowledge and acquiescence, or by a use so open, notorious, visible and uninterrupted that knowledge and acquiescence will be presumed. Each of these elements is essential. Acquiescence, here, means passive assent or submission. It is consent by silence. Where the adverse use has continued for twenty years without interruption or denial on the part of the owner, his/her acquiescence is conclusively presumed. But it was error for the judge to rule that proof of acquiescence was unnecessary. Now it is necessary to decide whether Dartnell's (P) letter disproves acquiescence. It is important to remember the distinction between prescriptive easement and adverse possession. In the latter the title arises out of the adverse possession, and nothing short of entry or legal action will break the continuity of the possession. In the former the title arises out of use. Nonacquiescence will defeat an easement, but it alone will not defeat a title by adverse possession. If acquiescence is consent by silence, to break the silence, as Dartnell (P) did here, by denials and remonstrances affords evidence of nonacquiescence. Dartnell's (P) letter to Bidwell (D) expressly denying the latter's right, protesting its present and forbidding its future, ought to be sufficient evidence of Dartnell's (P) nonacquiescence, and of an interruption of Bidwell's (D) inchoate easement.

EDITOR'S ANALYSIS: It is said that the foundation of a right by prescription is acquiescence of the owner. In the absence of a statute providing otherwise, however, if the owner has actual or constructive knowledge of the user and takes no steps to prevent the use, he will be considered to have acquiesced to that use. Further it is presumed that every person knows the condition and status of his land. If anyone enters into an open and notorious possession of an easement therein under claim of right, the owner is charged with knowledge and actual knowledge is unnecessary. In such a case, the law implies both knowledge of the user and consent thereto on the part of the owner.

NOTES:

ROMANS v. NADLER
SUP. COURT OF MINNESOTA, 1944.
217 Minn. 174, 14 N.W. 2d 482

NATURE OF CASE: Action for the establishment of a property boundary line.

FACT SUMMARY: Romans (P) claims to have acquired title by prescription in parts of Nadler's (D) property and easements in other parts.

CONCISE RULE OF LAW: In cases of easements, the requirement of continuity depends upon the nature and character of the right claimed.

FACTS: Romans (P) and Nadler (D) have owned adjoining lots since 1921. Romans' (P) house is close to the property line between the lots. His garage encroaches on Nadler's (D) lot. The eaves and gutters of Romans' (P) house and garage project over and drip onto Nadler's (D) land. Since, at least, 1924, a portion of Nadler's (D) land has been fenced and used by Romans (P). Romans (P) went onto Nadler's (D) lot to put on and take off storm windows every six months, and each time Romans' (P) house was painted, which was every six or seven years, painters set up ladders on Nadler's lot. The trial court adjudged Romans (P) as owner by prescription of the areas encroached by the garage, fenced and occupied by Romans (P), and beneath Romans' (P) eaves and gutters, and to own an easement to go upon Nadler's (D) lot as much as necessary to paint or put on or take off storm windows. Nadler (D) appeals.

ISSUE: Does the continuity of use required in cases involving easements depend upon the nature and character of the right claimed?

HOLDING AND DECISION: Yes. The same continuity of user is not required in cases of prescriptive easements as in those of title by adverse possession. In cases of easements there must be such continuity of use as the right claimed permits. However, if the rules of adverse use are to be maintained, there must be limits upon the extent to which the requirement of continuity of use can be relaxed. That limit is reached where the use is only occasional and sporadic. Since adverse possession requires greater continuity than do easements, occasional and sporadic use for temporary purposes will not constitute adverse possession, even where they continue throughout the statutory period. This is because such uses do not indicate permanent occupation and appropriation of land. In this case, Romans (P) acquired title by adverse possession to those parts of Nadler's (D) lot which he enclosed with the fence and occupied, and which he occupied and possessed by the encroachment of the garage. But he did not acquire any title to the parts under the eaves and gutters of the house and the garage, because those parts were in the actual possession of Nadler (D). The projection of the eaves and gutters of the house and garage and the dripping were of such a character as to satisfy the rules of adverse use, and hence, Romans (P) did acquire by prescription an easement in Nadler's (D) land to have the eaves and gutters project and to have the gutters drip. The periodical entries for putting on and taking off storm windows and painting were occasional trespasses, and consequently could not give rise to any prescriptive rights. Under such circumstances as are present here, something more than occasional uses of land should be required to give rise to prescriptive rights. The trespasser should be required to show by some additional acts that the entry is hostile and under claim of right, so as to warn the owner that, if he acquiesces, adverse rights will be established against him. Here there was no continuity of use to give such warning in regard to the areas entered for painting, etc.

EDITOR'S ANALYSIS: Generally , if whenever the claimant needs, from time to time, he makes use of the area, and the acts constituting the use are of such nature and frequency as to give notice to the landowner of the right being claimed against him, the use will be considered continuous. But there must be such repeated acts of such character and such frequency as to sufficiently indicate to the owner that an easement is claimed. As demonstrated here, mere occasional acts of trespass do not satisfy this requirement of continuity, even though the acts are repeated over a long period of time, because such acts do not give the owner the required notice.

NOTES:

CRIMMINS v. GOULD

FIRST DISTRICT CT. OF APPLS. OF CAL., 1957.
149 Cal. App. 2d383, 308 P.2d 786

NATURE OF CASE: Action to determine whether Gould (D) has any rights in a certain roadway.

FACT SUMMARY: Gould (D) had an easement over a lane owned by Crimmins (P). Gould (D) extended the lane by two public roads across land owned by him. The roads connected with another public road, and use and wear and tear on the lane was greatly increased.

CONCISE RULE OF LAW: An easement will be extinguished where the burden of the servient estate is increased through changes in the dominant estate which increase the use and subject it to use of non-dominant property, and it is impossible to sever the unauthorized use.

FACTS: In 1929 McCormick built McCormick lane over certain of his property. The lane runs from Fair Oaks Lane on the south to the junction of parcels 1 and 2 on the north. McCormick also owned parcel 1. The McCormick land other than parcel 1 is now subdivided and owned by Crimmins (P), Gould (D) and three others. Rights of way over McCormick lane were given to all of these owners. In 1931, McCormick deeded the lane to Crimmins (P) in fee. Gould (D) now owns parcels 1 and 2. In 1926, McCormick conveyed parcel 1 and an easement for ingress and egress to and from McCormick Lane to a predecessor of Gould (D). In 1954, Gould (D) subdivided parcels 1 and 2 into 29 residential lots. He also constructed two public roads across parcels 1 and 2, both of which extend McCormick Lane to Watkins Avenue, a public road, on the north. Crimmins (P) posted signs on McCormick Lane a few times declaring that it was not a public road. These were torn down and none have been posted since 1942. Since 1948, taxes for the lane have been assessed to Crimmins (P). In 1935, Crimmins (P) offered to deed the lane to the town. The offer was refused unless the road was rebuilt. Crimmins (P) and three other surrounding property owners (including one of Gould's [D] predecessors, but not including his predecessor in title to parcel 1) paid the cost of resurfacing the road and thereafter maintained the road at their expense. Prior to 1954, the land was used by persons not connected with the surrounding properties. The police patrol it occasionally, public utilities were granted rights of way in it, guard rails and street lights were installed there by the town. Crimmins (P) notified Gould (D) that the lane was not to be connected to the subdivision. Since the connection was made in 1954, the use and wear and tear on the lane have greatly increased. Crimmins (P) contends that Gould's (D) extension of the lane by public streets to Watkins Avenue extinguished the easement of parcel 1; Gould (D) thereby attempted to use the easement of parcel 1 for the benefit of all owners in parcel 2 and the public generally.

ISSUE: Where the burden of the servient estate is increased through changes in the dominant estate which increase the use and subject it to use of non-dominant

property, and it is impossible to sever the unauthorized use, will an easement be extinguished?

HOLDING AND DECISION: Yes. The controlling statute provides that a servitude is extinguished by any act upon either tenement, by the owner of the servitude, which is incompatible with its nature or exercise. Generally, misuse or excessive use is not sufficient for extinguishment of an easement. But where the burden of the servient estate is increased through changes in the dominant estate which increase the use and subject it to use of non-dominant property, an extinguishment will be justified if the unauthorized use may not be severed. Here, the easement of ingress and egress of parcel 1, although acquired at a time of single ownership of that parcel, would be extended to the subdivisions of that parcel. Further, Gould (D) attempted to extend the easement to all parts of parcel 2 which had no easement and also attempted to extend it to two public streets. This is not a case of merely "some increase in burden" upon a servient tenement by permitting an easement appurtenant to attach to each of the parts into which a dominant tenement may be subdivided. Rather, it is one of the acts by the owner of the servitude which are incompatible with its nature or exercise. The court also decided that McCormick Lane never became a public road. While there is a general presumption that a use by other than the owner is adverse and not permissive, the sporadic use by the public of McCormick Lane is not the type of use required. The court also decided that Gould's (D) contention that lesser relief than a declaration that Gould (D) no longer had any right to use McCormick Lane was without merit. A sign would not protect Crimmins' (P) rights. Nor would an injunction attempting to restrain all persons from using McCormick Lane other than owners or residents fronting on the lane or their invitees be practicable or enforceable. Such a sign and injunction would not prevent all or any of the residents of parcel 2 as well as the general public from using the lane. The only practical way of preventing this is to close the lane at its junction with parcels 1 and 2. This compels the extinguishment of Gould's (D) easement in the lane. This extinguishment does not constitute a taking of Gould's (D) property without due process. It is not a taking at all, but merely a determination that by his own acts, Gould (D) has made it impossible for either himself or Crimmins (P) to confine the use of the easement to the owners of lots in parcel 1 only. Hence, the easement must be extinguished.

EDITOR'S ANALYSIS: The rights of any person having an easement in the land of another are measured and defined by the purpose and character of the easement. A principle underlying the use of all easements is that the owner of the easement cannot materially increase the burden of the servient estate or impose on it a new and additional burden. The owner of an easement is said to have all rights incident or necessary to its proper enjoyment, but nothing more. And if he exceeds these rights either in the manner or in the extent of use, he becomes a trespasser to the extent of the unauthorized use.

BANG v. FORMAN

SUPREME COURT OF MICHIGAN, 1928.
244 Mich. 571, 222 N.W. 96

NATURE OF CASE: Action to enjoin resubdivision of certain plats.

FACT SUMMARY: Forman (D) has resubdivided three plats of land which materially increased the burden on a beach area to which owners of the subject property had an easement.

CONCISE RULE OF LAW: The grantee of any part of an estate is entitled to any easement appurtenant to it; but, under no circumstances will he be allowed to burden the servient estate to a greater extent than was contemplated at the time of the creation of the easement.

FACTS: Bang (P) and Forman (D) are owners of lots in a development known as Shady Shore. Twenty-five of the twenty-seven lots in the development have fronts on the beach. The beach area was dedicated by the original owners "... to the sole and only use of the lot owners." A provision intended to maintain the quality of the housing in the area was contained in all of the deeds to the lots: "The said lot to be used for dwelling purposes only ... and any dwelling house erected thereon shall not be of less value than fifteen hundred dollars." Forman (D) bought three lots and then subdivided them into 26 smaller lots "with beach privileges to all owners." Bang (P) and the other lot owners sued Forman to enjoin the sales of the resubdivided lots, and the construction of a road through the property to the beach. At trial, it was proved that the increased number of inhabitants had disturbed the peace and quiet of the holders of the other lots and that some of the smaller houses were being rented out for weekends, etc. From a decree in favor of Bang (P), Forman (D) appeals.

ISSUE: Is the grantee of an estate limited in the burden he may permissibly place on a servient estate?

HOLDING AND DECISION: Yes. The grantee of any part of an estate is entitled to any easement appurtenant to it; but, under no circumstances will he be allowed to burden the servient estate to a greater extent than was contemplated at the time of the creation of the easement. It is well settled that where land is granted with a right of way (easement) over other lands, the right is appurtenant to every part of the land so granted; and the grantee of any such part, no matter how small, is entitled to this right. Furthermore, this right will pass to a grantee of the estate, or any subdivision thereof, regardless of whether or not the easement is mentioned in the grant or is really necessary to the enjoyment of the estate. But it is just as well settled that the servient estate is not to be burdened to a greater extent than was contemplated at the time of the creation of the easement. Of course, whether this right has been exceeded is a question of fact for the trier of fact. Here, by resubdividing three lots of the original plat into 26 small lots, and granting beach privileges to each, Forman (D) has abused the easement and materially increased the burden on the servient estate. In addition, the driveway he built has provided public access to the beach where none before could be had. As both of these abuses were found by the trier of fact, its decree must be affirmed.

EDITOR'S ANALYSIS: This case points up the general rule for use by the grantee of an easement appurtenant. An easement appurtenant is one created for use in connection with specific land. The extent of its use may be no greater than that intended by the grantor. An easement is a non-possessory interest in land. An affirmative easement authorizes the doing of an act on the land of another (the servient estate), such as a right of way, maintenance of a ditch, etc. A negative easement places a restriction upon the activities of the servient owner, such as not erecting a structure which might interfere with an easement for light and air.

An action for damages or for an injunction may be maintained on an easement. An action of ejectment is not maintainable, however, since an easement is not a possessory interest.

NOTES:

CITY OF PASADENA v. CALIFORNIA-MICHIGAN LAND AND WATER CO.

SUPREME COURT OF CALIFORNIA, 1941.
17 Cal. 2d 576, 110 P. 2d 983

NATURE OF CASE: Action for injunction and damages for invasion of an easement.

FACT SUMMARY: California-Michigan (D) constructed water pipes in the same five-foot easements which Pasadena (P) had contracted for previously.

CONCISE RULE OF LAW: The intention to convey an exclusive easement will never be imputed to the owner of a servient estate in the absence of a clear indication of such intention; and, the mere grant of an unrestricted easement, not specifically defined as to the burden imposed on the servient estate, entitles the owner to make any use of the land that does not unreasonably interfere with the easement.

FACTS: Pasadena (P) and California-Michigan (D) are competing vendors for the water service for an unincorporated area outside of Pasadena. The original grant to Pasadena (P) created " ... Easements for the purpose of installing and maintaining water mains and connections thereto ... all of said easements being five feet in width, to wit: "In lots 1 to 12..." Subsequently, with the permission of the same servient owners, California-Michigan installed water lines in the same easement areas as Pasadena (P) had used. Pasadena (P) sues to enjoin this, claiming that the specificity of the original grant gave them exclusive rights to the easement.

ISSUE: Does the specificity of one material provision of an unrestricted easement make that easement an exclusive one for the grantee?

HOLDING AND DECISION: No. The intention to convey an exclusive easement will never be imputed to the owner of a servient estate in the absence of a clear indication of such intention; and, the mere grant of an unrestricted easement, not completely and specifically defined as to the burden imposed on the servient estate, entitles the owner to make any use of the land that does not unreasonably interfere with the easement. Specificity of some elements is not enough. It is true that an easement which grants a surface right of way, with a specified width, gives the grantee an absolute and exclusive right to occupy the surface to that width; but, such is not true with water pipes where the factors of the number and size of pipes, the right to shift pipes, etc., must be considered by the courts. Here, the grant to Pasadena (P), though unrestricted and specific as to the width of the easement, was not specific enough to justify the finding of an exclusive easement. Judgment for California-Michigan must be affirmed.

EDITOR'S ANALYSIS: This case points up the general rule that an exclusive easement is an unusual interest in land. Only with a clear indication of intent will such an exclusive easement be found. Nevertheless, it is also true that, between the easement owner and the servient estate owner, priority is given to the easement owner. The owner of the servient estate may put that estate to any use which does not unreasonably interfere with the easement.

NOTES:

GEFFINE v. THOMPSON

COURT OF APPEALS OF OHIO, 1945.
76 Ohio App. 64, 62 N.E. 2d 590

NATURE OF CASE: Action of ejectment.

FACT SUMMARY: Thompson (P) complains about a right of way for a gas pipe line which his predecessor in title assigned to Geffine's (D) predecessor in title.

CONCISE RULE OF LAW: The right of way to construct a gas pipe line is necessary and, therefore, appurtenant to the enjoyment of an entire entity (gas company); and, being analogous, thereby, to a right of way appurtenant to real estate, it is alienable with the entity to which it is appurtenant.

FACTS: Thompson's (P) predecessor in title granted a right of way for a gas pipeline to Geffine's (D) predecessor in title. Now, some twenty years after acquiring title, Thompson (P) complains about the right of way. He sues now to eject Geffine (D) from the right of way on the grounds that the right of way involved here is personal in nature and therefore could never have been properly assigned to Geffine (D). Geffine (D) cross-complains seeking to quiet title to his right of way. From judgment for Thompson (P), Geffine (D) appeals.

ISSUE: Is the right of way to construct a gas pipeline necessarily personal, and, therefore, non-assignable because it is not appurtenant to any real property?

HOLDING AND DECISION: No. The right of way to construct a gas pipeline is necessary and, therefore, appurtenant to the enjoyment of an entire entity (gas company); and, being analogous, thereby, to a right of way appurtenant to real estate, it is alienable with the entity to which it is appurtenant. The right to construct a gas pipeline is analogous to the right to construct a railroad track to transport passengers and freight, not to a right granted to an individual to pass over land. A railroad is an entire entity; and the entire right of way for a railroad is made up of a union of many rights derived from many individual owners (some by contracts, others by a delegated right of eminent domain). Any one right is appurtenant and necessary to all of the rest. By analogy, therefore, to real property, such rights must necessarily be alienable with the rest. Here, the right of way to construct a gas pipeline is necessary to the enjoyment of the rights of the gas company. Being so appurtenant, it must therefore be alienable as well. Geffine (D) took assignment to it properly. His title to it must be quieted. The judgment of the trial court must be reversed.

EDITOR'S ANALYSIS: This case points up the modern trend of authority that commercial easements, though technically easements in gross, are assignable interests in property. The rationale is that they are so necessary to the enjoyment of other rights (contract rights above) that they are, in effect, no different than easements appurtenant to real property rights. This is, of course, also consistent with the trend of authority that real property is no more "sacred" than any other property (contract rights, etc.), and may be treated as a commodity for sale like any other form of property.

HOPKINS, THE FLORIST INC. v. FLEMING
SUPREME COURT OF VERMONT, 1942.
112 Vt. 389, 26 A. 2d 96

NATURE OF CASE: Action seeking a declaratory judgment as to an easement.

FACT SUMMARY: Fleming (D) moved his house which his predecessor in title had covenanted with the predecessor in title of Hopkins The Florist (P) would always have a certain view.

CONCISE RULE OF LAW: The substantial change in a dominant estate may result in the extinguishment of an easement of light and air; and, where it is clear from the language used in creating such easement that it was to be appurtenant to a certain house which is no longer in the (original) position to enjoy it, such easement is extinguished.

FACTS: Fleming's (D) predecessor in title had, by deed and by independent instrument, exacted from the predecessor in title of Hopkins The Florist (P) on easement for light and air. Briefly, the easement guaranteed that Hopkins' (P) predecessor would do nothing to obstruct the southerly view from Fleming's (D) predecessor's house on the adjoining lot for 32 feet from Main Street into Hopkins' (P) predecessor's lot. Fleming (D) has since moved the subject house from the front of the lot to the back. Hopkins The Florist (P) now sues to have the easement for light and air declared extinguished. From decree in favor of Hopkins (P), Fleming (D) appeals.

ISSUE: May an easement for light and air be extinguished by the moving of a house which was designated as the dominant estate?

HOLDING AND DECISION: Yes. The substantial change in a dominant estate may result in the extinguishment of an easement of light and air; and, where it is clear from the language used in creating such easement that it was to be appurtenant to a certain house which is no longer in the (original) position to enjoy it, such easement is extinguished. The court accepts both parties' stipulation that the right involved was an easement. While the interest to which an easement may attach is usually real estate, it is well established that it may be a structure erected upon the real estate, as well. Where the easement is limited to such a structure, the moving of such structure will, of course, extinguish it. Here, the easement of light and air was intended to attach to the house where originally constructed. The subsequent moving of the house, not within the contemplation of the original parties, destroys the intended easement. The decree must be affirmed.

EDITOR'S ANALYSIS: The easement can only be used for what it was intended for in the grant. A change in use cannot be justified, even if it is shown to place no increased burden on the servient estate. This does not mean, however, that the owner of an easement will be arbitrarily held to only the actions sanctioned by the grant in his exercise of such easement. Easement owners have secondary rights, called secondary easements, which guarantee the right to do whatever they feel is necessary for the proper exercise of the primary easements.

UNION NATIONAL BANK v. NESMITH
238 Mass. 247, 130 N.E. 251 (1921)

NATURE OF CASE: Appeal from denial of registration of land.

FACT SUMMARY: Union National (P) sought to tear down a building and erect a new one without the common entrance to Nesmith's (D) building that the existing structure shared.

CONCISE RULE OF LAW: An easement may be destroyed when the owner of the servient estate destroys the building within which the easement rested.

FACTS: John Nesmith (D) and Thomas Nesmith owned adjacent parcels of land upon which they built buildings which had a common entrance. Thomas conveyed his interest to Union National (P) who proposed to tear down the building on its land and erect another without a common entrance. John Nesmith (D) contested Union's (P) petition to register the land asserting an easement in the existing building would exist wntil the building was destroyed or removed without the fault or voluntary act of the owner. The trial court denied an order of registration, and Union (P) appealed.

ISSUE: Can the owner of a servient estate voluntarily destroy an easement by voluntarily destroying the building within which it rests?

HOLDING AND DECISION: (J. Jenney) Yes. An easement in a building may be terminated through the voluntary destruction of the building by its owner. The owner of the easement cannot compel the owner of the land to maintain a building on it. This would be an improper restraint on the owner's ability to use his land as he wishes. As a result, Union (P) could destroy the building notwithstanding the easement. Reversed.

EDITOR'S ANALYSIS: This case illustrates the general rule that an easement through a building exists only so long as the building exists. This is based on the logical rationale that this was the implied intention of the parties when the easement was created.

NOTES:

NECTOW v. CITY OF CAMBRIDGE
277 U.S. 183, 48 Sup. Ct. 447 (1928)

NATURE OF CASE: Appeal from dismissal of action to compel issuance of a building permit.

FACT SUMMARY: Nectow (P) contended a zoning ordinance precluding the maintenance of certain buildings on a portion of his property was invalid as it deprived him of his property without due process.

CONCISE RULE OF LAW: Zoning power is restricted to ordinances which bear a substantial relation to the public health, saftey, morals, or general welfare.

FACTS: Nectow (P) challenged the validity of a zoning ordinance enacted by Cambridge (D) which restricted the use of a portion of the land to residential purposes. He contended that due to its proximity to an automobile factory and soap factory, it could not be used residentially, and therefore the ordinance deprived him of his property without due process. The case was assigned to a special master who found that because the areas surrounding the restricted parcel were unrestricted, and because of the two factories, the ordinance did not promote the health, saftey, convenience, or welfare of the city. The trial court confirmed the master's report, yet sustained the validity of the ordinance. Nectow (P) appealed.

ISSUE: Is a zoning ordinance valid even though it is not substantially related to the public health, saftey, or welfare?

HOLDING AND DECISION: (J. Sutherland) No. The governmental power to interfere with property rights through zoning is limited and such restrictions cannot be imposed if they do not bear a substantial relation to the public health, saftey, morals, or general welfare. In this case, the findings of the master were accepted and were not clearly erroneous. They found that the ordinance did not relate to the health and saftey of the city. Therefore, the ordinance could not be validated. The use of the land for non-residential purposes would not destroy any general plan. Therefore it should not have been upheld. Reversed.

EDITOR'S ANALYSIS: This case illustrates the scope of use zoning regulations. The constitutionality of these zoning ordinances which divide a municipality into districts and prescribe the use to which land within the district may be put was upheld in Village of Euclid v. Ambler Realty Co., 272 U.S. 365 (1926). The Nectow case illustrates that the validity of such ordinances may depend upon their application in a particular area.

NOTES:

Noted

PEOPLE v. STOVER

COURT OF APPEALS OF NEW YORK, 1963. 12 N.Y. 2d
462, 192 N.E. 2d 272. Appeal Dismissed 375 U.S. 42

NATURE OF CASE: Appeal of criminal conviction for violation of a zoning ordinance.

FACT SUMMARY: Stover (D) hung old rags and clothes on a clothesline in the frontyard as a protest of high taxes, despite a city ordinance prohibiting clotheslines in frontyards.

CONCISE RULE OF LAW: As it is well settled that aesthetic considerations may be a valid subject of legislative concern, whether or not a zoning ordinance should be voided as unconstitutional must depend on whether the restriction is an arbitrary and irrational means of achieving the end of an attractive community, not whether its objectives are primarily aesthetic.

FACTS: As a protest against high taxes, the Stovers (D) hung a clothesline across their frontyard, with old clothes and rags displayed on it. They added one new clothesline a year for five years until the city of Rye passed an ordinance banning the hanging of clotheslines in frontyards. The People (P) charged the Stovers (D) with violation of this ordinance. They now appeal their conviction on the grounds that (1) it is outside the permissible scope of the police power as concerned with mere aesthetics, and (2) as applied, it deprives them of the right of symbolic speech guaranteed by the First Amendment. The People contend that the ordinance was passed to prevent the blocking of the view of intersections for drivers.

ISSUE: May a zoning ordinance be sustained on purely aesthetic grounds?

HOLDING AND DECISION: Yes. As it is well settled that aesthetic considerations may be a valid subject of legislative concern, whether or not a zoning ordinance should be voided as unconstitutional must depend upon whether the restriction is an arbitrary and irrational means of achieving the end of an attractive community, not whether its objectives are primarily aesthetic. It is true that early decisions of this court held that aesthetic considerations alone are not sufficient to justify the exercise of the police power, but this view is now out of date. The desire to protect the residential appearance of a neighborhood by outlawing frontyard clotheslines is clearly not so unreasonable as to be unconstitutionally void. Furthermore, the right of symbolic speech, protected by the First Amendment, is not unlimited. Surely, for example, a person could not exercise his freedom of speech by taking his stand in the middle of a crowded street, contrary to traffic regulations. The ordinance here bears no necessary relationship to the dissemination of ideas. Either way, the ordinance is valid and the convictions must stand.

DISSENT: The dissenting justice contends that this exercise of the police power is void as too great an intrusion on the right of the Stovers (D) to be different. Zoning, he contends, is too rapidly becoming a device to prevent property owners from doing things which their neighbors dislike. Here, the Stovers (D) were hanging rags on their clothesline as a protest. In political retaliation, the city passed the ordinance in question. Aesthetics were merely secondary to these political concerns. Protection of such minority rights are as essential to democracy as the majority vote. Zoning ordinance must not be allowed to subvert these rights.

EDITOR'S ANALYSIS: This case superficially appears to point up a departure from the general rule that mere aesthetics may not serve as the basis for sustaining a zoning ordinance as a proper exercise of the police power. As the dissent points out, however, the underlying purpose is not aesthetics but really neighborhood politics, inspired by the desire of a community to censor a neighborhood iconoclast. The underlying considerations for prohibiting mere aesthetic zoning are no less valid today than they were originally. Definitions of "aesthetic" and/or "beastly" are no easier.

This case also points up the use of zoning ordinances to abate nuisances. Note, however, that the mere fact that a use is prohibited by a zoning ordinance does not make it a nuisance. Alternatively, the mere fact that a use is permitted by a zoning ordinance does not preclude its being enjoined as a nuisance.

NOTES:

PENN CENTRAL TRANSP. v. CITY OF NEW YORK

— Landmark Regulation

42 N.Y.2d 324, 397 N.Y.S.2d 914 (1977)

NATURE OF CASE: Appeal from an action seeking an injunction and a declaratory judgment.

FACT SUMMARY: Penn Central Transportation Co. (P), owner and proposed developer of the air rights above Grand Central Terminal, brought this action seeking a declaration that a landmark regulation as applied to the terminal property is unconstitutional.

CONCISE RULE OF LAW: Although governmental regulation is invalid if it denies a property owner all reasonable return on his property, there is no constitutional imperative that the return embrace all attributes or contributing external factors derived from the social complex in which the property rests.

FACTS: Penn Central Transportation Co. (P), owner and proposed developer of the air rights above Grand Central Terminal brought this action against the City of New York (D) seeking a declaratory judgment that the landmark preservation provisions as applied to the terminal property, are unconstitutional. Penn (P) also seeks to enjoin the City of New York (D) from enforcing the landmark regulation against the subject property. Penn (P) desires to construct an office building atop the terminal and contends that the landmark regulation deprives it from realizing a reasonable return on the property in violation of the Due Process Clause of the constitution. Trial Term granted the requested relief, but the Appellate Division reversed. Penn (P) appealed.

ISSUE: Is a government regulation invalid if it denies a property owner of all reasonable return on his property?

HOLDING AND DECISION: Yes. Although government regulation is invalid if it denies a property owner all reasonable return, there is no constitutional imperative that the return embrace all attributes or contributing external factors derived from the social complex in which the property rests. So many of these attributes are not the result of private effort or investment but of opportunities for the utilization or exploitation which an organized society offers to any private enterprise, especially to a public utility, favored by government and the public. It is enough, for the limited purposes of a landmarking statute that the privately created ingredient of property receive a reasonable return. All else is society's contribution. Moreover, in this case, the challenged regulation provides Penn Central (P) with transferable above-the-surface development rights which, because they may be attached to specific parcels of property, some already owned by Penn Central (P), may be considered as part of the owner's return on the terminal property. Thus, the regulation does not deprive Penn (P) of property without due process of law, and should be upheld as a valid exercise of the police power. Absent past heavy public governmental investment in the terminal, the railroads, and connecting transportation, it is indisputable tht the terminal property would be worth but a fraction of its current economic value. Penn Central (P) may not now frustrate legitimate and important social objectives by complaining, in essence, that government regulation deprives them of a return on so much of the investment made not by private interests but by the people of the city and state through their government. The judgment of the Appellate Division is affirmed.

EDITOR'S ANALYSIS: Landmark regulation is not a zoning problem. Restrictions on alteration of individual landmarks are not designed to further a general community plan, but to prevent the alteration or demolition of a single piece of property. To this extent, such restrictions resemble discriminatory zoning restrictions. There is, however, a significant difference. Discriminatory zoning is condemned because there is no acceptable reason for singling out one particular parcel for different and less favorable treatment. When landmark regulation is involved, there is such a reason: the cultural, architectural, historical or social significance attached to the property.

NOTES:

CONSTRUCTION INDUSTRY ASSOCIATION OF SONOMA COUNTY v. CITY OF PETALUMA

U.S.CT.OF APPLS., 9th Cir.,1975. 522 F.2d 897

NATURE OF CASE: Appeal from a finding of unconstitutionality of a zoning plan.

FACT SUMMARY: Petaluma (D) devised a zoning ordinance which was designed to allow the city to grow in an orderly manner after several years of startling and haphazard growth, but the plan was found unconstitutional by a district court as a violation of the right to travel.

CONCISE RULE OF LAW: This concept of public welfare in zoning is sufficiently broad to uphold a municipality's desire to preserve its character and to grow at an orderly and deliberate pace.

FACTS: Petaluma (D), located about 40 miles north of San Francisco, experienced dramatic increases in housing starts and population growth from 1964 to 1971. Petaluma (D), in order to control its haphazard eastward sprawl, temporarily froze development in 1971, studied the situation, and created a growth plan. The plan for five years limited construction starts of five unit or more buildings to 500 a year. Permits were to be awarded on a point system with more points to be given for good design, recreational facilities, and providing low- and moderate-income dwellings. Permits were to be allocated between east and west sections and to fill in vacant land closer to the city center. Industry (P) opposed the plan as an economic threat to its interest and business. The district court found that the plan was to limit immigration of new residents. (While the district overturned the plan as a violation of the right to travel, the Court of Appeals considered other grounds on appeal also.) Petaluma (D) appealed.

ISSUE: Is the concept of public welfare in zoning sufficiently broad to uphold a municipality's desire to preserve its character and to grow at an orderly and deliberate pace?

HOLDING AND DECISION: Yes. The concept of public welfare in zoning is sufficiently broad to uphold a municipality's desire to preserve its character and to grow at an orderly and deliberate pace. While Industry (P) contended that the plan was arbitrary and unreasonable, the plan bore a rational relationship to a legitimate state interest. "Zoning regulations must find their justification in some aspect of the police power, asserted for the public welfare." A community can determine that it "should be beautiful as well as healthy, spacious as well as clean, well-balanced as well as carefully patrolled." The Petaluma (D) plan was not as restrictive as others which have been upheld. It was designed to restrict uncontrolled growth, not all growth. It will increase density, allow for all income levels, and admit minorities. Due process is not necessarily violated because a municipality exercises police power in its own self-interest. Furthermore, as the plan was found to be valid as a reasonable and legitimate exercise of police power, it became unnecessary to consider the claim that the plan unreasonably burdened interstate commerce. ". . . . a state regulation validly based on the police power does not impermissibly burden interstate commerce where the regulation neither discriminates against interstate commerce nor operates to disrupt its required uniformity." Reversed.

EDITOR'S ANALYSIS: The court did not consider the right to travel question because the party who raised it was found on appeal not to have standing. The court's decision was not an endorsement of the plan as for its long-range effectiveness. Petaluma (D), as circumstances warranted, was not prohibited from amending the plan. As for the commerce clause issue, other illustrations of a reasonable effect upon interstate commerce include air pollution statutes, bans on phosphate detergents, and bans on non-returnable beverage containers. Notice that these examples are all types of environmental legislation.

NOTES:

BERMAN v. PARKER

SUP. COURT OF THE UNITED STATES, 1954.
348 U.S. 26, 75 S.Ct. 98, 99 L. Ed. 27

NATURE OF CASE: Action seeking to enjoin the condemnation of certain property.

FACT SUMMARY: Berman (P) challenges the constitutionality of the District of Columbia Redevelopment Act, particularly as applied to the taking of his property. The act declares the acquisition of real property and the leasing or sale thereof for redevelopment to be a public use.

CONCISE RULE OF LAW: It is within the legislature's power to take into account aesthetic considerations in enacting redevelopment legislation and to provide that a whole area should be redesigned notwithstanding a property owner's contention, that his building standing by itself was innocuous and unoffending.

FACTS: By the District of Columbia Act, Congress made a legislative determination that substandard housing and blighted areas in the District of Columbia were injurious to the public welfare and should be eliminated. The act states that Congress found that these ends could only be accomplished by a comprehensive and coordinated planning of the whole area. The act created a D.C. Redevelopment Land Agency and authorized it to acquire by eminent domain and, otherwise, real property for the redevelopment of the blighted territory and the prevention, reduction, or elimination of causes of blight. The act also authorizes a planning commission to develop a comprehensive plan for the area. Once the real property has been acquired the land agency is authorized to transfer to public agencies the land to be used for public purposes and to lease or sell the remainder to a redevelopment company or individual. Preference is to be given to private enterprise over public agencies in executing the redevelopment plan. Berman (P) owns property in the area to be redeveloped. It is not used as a dwelling house. A department store is on it. It is not slum housing and is not innocuous or offensive. It will be put into the project under the management of a private, not a public, agency and redeveloped for private, not public, use.

ISSUE: Is it within the police power of the legislature to take into account aesthetic considerations in enacting redevelopment legislation?

Is it within the legislature's power to provide for the redesigning of a whole area, notwithstanding a property owner's contention that his building, standing by itself, is innocuous and unoffending?

HOLDING AND DECISION: Yes. Public safety, public health, morality, peace and quiet, law and order do not constitute the entire scope of police power, and the court's role in determining whether the police power is being exercised for a public purpose is an extremely narrow one. The court does not sit to determine whether a particular housing project is or is not desirable. The concept of the public welfare is broad and inclusive. It represents spiritual and aesthetic values as well as physical and monetary ones, and it is within the legislature's power to consider the former values. In this case, Congress has taken a wide range of values in making its determination, and it is not for the court to reappraise them. "If those who govern the District of Columbia decide that it should be beautiful as well as sanitary, there is nothing in the Fifth Amendment to stand in its way." And once the object is within Congress' authority the right to exercise it through eminent domain is clear.

Yes. Congress has determined that the area as a whole must be redesigned to eliminate the conditions that cause slums: the overcrowding of dwellings, the lack of parks, the lack of adequate streets and alleys, recreational areas, the presence of outmoded street patterns. Property which standing by itself is innocuous or unoffending may be taken for this redevelopment. If owner after owner were permitted to resist these redevelopment programs on the ground that his particular property was not being used against the public interest, integrated plans for redevelopment would suffer greatly. Berman (P) argues that his property is being taken for the benefit of another private business person, since private enterprise is to be utilized. However, once the public purpose has been established, as it has been here, it is for the legislature alone to determine the means of executing it, and here it has chosen private enterprise as a means. In this case, Berman's (P) rights as a property owner are satisfied when he receives just compensation required by the Fifth Amendment.

EDITOR'S ANALYSIS: As a general rule the taking of private property for slum clearance or public housing projects, or for community redevelopment, is a taking for a public use or purpose within the law of eminent domain. The taking for such purposes is a taking for a public use, although the dwelling may not, and cannot, be occupied by all members of the community, but only by a few having the necessary qualifications, such as poverty. Also, an area does not have to be a slum to make its redevelopment a public use.

NOTES:

MILLER v. CITY OF TACOMA
SUPREME COURT OF WASHINGTON, 1963.
61 Wash. 2d 374, 378 P. 2d 464

NATURE OF CASE: Action for a declaratory judgment to challenge constitutionality of state urban renewal law and for injunction.

FACT SUMMARY: Miller (P), owner of real property within the boundaries of a municipal urban renewal project, arguing that his house is in good condition, seeks to halt redevelopment of the area.

CONCISE RULE OF LAW: The acquisition, elimination and redevelopment of blighted areas, and the subsequent resale of a portion of these areas to private persons, with use restrictions under an urban renewal law is a public use that warrants the exercise of the power of eminent domain and a public purpose that justifies the expenditure or loan of public funds.

FACTS: The federal government enacted legislation authorizing it to contribute two-thirds of the costs of urban renewal and redevelopment of slum or blighted areas to be matched by a one-third contribution from local funds. Washington state law empowered cities to determine the existence of blighted areas within their environs, to acquire such lands by purchase or condemnation, and, after acquisition, to hold, improve, clear or prepare the property for redevelopment. State law also generally defines "blight" and permits municipalities to sell, lease or otherwise transfer real property. In accordance with these provisions, the city of Tacoma (D) approved and adopted a comprehensive plan, and acquired land for redevelopment purposes. Miller's (P) property is within the boundaries of an urban renewal project and he seeks to enjoin the city (D) from exercising its powers of eminent domain in claiming his land.

ISSUE: Is urban renwal constitutional?

HOLDING AND DECISION: Yes. If the city (D) sought land merely for the establishment of industrial development districts, this would clearly be, as an earlier state supreme court decision held, unconstitutional. Here the test is whether a rational connection exists between the evil sought to be cured (blight) and the means adopted by the legislature to cure it. The statutory definition of a "blighted area" is sufficient to support a conclusion that the area is being acquired for a public use since it goes directly to preserving public health, safety, welfare and morals. The state has an interest in eradicating "unsanitary or unsafe conditions," fire hazards, and "conditions ... conducive to ill health, transmission of disease, infant mortality, juvenile delinquency and crime." Furthermore, the subsequent transfer of land to private parties is merely incident to the main purpose of eradicating blight since restrictions are placed in the deeds of reconveyance.

EDITOR'S ANALYSIS: In addition, land may not be condemned solely for revenue-producing purposes.

NOTES:

COURTESY SANDWICH SHOP v. PORT OF NEW YORK AUTHORITY

COURT OF APPEALS OF NEW YORK, 1963.
12 N.Y. 2d 379, 190 N.E. 2d 402, Appl. Dismissed 375 U.S. 78

NATURE OF CASE: Condemnation proceeding.

FACT SUMMARY: A state statute authorizes the port of New York Authority (P) to effectuate a port development project to be known as the World Trade Center. Courtesy Sandwich Shop (D) contends the statute is unconstitutional in that it authorizes a taking for other than public use.

CONCISE RULE OF LAW: Improvement of a city's port by facilitating the flow of commerce and centralizing all activity incident thereto is a public purpose.

Where a statute, authorizing the condemnation of property to develop a World Trade Center authorized only portions of structures, otherwise devoted to project purposes, to be used for production of incidental revenue for expenses of the port development, it is constitutional since this use does not vitiate the public purpose of the project as a whole.

FACTS: A state statute authorizes the Port of New York Authority (P) to condemn property to develop the World Trade Center. The center is defined as a facility of commerce for the centralized accommodatiion of functions, activities and services for, or incidental to, the transportation of persons, the exchange, buying, selling and transportation of commodities in world trade and commerce. It also includes structures, portions of which are not functionally related to the project's purpose and are used solely for the production of incidental revenue for the expenses of the port development project. Courtesy (D) contends that the statute authorizes the taking of private property for other than a public use.

ISSUE: Is a statute, authorizing the condemnation of property to develop a World Trade Center, which authorizes portions of structures otherwise devoted to project purposes to be used for production of incidental revenue for expenses of all or part of the port development unconstitutional as authorizing condemnation for the production of revenue without subordination to any public purpose?

HOLDING AND DECISION: No. Fostering harbor facilities has long been recognized by the courts as the legitimate concern of government. The centralization of inland trade has been held to be a public purpose and has been held to support the exercise of eminent domain for the establishment of public markets where private merchants traded. The improvement of the Port of New York by facilitating the flow of commerce and centralizing all activity incident thereto, as this statute seeks to do, is a public purpose which will support the condemnation of property for any activity functionally related to that purpose. The lower court held the statute to be unconstitutional because it wrongly read the statute to allow the unfettered erection of structures that are solely revenue producing. The act may properly be read to

authorize only incidental extensions of a site required for public use. It allows only "portions" of structures otherwise devoted to project purposes to be used for the "production of incidental revenue." Thus considered, it does not vitiate the public purpose of the development as a whole, and is not unconstitutional.

DISSENT: The statute is unconstitutional as it grants the Port Authority (P) extensive and uncontrolled governmental power to condemn and manage private real property for private purposes as a major object of the act. Being engaged in foreign trade in some capacity will transform a private business into one conducting a public purpose if it is selected by the Port Authority (P) as one from among many to be housed in the project area. If this statute is constitutional, the Legislature could amplify the project area to include any larger area of the city.

EDITOR'S ANALYSIS: Private property can be taken only for a public use or purpose, and the legislature cannot authorize a taking for a strictly private use, even on making compensation. The basis for this rule is that the assertion of a right on the part of the legislature to take the property of one citizen and transfer it to another, even for full compensation, where the public interest is not promoted, is "claiming a despotic power, and one inconsistent with every just principle and fundamental maxim of a free government." A statute or ordinance which provides that private property may be taken for private use is invalid. This rule does not prevent, however, property taken for public use from being resold, leased, or assigned to private persons with restriction on them to carry out the public purpose.

NOTES:

POLETOWN NEIGHBORHOOD COUNCIL
v. CITY OF DETROIT
410 Mich.616,304 N.W.2d 455(1981)

NATURE OF CASE: Appeal in condemnation action.

FACT SUMMARY: Detroit (D) sought to condemn certain property for transfer to General Motors Corporation (GM) for construction of an assembly plant.

CONCISE RULE OF LAW: A condemnation action which is authorized primarily for the benefit of the public will not be invalidated by the fact that an incidental private benefit also occurs.

FACTS: The City of Detroit (D), through its Economic Development Corporation, approved a plan to acquire, by condemnation if necessary, a large tract of land to be conveyed to GM as a site for construction of an assembly plant. Such a plan was authorized by the Michigan Legislature, which provided that municipal condemnation powers may properly be used to stimulate economic recovery in such a fashion. The Poletown Neighborhood Council (Council) (P), a group of affected homeowners, objected to the City's (D) plan, contending that it was an unconstitutional use of the powers of eminent domain for the benefit of a private entity. The trial court found that the primary purpose of the proposed condemnation action was the benefit of the public and dismissed the Council's (P) complaint. The Council (P) appealed.

ISSUE: May a condemnation action, which is authorized primarily for the public good, convey an incidentally private benefit as well?

HOLDING AND DECISION: (Per Curiam) Yes. It is clear that a condemnation action which is primarily intended to benefit the public at large will not be rendered unconstitutional merely because it also happens to convey a benefit to a private entity as well. Accordingly, the sole focus of inquiry is whether the primary benefit of the instant condemnation proceeding accrues to the people of Detroit or to GM. The City (D) asserted that the controlling purpose in taking the land is to create an industrial site which will be used to alleviate conditions of unemployment and fiscal distress. As the determination of what constitutes a public purpose is primarily a legislative function, the courts may only reverse such a determination where it is clearly arbitrary and incorrect. There is no showing in the instant action that the legislative determination of a primary public purpose is arbitrary or incorrect. Accordingly, the condemnation action is not unconstitutional. Affirmed.

DISSENT: (Fitzgerald, J.) The condemnation contemplated in the present action goes beyond the scope of the power of eminent domain in that it takes private property for private use. As such, it cannot be permitted.

DISSENT: (Ryan, J.) Eminent domain is an attribute of sovereignty. When individual citizens are forced to suffer dislocation to permit private corporations to construct plants where they deem it most profitable, it becomes questionable as to who the sovereign is. This purported condemnation actions is a clearly unconstitutional taking of property.

EDITOR'S ANALYSIS: The name Poletown refers to the fact that many of the residents of the affected neighborhood in the principal case were of Polish descent. The ethnic "flavor" of the neighborhood was asserted in the complaint as an additional reason for not allowing condemnation, since it would have "a major adverse impact on the. . .social and cultural environment which is referred to as Poletown." Both the trial court and Supreme Court rejected the claim, contending that the maintenance of a "social and cultural environment" was outside the legislative intent of the controlling statute.

NOTES:

GORTON v. SCHOFIELD
SUP. JUDICIAL COURT OF MASSACHUSETTS, 1942.
311 Mass. 352, 41 N.E. 2d 12

NATURE OF CASE: A bill in equity by which Gorton (P) seeks to compel Schofield (D) to rebuild or repair a retaining wall on Schofield's (D) land.

FACT SUMMARY: After Schofield (D) removed a stable on his land that supported a retaining wall on his land which provided lateral support to Gorton's (P) land, large holes developed on Gorton's (P) land.

CONCISE RULE OF LAW: Where a lateral support has been withdrawn by a predecessor in title, and the condition caused by the lack of support has caused injury to a neighbor's land, the owner of the land at the time of the injury will be held liable.

FACTS: Gorton (P) owns land adjacent to Schofield's (D). Originally both lots were on a slope. Due to excavations, Schofield's (D) land is now flat. Gorton's (P) land is still sloped, and slopes to a retaining wall on Schofield's (D) land. The wall is in disrepair. A well-built stable supported the wall. The stable was on Schofield's (D) land. After it was demolished, Gorton's (P) land sunk, forming large holes on her land. Gorton (P), with Schofield's (D) permission, repaired the most unstable part of the wall. It was found that it would cost an additional $1,000 to $1,5000 to repair the wall fully. The excavations and wall had been made by the former owner of Schofield's (D) land.

ISSUE: Where the predecessor in title had withdrawn lateral support from plaintiff's land and had built a retaining wall, is the present owner bound to maintain the wall in such condition as to prevent damage to plaintiff's land?

HOLDING AND DECISION: Yes. The burden of providing lateral support to the adjacent land in its natural condition is one of continued support running against the servient land. Where a predecessor in title has made an excavation which withdrew support from a neighbor's land, and has built a retaining wall, the subsequent owner's failure to continue to provide necessary support by allowing the wall to decay is a continual withdrawal of support for which he'll be held liable. In this case, Schofield's (D) failure to repair the wall was such a withdrawal. Gorton (P) has shown irreparable damage in that the holes occur after heavy rains, and it can be assumed that they will continue to occur. An award of damages would not give her adequate relief, since it would not prevent future damage.

EDITOR'S ANALYSIS: This case demonstrates the problem of excavations done by one who owned land previously, which later cause damage to adjacent land. Many states and municipalities have enacted legislation concerning lateral or subjacent support. Lateral support is the right o have surface land supported by adjoining land. Subjacent support is the right to have land supported by underlying strata.

UNITED STATES v. WILLOW RIVER POWER CO.
324 U.S. 499, 65 Sup. Ct. 761 (1945)

NATURE OF CASE: Appeal from determination of riparian rights.

FACT SUMMARY: Willow River (P) asserted an ownership right in the use of water running alongside its property for the development of power.

CONCISE RULE OF LAW: A riparian owner has no private ownership right to the use of the water superior to that of the general public.

FACTS: Willow River (P) claimed that as a riparian landowner, it had a right to a set level of water flow by its land for use in power production, and that the government (D) had an inferior right to impound a portion of the flow to improve navigation.

ISSUE: Does a riparian land owner have an ownership right in the water flowing by his land?

HOLDING AND DECISION: No. A riparian landowner has no private ownership rights in the water flowing by his land. His rights are no different from that of the general public and must yield to the overriding right of the federal government to regulate navigation. Therefore, in this case, Willow River (P) had no assertable right to a minimum water flow.

EDITOR'S ANALYSIS: This case illustrates the preeminence of the power of the federal government over the maintenance of navigable waters. Because navigation was so important to commerce during the early years of the country, the federal power over navigable waterways was closely tied to the almost limitless power to regulate commerce.

NOTES:

FERGUSON v. CITY OF KEENE

SUP. CT. OF N.H., 1968.

238 A. 2d 1

NATURE OF CASE: Action to recover compensation for a governmental taking.

FACT SUMMARY: Noise from planes at City of Keene's (D) airport have caused windows to break in Ferguson's (P) house and make conversation or sleep in the house impossible.

CONCISE RULE OF LAW: There has been no taking requiring compensation where noise from a government airport causes damage to nearby land, but such damage is not caused by flights over the land, and no such overflights occur.

FACTS: City of Keene (D) took part of Ferguson's (P) land in order to lengthen its airport runway. The runway was extended to a few hundred feet from Ferguson's (P) house. Ferguson (P) alleges that the use of a "warmup apron" located opposite her house resulted in such noise and vibration as to cause twenty windows to break in one winter, and to make conversation or sleep in the house impossible and life there generally unbearable. Ferguson (P) contends that the use of the airport constitutes a taking and a nuisance.

ISSUE: Has there been a taking where noise from a government airport causes damage to nearby land, but planes do not fly over the land?

HOLDING AND DECISION: No. Inverse condemnation is a cause of action to recover the value of property which has been taken in fact by the government, even though no formal exercise of the power of eminent domain has been attempted. The U. S. Supreme Court has not gone beyond the point of holding that there may be recovery in inverse condemnation for damages occasioned by direct flights over a claimant's property. The few decisions that have permitted recovery where no overflight was involved have been criticized. There is a genuine difference between the nature of the injury of one whose land is subjected to overflights and one whose land is not. The former has lost the air space above his land, and is subjected to risks of physical damage not shared by the latter. The question of whether inverse condemnation should be extended to cases which do not involve overflight is one for the legislature. In this case Ferguson (P) has failed to state a cause of action in inverse condemnation because there was no allegation of overflights. She has, however, alleged a cause of action in nuisance.

EDITOR'S ANALYSIS: The dissenting Justice feels that Ferguson (P) has stated a cause of action in inverse condemnation and should be allowed to recover for a governmental taking. He states, "A person's property rights can be damaged as greatly by sound waves traveling horizontally as by those traveling vertically, and to draw a distinction is to ignore reality." He does not agree with the majority's refusal to grant recovery because there was not an overflight.

TUCKER v. BADOIAN

Sup.Jud.Ct. of Mass.,1978. —Mass.—, 384 N.E.2d 1195

NATURE OF CASE: Action for damages for negligence.

FACT SUMMARY: Tucker (P) contended that a neighbor negligently made certain changes on its land and thus caused large quantities of water to collect on Tucker's (P) land and in his cellar.

CONCISE RULE OF LAW: Liability for surface-water runoff onto another's land does not exist in the absence of proof that the defendant caused surface water which might otherwise have been absorbed or have flowed elsewhere to be artificially channeled and discharged onto plaintiff's land so as to cause damage.

FACTS: Tucker (P) purchased a house and land adjoining property owned by Morningside Realty (D). Morningside (D) filled in a pothole and ditch that crossed its lot when filling and grading a strip of its land for a proposed road to connect to the main road. Tucker (P) brought suit, claiming this negligent action had resulted in surface water draining onto his land and flooding it and his cellar. From a jury verdict in favor of Tucker (P), an appeal was taken. The appeals court held it was error for the judge to deny Morningside's (D) motion for directed verdict and reversed the judgment. It ruled liability existed only for artificially channeled water discharged onto another's land.

ISSUE: Does liability exist only for artificially channeled water discharged onto another's land?

HOLDING AND DECISION: (J. Quirico) Although many jurisdictions have abandoned rigid approaches like our own in favor of a more flexible "reasonable use" doctrine, this jurisdiction continues to follow the "common enemy" approach to surface water problems. A landowner is not liable for surface water discharge onto another's land unless he uses definite, artificial channels so as to harm his neighbor. Such was not done in this case, so there is no basis for holding Morningside (D) liable. Affirmed.

CONCURRENCE: (J. Kaplan) While the result is proper when the "common enemy" rule is applied, those subscribing to this concurrence desire to state their intention to change that doctrine in the future and move to the standard of "reasonable use" in surface water situations.

EDITOR'S ANALYSIS: Many jurisdictions simply abandoned the "common enemy" rule as archaic, but others chose to "civilize" it by allowing various "exceptions" thereto. On the other end of the spectrum, some jurisdictions adopted the "natural flow" rule and imposed liability for interfering with the drainage of surface waters in their natural course in any way to the detriment of a neighbor. The "reasonable use" standard adopts a middle ground and is favored by a majority of commentators.

NOTES:

MEEKER v. CITY OF EAST ORANGE

Ct. of Errors and Appeals of N.J., 1909.
77 N.J.L. 623, 74 A. 379

NATURE OF CASE: Action to recover damages for diversion of percolating underground water.

FACT SUMMARY: By its artesian wells on its land, City of East Orange (D) has diverted underground water which would have reached Meeker's (P) well and spring. City of East Orange (D) has also taken underground water from beneath Meeker's (P) land, thereby causing damage to his crops.

CONCISE RULE OF LAW: There are correlative rights in percolating underground waters, and no landowner has the absolute right to withdraw such waters from the soil to the detriment of other owners, and is limited to reasonable uses.

FACTS: Meeker (P) owned a farm through which flowed two streams. There was also a well and a spring on the farm, which he used for drinking and domestic purposes. His cattle drank from the streams. To provide water for its inhabitants, City of Orange (D) acquired land and installed on it a water plant consisting of twenty artesian wells. City of Orange (D) took water from these wells, which but for its interception would have reached Meeker's (P) spring, streams and well. City of Orange (D) has also taken underground water from beneath the surface of Meeker's (P) land thereby causing damage to his crops.

ISSUE: Does a landowner have an absolute right to underground percolating water beneath the surface of his land and to withdraw such water for distribution or sale for uses not connected with any beneficial ownership or enjoyment of the land?

HOLDING AND DECISION: No. The rights of each landowner to underground water are similar, and their enjoyment is dependent upon the action of other landowners. Hence, their rights must be correlative, and each landowner's use must be reasonable in view of the rights of others. Such reasonable use is the use of the water for some purpose connected with ordinary operations of agriculture, mining, domestic use or improvements either public or private. This is the "reasonable use" doctrine. It does not prevent any reasonable development of one's land such as by mining, even though a neighbor's underground water may be diverted or interfered with by such development. It does prevent, however, the withdrawal of underground water for distribution or sale for uses not connected with any beneficial ownership or enjoyment of the land where such taking results in the interference with a neighbor's reasonable use of sub-surface water on his land. Nor will such withdrawal be allowed where it causes a neighbor's wells, springs, or streams to be materially diminished or his land to be made so arid as to be less valuable for agriculture, pasturage, or other legitimate purposes. City of East Orange (D) may not take the underground water by means of artesian wells and convey it away from the land for sale when such taking interferes with Meeker's (P) reasonable use and enjoyment of his land by causing his well, spring, and streams to be diminished and his land to become arid. Hence, Meeker (P) may recover damages from City of East Orange (D).

EDITOR'S ANALYSIS: In adopting the reasonable use doctrine, here, the court rejected the older absolute right doctrine. Under that doctrine the landowner had an absolute right to appropriate underground water found beneath his land. If such appropriation resulted in the drying up of a neighbor's spring, well, and stream, or rendered his land so arid as to be worthless, it was damnum absque injuria (damage for which there is no recovery).

NOTES:

UNITED STATES v. CAUSBY
Supreme Court of the United States, 1946
328 U.S. 256, 66 S.Ct. 1062, 90 L.Ed. 1206

NATURE OF CASE: Suit seeking compensation for an alleged taking of property.

FACT SUMMARY: United States (D) planes, using a nearby airport, disturbed the Causbys (P) in their home and forced the discontinuation of their chicken farming business.

CONCISE RULE OF LAW: The use of a landowner's airspace by low-flying government planes constitutes a partial taking for which, under the Fifth Amendment, the landowner is entitled to be compensated.

FACTS: The United States (D), during World War II, leased an airport located near a farm owned by Causby (P) and his wife (P). One of the airport's runways was located less than half a mile from the Causbys' (P) house and barn, and this runway was, from time-to-time, used by the United States (D) for the landing and taking off of airplanes. These planes sometimes passed over the Causbys' (P) property at altitudes as low as 83 feet, making sleep impossible and causing acute nervousness. The low-flying planes also proved so frightening to the chickens that the Causbys (P) were eventually forced to give up their chicken business. Presented with these facts, the United States Court of Claims ruled that there had been a taking of the Causbys' (P) property through the acquisition by the United States (D) of an easement. The United States (D) was ordered to pay $2,000 in compensation. The United States (D) then petitioned the Supreme Court, which granted certiorari.

ISSUE: Is a private landowner entitled to compensation for a reduction in property value which results from the disturbance created by low-flying government aircraft?

HOLDING AND DECISION: Yes. The use of a landowner's airspace by low-flying government planes constitutes a partial taking for which, under the Fifth Amendment, the landowner is entitled to compensation. In this day and age, aircraft operators obviously enjoy at least a limited privilege to utilize the airspace above a private landowner's property. But, despite the United States' (D) argument that the path of glide followed by the planes had been approved by the Civil Aeronautics Authority, this is not the standard to be used in evaluating the legality of a plane's altitude. Minimum safe altitudes are prescribed by law, and the flights over the Causbys' (P) land did not comply with the statutory standards. Therefore, the United States (D) did, in effect, usurp an easement in the Causbys (P) property, and should be required to pay compensation for this taking. However, since the court of claims failed to make a finding as to the extent and duration of this easement, the case must be remanded to that court so that the propriety of the amount of the compensation award may be determined.

DISSENT: (J. BLACK) The mere making of noise or reflection of glare onto a person's land does not constitute a taking of the land in a constitutional sense. The airspace of the United States is necessary for navigational purposes, and the flying of a plane above private land does not constitute a constitutional taking either. The power of Congress to keep the air free must be viewed as preeminent.

EDITOR'S ANALYSIS: Courts are inclined to be generous in their treatment of landowners who are disturbed by aircraft flying over their property. Although plane flights are regarded as qualifiedly privileged, abuses are readily found to have occurred. The rule of the *Causby* case has been applied even to flights which were not violative of Civil Aeronautics Authority regulations and were no lower than necessary for landings or take-offs. (*Griggs v. Allegheny County,* 369 U.S. 84, 82 S.Ct. 531, 7 L.Ed. 2d 585 (1962), reh. den. 369 U.S. 857, 82 S.Ct. 931, 8 L.Ed. 2d 16.)

NOTES: